Beckett's Dying Words

Most people most of the time want to live for ever. But there is another truth: the longing for oblivion. With pain, wit, and humour, the art of Samuel Beckett variously embodies this truth, this ancient enduring belief that it is better to be dead than alive, best of all never to have been born.

But how does a writer give life to dismay at life itself, to the unwelcome encroachments of death? After all, it is for the life, the vitality, of their language that we value writers.

Beckett became himself as a writer when he realized in his very words a principle of death. In clichés, which are dead but won't lie down. In a dead language and its memento mori. In words which mean their own opposites, cleaving and cleaving. In the self-stultifying or suicidal turn dubbed the Irish bull. In what Beckett called a syntax of weakness.

This book explores the relation between deep convictions about life or death and the incarnations which these take in the exact turns of a great writer—the realizations of an Irishman who wrote in English and in French, two languages with different apprehensions of life and of death.

Christopher Ricks is Professor of English, Boston University.

D1324246

Beckett's Dying Words

The Clarendon Lectures

1990

CHRISTOPHER RICKS

Oxford   New York

OXFORD UNIVERSITY PRESS

1995

Oxford University Press, Walton Street, Oxford OX2 6DP

Oxford New York
Athens Auckland Bangkok Bombay
Calcutta Cape Town Dar es Salaam Delhi
Florence Hong Kong Istanbul Karachi
Kuala Lumpur Madras Madrid Melbourne
Mexico City Nairobi Paris Singapore
Taipei Tokyo Toronto
and associated companies in
Berlin Ibadan

Oxford is a trade mark of Oxford University Press

First published by Clarendon Press 1993
First issued as an Oxford University Press paperback 1995

British Library Cataloguing in Publication Data
Data available

Library of Congress Cataloging in Publication Data
Data available
ISBN 0-19-282407-4

1 3 5 7 9 10 8 6 4 2

Printed in Great Britain by
Biddles Ltd
Guildford and King's Lynn

CONTENTS

1. *Death*

We know about our wish to go on being, we human beings, our wish not to die. Samuel Beckett, who rigged nothing, fashioned for himself and for us a voice, Malone's, at once wistful and wiry:

Yes, there is no good pretending, it is hard to leave everything.[1]

These are the accents of a consciousness, imagining and imagined, which braves the immortal commonplace of mortality.

Most people most of the time want to live for ever. This truth is acknowledged in literature, including Beckett's. But like many a truth, it is a half-truth, not half-true but half of the truth, as is the truth of a proverb. For, after all, most people some of the time, and some people most of the time, do not want to live for ever.

This counter-truth—that, on occasion and more than moodily, we want oblivion, extinction, irreversible loss of consciousness—is insufficiently, or is mostly prophylactically, rendered by literature. Authorities, sacred and secular, do not care for the thought; they do not want you to want to be dead. Except, perhaps, as a martyr, and even this they have their doubts about.

Yet who would maintain, through thick and thin, that the energy which is consciousness is eternal delight? Consciousness does not have to be pained to be a burden or to be a perturbation of mind in endless prospect.

The young T. S. Eliot insisted that

Poetry is not a turning loose of emotion, but an escape from emotion; it is not the expression of personality, but an escape from personality. But, of course, only those who have personality and emotions know what it means to want to escape from these things.[2]

---

[1] *Malone Dies* (1956), 107. Following *Malone meurt* (1951), 172: 'Oui, on a beau dire, il est difficile de tout quitter'. I give always both the French and the English of Beckett. 'Following' and 'Preceding' are specified in the references to indicate the priority of the French or the English.

[2] 'Tradition and the Individual Talent' (1919); *Selected Essays* (1932; 3rd edn., 1951), 21.

'And that's true too', even though Eliot has his vibratory coercions (his 'of course' is exquisite). For Beckett, tradition and the individual talent converge upon an escape yet more total and more final than that escape from personality and emotions which Eliot envisaged. (The paradoxes, courting solecism, would be to Beckett's liking: *more* total? *more* final?) For, last-trumping even the escape from personality and emotions, and constituting the only entire escape from them, must be the escape from consciousness, and in particular the guaranteed form of this, the escape into death.

Waiting for imminent and immanent death, Malone muses:

I have lived in a kind of coma. The loss of consciousness for me was never any great loss.[3]

It is the consciousness of this (of the relief and release which a permanent, not just a temporary, loss of consciousness may be trusted to be) which grounds a lethally level death-sentence by Stevie Smith, a graffito spelt out gravely enough for the walls of Belshazzar: 'There are some human beings who do not wish for eternal life'.[4]

Philip Larkin, admirer of Stevie Smith, differed from her in wishing never to die, as is clear from the hooded anguish of his last months; but, with an artist's independence of himself, he had given enduring expression to that other half of the truth which he could conceive but not personally possess.

Wants

Beyond all this, the wish to be alone:
However the sky grows dark with invitation-cards
However we follow the printed directions of sex
However the family is photographed under the flagstaff—
Beyond all this, the wish to be alone.

Beneath it all, desire of oblivion runs:
Despite the artful tensions of the calendar,
The life insurance, the tabled fertility rites,
The costly aversion of the eyes from death—
Beneath it all, desire of oblivion runs.

---

[3] *Malone Dies*, 6. Following *Malone meurt*, 14: 'J'ai vécu dans une sorte de coma. Perdre connaissance, pour moi, c'était perdre peu de chose.'

[4] With a sketch by her, in *New Departures*, Nos. 7–8 and 10–11 (1975), 19.

'The wish to be alone' is set against—even while it cannot but concede as it passes—the wish to *be*. Or not to be. Period. Will one ever be alone except in the grave?

> Now with his love, now in his colde grave
> Alone, withouten any compaignye.
> (*The Knight's Tale*, 2778–9)

Despite the word 'wish' framing the first stanza, Larkin's title is *Wants*, not 'Wishes', and this summons what is wanting as well as what is wanted. The first stanza launches out, and at the end rounds itself out, without verb or declaration exactly ('Beyond all this, the wish to be alone'). But the second stanza finds itself desiring the undercurrent of a verb: 'Beneath it all, desire of oblivion runs'—the verb 'runs' the more marked because, though entirely at home and enacting its own meaning (the syntax runs on, past its sibling-syntax of the first stanza's refrain, to the end), neither the sense nor the rhythm actually demands the verb. The repeated line might perfectly well have been (much less perfectly), in an entirety of parallelism with the first stanza's refrain, 'Beneath it all, desire of oblivion'. No, see how it runs. Oblivion will be without movement; the desire of it moves, and moves us.

In his early book on *Proust*, his first book (1931), in his mid-twenties, Beckett considered 'our first nature' (as against what has become second nature), and wrote of 'a deeper instinct than the mere animal instinct of self-preservation'.[5] This intimated darkly the depths of death's oblivion.

The desire of oblivion is marked in the strangest of Beckett's novels, the one which makes as if—feints as if—to convert his trilogy (*Molloy, Malone Dies, The Unnamable*) into a tetralogy: *How It Is*. A modern vision of ancient eternal torment, where Dante's sufferers are newly scored with tin-openers, *How It Is* longs to put a stop—and has no stops or punctuation at all other than white line spacing:

thump on skull no point in post mortems and then what then what we'll try and see last words cut thrust a few words DO YOU LOVE ME CUNT no disappearance of Pim end of part two leaving only part three and last one

---

[5] *Proust* (1931), 11.

can't go on one goes on as before can one ever stop put a stop that's more like it one can't go on one can't stop put a stop[6]

In translating his French ('s'arrêter arrêter'), Beckett falls upon punctuation's counterpoint:

one can't stop put a stop

Time must have a stop. Eternity must not. The French verb 'arrêter' refuses to be intransitive despite this beetling of reflexive brows at it ('s'arrêter arrêter'). And there's the rub. You cannot, however, much you may long to, *arrêter, tout court*. In parallel, but even more hauntingly, the English 'put a stop' aches to consummate itself with a *to* of some sort: put a stop *to* . . . As it is, the vista opens horribly up:

one can't go on one can't stop put a stop

—opens up not only because of the white space (no stop vouchsafed) after 'stop' but because you can't put a stop to anything whatsoever with the phrase 'put a stop', for ever reaching out as it does for a completion denied to it.

one can't stop

—ah, for this moment at least it isn't the very language which stops one ('stop' can be transitive or intransitive), and where there's death there's hope. Whereupon this brief hope of cessation is dashed, for hard on the heels of 'one can't stop' treads the infinite indefatigability:

one can't stop put a stop

As often in Beckett, his original French reads like a highly talented translation of a work of genius, and not as the thing itself.

---

[6] *How It Is* (1964), 99. Following *Comment c'est* (1961), 110:

coup sur le crâne à quoi bon l'autopsie puis quoi puis quoi nous allons essayer de voir puis derniers mots du tac au tac quelques mots M'AIMES-TU CON non disparition de Pim fin de la deuxième plus que la troisième et dernière on ne peut continuer on continue la même chose pourra-t-on s'arrêter arrêter c'est là plutôt on ne peut continuer on ne peut s'arrêter arrêter

Given here and above is the entire unit (for which we don't have a word, since it is not a paragraph); there is white space before and after it, and no punctuation within it though its phrasing and clausing are not hard to reconstitute, with something of the need, in reading, to thread and brake which is now incited by a medieval manuscript such as wastes no space on lineation.

The English language is more inclined to share its cravings with Beckett. Where *Comment c'est* lets slip the brusque acknowledgment 'ça c'est vrai', *How It Is*[7] substitutes for this a turn suppurating with supplication:

> give me my due

Only one thing is altogether and for ever due.

Oblivion may be as distant as our destiny and as homely as our destination. Ancestral voices prophesying oblivion are heard 'beneath it all' in the novel *Watt*; the second, final, verse of the song (infantile, spooky, and cretinous) comes home:

> *oh a bun a big fat bun*
> *a big fat yellow bun*
> *for Mr Man and a bun*
> *for Mrs Man and a bun*
> *for Master Man and a bun*
> *for Miss Man and a bun*
> *a big fat bun*
> *for everyone*
> *four two eight five seven one*
> *four two eight five seven one*
> *till all the buns are done*
> *and everyone is gone*
> *home to oblivion.*

The singing then ended.
Of these two verses Watt thought he preferred the former. Bun is such a sad word, is it not? And man is not much better, is it?[8]

Death, though, is a less sad word than unthinking people think. Yet when Larkin reviewed *The Oxford Book of Death*, he found no room for his own admission, his alms for oblivion:

Several recognisable attitudes emerge from his [D. J. Enright's] chorus of voices. First, of course, death isn't going to happen ('One short sleep past, we wake eternally'). Or, if it does happen, it is by definition something we needn't worry about ('so long as we exist, death is not with us; but when death comes, then we do not exist'). Or, if it does happen,

---

[7] *How It Is*, 52. Following *Comment c'est*, 57.
[8] *Watt* (1953), 35. Preceding *Watt* in French (translated by Ludovic and Agnès Janvier in collaboration with Beckett, 1968), 35, which is without the songs and the closing comment.

it is jolly nice and comfortable ('in a sleep deeper and calmer than that of infancy, wrapped in the finest and softest dust'). Or, finally, life would be very dull without death ('it is immeasurably heightened'), to me a view that fails to grip even more conspicuously than the others. It was thoroughly torpedoed by Kingsley Amis in 'Lovely' ('Look thy last on all things lovely / Every hour, an old shag said'), a poem I am sorry not to see included.

What might with some justice be called the majority view, however—death is the end of everything, and thinking about it gives us a pain in the bowels—is poorly represented.[9]

The calculated débâcle of the end, 'is poorly represented', deliciously effects what Beckett called a 'syntax of weakness'. Belated, obdurate, pursed, formal, and yet less a dying fall than all of a heap.

Of growing older, Larkin knew what he could only say: 'If you ask why does it bother me, I can only say I dread endless extinction.'[10] And in what was to be effectively his last published poem, 'Aubade' (1977), he returned, with the laconic indeflectibility of a QED, to what is to be demonstrated in death:

> Most things may never happen: this one will

Yet in contemplating *The Oxford Book of Death*, Larkin did not let his own writ run. He found no place, even when listing 'attitudes', for the thought, once his own, that 'Beneath it all, desire of oblivion runs', or for the age-old conviction that it is better to be dead than alive.

Beckett's first separate publication was *Whoroscope* (1930), and in his first novel, *Murphy* (1938),[11] the hero reaches the last words of his horoscope:

> Lucky Years. 1936 and 1990. Successful and prosperous, though not without calamities and set-backs.

And Beckett's own luck? 1936 had been the year that saw the writing of this very *Murphy*. As for 1990, it was to prove the first year of Beckett's no longer living (he died on 22 December 1989), 1990 being a year in which once again Good Friday, as in 1906,

---

[9] *The Observer*, 24 Apr. 1983.
[10] 'An Interview with the *Observer*' (1979): *Required Writing* (1983), 55.
[11] *Murphy* (1938), 33. Preceding *Murphy* in French (1947), 31: '*Années Propices*: 1936 et 1990. Heureuses et Prospères, quoique non sans Calamités et Rebuffades.'

the year and the day when Beckett first saw the light of day, happened to be a Friday the Thirteenth.[12]

'Lucky Years, 1936 and 1990. Successful and prosperous, though not without calamities and set-backs.' It made a fine prognostication of what was for Beckett the only true, and only truly desirable, *afterlife*. Set-backs? Calamities? Come now. Rather, at last, the thoroughly 'successful and prosperous'. For where, if Hamlet is misguided and no dreams are to be feared in that sleep of death, is now 'The respect | That makes Calamity of so long life'?

1990. A fluke of prescience? A shrewd calculation? Beckett, who famously became the Nobel Prize winner who appears in Wisden, may have calculated that (born 1906) he would by 1990 have had his good innings.

As to luck, there is Berryman:

> —What happen then, Mr Bones?
> —I had a most marvellous   piece of luck. I died.[13]

It was Robert Lowell who performed the emergency amputation 'All's well that ends'. This acknowledgement, life yielding to

[12] Some scholars, though, scent something fishy about this Good Friday. Alice and Kenneth Hamilton noted: 'The date always given, on Beckett's own authority, is the thirteenth of April, 1906. In that year, the day happened to be Good Friday. Yet this is perhaps not the actual historical date, since the Irish birth certificate of "Samuel Barely Beckett" is dated the thirteenth of May, 1906. That day was Rogation Sunday in 1906'. Samuel *Barely* Beckett is an inspiration, whether the Hamiltons' or another's; read Samuel Barclay Beckett. A note adds: 'The writers have seen copies of Beckett's birth certificate and of the registration of his birth. Both show the date of his birth as being the thirteenth of May, 1906, registration of the birth being on the fourteenth of June' (*Condemned to Life* (1976), 17, 197). Deirdre Bair comments: 'He insists that he was born on Good Friday, April 13, 1906, a date to which he has not discouraged scholars of his writing from attaching undue importance, but his birth certificate gives the date as May 13, 1906. Since it was the custom in Ireland for live births to be recorded when the infant had survived the first month of life, and since Beckett's was officially entered on June 14, 1906, there is a certain validity to the question of the actual date' (*Samuel Beckett: A Biography* (1978), 3).

Those who think, as I do not, that Beckett told a lifetime's untruth might like to add to the criss-cross of Good Friday and Friday the Thirteenth the thought that by plumping for April instead of May, Beckett furthermore at birth got out from under his mother, May. 'I am what her savage loving has made me' (Beckett, 6 Oct. 1937; Bair, *Samuel Beckett*, 263). 'Like her namesake, May, in the play *Footfalls*, which Samuel Beckett wrote almost seventy years later, she removed the carpets in some areas of the house because she "... must hear the feet, however faint they fall"' (Bair, *Samuel Beckett*, 10–11).

[13] *77 Dream Songs* (1964), no. 26.

death, is a wording grimly glad to be suddenly cut short. He was presumably not unaware that Lowell chances to be a name that ends 'well'.

When Beckett in *Murphy* reminds us, 'But all good things come to an end',[14] he brings home the reminder that there is a perspective within which coming to an end may be judged—for all the fears and pains which attend upon it—the best of all good things. His adopted tongue, when he translated the book into French, could not do as well by him, since our factitiously blithe 'all good things' is their laconic 'tout': 'Mais tout ayant une fin'.

Naturally there are paradoxes in all this (in what are there not?), for the artist presumably wants to live long enough to fulfil his art. Even Beckett must on occasions have had fears that he might cease to be before his pen had gleaned his teeming brain. There are contradictions, then, in any such dicta. But as Empson insisted, 'Life involves maintaining oneself between contradictions that can't be solved by analysis',[15] and among these contradictions in life there are those of death.

So that to put an emphasis on Beckett's giving voice to the longing for oblivion is not to deny that another emphasis is possible, not least because Beckett makes light of no longings, even the well-acknowledged longing not to end. He is a catholic writer. And he is, for Eric Griffiths, a writer open to Catholic understanding. In the month of Beckett's death, Griffiths wrote with respectful poignancy:

Catholics pray for the dead that they be granted '*refrigerii sedem, quietis beatitudinem, et luminis claritatem*'—'a place of cool refreshment, the blessing of calm, and radiant light'. I do not know (yet) what these words exactly mean, but these words are what I wish for Samuel Beckett. Perhaps I wish this against his wishes, because his writing eloquently often seems to long for absolute cessation, the pulse dropped away to nought. Thus, the last words of the tale he has last published: 'Oh all to end' (*Stirrings Still*). Yet even there, giving up on breath, his words work overtime, mean ever more at the edges of the meaningless. The four monosyllables 'Oh all to end' express both a hope and a regret: 'if only the whole thing would be over', 'how sad that it should stop'.[16]

[14] *Murphy*, 89. Preceding *Murphy* in French, 69. Stevie Smith in 1936 had given the thought quite a turn: 'But all good things come to an end, and the same goes for all bad things' (*Novel on Yellow Paper* (1951 edn.), 155).
[15] In Empson's note to 'Bacchus', *Collected Poems* (1955), 104–5.
[16] *The Independent*, 27 Dec. 1989.

DEATH AS EASE

Beckett has his predecessors, these being at root the same thing etymologically as predeceasers.

In the old days, at least from Spenser to Tennyson, writers who did not wish to be convicted were well advised to put certain convictions into the mouths of figures who were manifestly deluded or corrupt or *in extremis*. The writer could honourably lurk, watching from the hide of a myth or of a dramatization. Then his or her words were allowed to be alive with the disreputable desire for oblivion. Half in love with easeful death, such writers summoned the supreme illicit vision of ease.

There are the artful solicitations of Spenser's Despair, tempting the Redcrosse knight to emulate the suicide before his eyes:

> He there does now enjoy eternall rest
>> And happie ease, which thou doest want and crave,
>> And further from it daily wanderest:
>> What if some litle paine the passage have,
>> That makes fraile flesh to feare the bitter wave?
>> Is not short paine well borne, that brings long ease,
>> And layes the soule to sleepe in quiet grave?
> Sleepe after toyle, port after stormie seas,
> Ease after warre, death after life does greatly please.

> *(The Faerie Queene*, I. ix. st. 40)

Ease preys too upon the mind of the deposed and captive Richard II, near sudden death:

> Then am I king'd againe: and by and by,
> Thinke that I am un-king'd by Bullingbrooke,
> And straight am nothing. But what ere I am,
> Nor I, nor any man, that but man is,
> With nothing shall be pleas'd, till he be eas'd
> With being nothing.

> *(Richard II*, v. v)

Greatest in giving equal voice to both of the counter-truths is *Measure for Measure*, where the Duke-Friar enters into 'Be absolute for death', with all its consolations genuine and not enough, and where later in the same scene (III. i) Claudio breaks into 'Ay, but to die, and go we know not where'.

Or there is Tennyson's 'Tithonus', a poem drafted in respon-

sive 1833 but not published until responsible 1860, a tale of
eternal ageing such as can make not only understandable but
forgivable the death-longing incarnate in long-suffering Tithonus:

> The woods decay, the woods decay and fall,
> The vapours weep their burthen to the ground,
> Man comes and tills the field and lies beneath,
> And after many a summer dies the swan.
> Me only cruel immortality
> Consumes:

William Empson, who judged 'Tithonus' to be 'the best and
deepest' of Tennyson's poems, described it with acute bizarrerie
as 'a poem in favour of the human practice of dying',[17] for all the
world as if humans were the only ones to die. Ah, but they may be
the only ones who could be said to be in favour of it, and who can
muster the witty stoicism of dubbing it 'the human practice of
dying'. And assuredly Tithonus begs for death's favour,

> when the steam
> Floats up from those dim fields about the homes
> Of happy men that have the power to die,
> And grassy barrows of the happier dead.
> Release me, and restore me to the ground.

Among Beckett's truths, then, is one which had sometimes
been indirectly told. His art makes much of convictions, long held
not only by him but by others. None the worse for that. He would
have been the first to say 'Others, I am not the first', were it not
that A. E. Housman had already said as much. But such of
Beckett's immediate predecessors as Housman, Hardy, and
Edward Thomas undertook directness. Each of them found himself reprimanded for his pains: Housman for immaturity, Hardy
for morbidity, and Thomas for self-pity.

Randall Jarrell spiritedly defended a poem by Housman:

In other words, death is better than life, nothing is better than anything.
Nor is this a silly adolescent pessimism peculiar to Housman, as so many
critics assure you. It is better to be dead than alive, best of all never to
have been born—said a poet approvingly advertised as seeing life steadily
and seeing it whole.[18]

---

[17] From a BBC programme (1972) on Tennyson; excerpted in the *Tennyson
Research Bulletin*, 4/3 (Nov. 1984), 108.

[18] 'Texts from Housman' (1939); *Kipling, Auden & Co.* (1980), 27.

If Sophocles, or his chorus in *Oedipus at Colonus*, can be so 'approvingly advertised' by Matthew Arnold,[19] why has Housman been judged unsteady and partial?

> It nods and curtseys and recovers
>   When the wind blows above,
> The nettle on the graves of lovers
>   That hanged themselves for love.
>
> The nettle nods, the wind blows over,
>   The man, he does not move,
> The lover of the grave, the lover
>   That hanged himself for love.

> (*A Shropshire Lad*, XVI)

Jarrell recovers the diverse life of this poem in his supreme elicitings from it.[20] And Jarrell, his death, something between an accident and a suicide? He too was by way of being a lover of the grave, with all the equivocation of the English 'of'. A vintage detective-story *Murder of My Aunt* dextrously had the aunt in the end doing the murdering.

Housman endorsed the chorus in Sophocles. But when Beckett came to invoke the Sophoclean thought, there was an unexpected diversion of it, a settling for comparatively small mercies. In *Murphy*, Neary will escape the long arm of the law, thanks to his friend's resourceful pretence that Neary is an errant lunatic:

'Never fear, sergeant,' he said, urging Neary towards the exit, 'back to the cell, blood heat, next best thing to never being born, no heroes, no fisc, no—'[21]

Our old (best) friend, the 'next best thing to never being born'? But no, *not* death, which is unexpectedly not summoned, but the other lesser asylum, the amniotic padded cell. Not so much, then, the 'next best thing to never being born', as the next best thing to

---

[19] In 'To a Friend':

> Who saw life steadily, and saw it whole;
> The mellow glory of the Attic stage,
> Singer of sweet Colonus, and its child.

[20] *Kipling, Auden & Co.*, 25–8.
[21] *Murphy*, 44. Preceding *Murphy* in French, 37–8:

—Soyez tranquille, dit-il, tout en poussant Neary vers la sortie. Rien de tel que la cellule, chaleur du sang, le rêve faute de ne pas naître, pas de héros, pas de fisc, pas . . .

the next best thing to never being born. Beckett knows the soft
spot for the antepenultimate or rather for its approach: 'Premoni-
tion of the last but one but one'.[22]

Ultimately, though, there is nothing to compare with the ultimate
asylum; there is no substitute for nothing.

Hardy stood his ground:

People call me a pessimist; and if it is pessimism to think, with Sophocles,
that 'not to have been born is best', then I do not reject the designation.[23]

Michael Millgate has compiled a sombre comical dossier of
Hardy's wholehearted devotion to the death-enhancing:

Where he differed from so many of his contemporaries was in the
absoluteness, the literalness, with which he believed that not to be born
was best, that consciousness was a curse, and that while death might be
distressing to the bereaved the dead were not themselves to be pitied.
'*Heu mihi, quia incolatus meus prolongatus est!*'; so wrote Hardy inside the
back cover of his copy of *The Missal for the Use of the Laity*, marking
also the passage and its translation ('Woe is me, that my sojourning is
prolonged!') at the point at which they occurred within the volume. In
February 1896 he insisted in conversation with Clodd that he wished he
had never been born, and 'but for the effort of dying, would rather be
dead than alive'; on Christmas Day 1890 he made a note for a poem:
'*The amusement of the dead*—at our errors, or at our wanting to live on'.
He told the grieving Rider Haggards that a child's death was 'never
really to be regretted, when one reflects on what he has escaped', and
when writing to Mrs Henniker about the fighting in South Africa, at a
time when her husband was still on active service there, allowed himself
to remark: 'It is sad, or not, as you look at it, to think that 40,000 will
have found their rest there. Could we ask them if they wish to wake up
again, would they say Yes, do you think?'[24]

A central critical question about Hardy's art is whether he
achieved ways with words constitutive of such a conviction rather
than just respectful of it. For those of us to whom Hardy the poet
is incomparably greater than Hardy the novelist, the very words of
his poems more corporeally realize this engraining, this wish to be

---

[22] *Molloy* (1955), 8. Following *Molloy* (1951) in French, 9: 'C'est le sens de
l'avant-dernier'. How the original French lacks, in comparison, the syntax of weakness,
the halt and the lame: 'but one but one'.

[23] In conversation with William Archer in 1901; Michael Millgate, *Thomas Hardy: A
Biography* (1982), 410.

[24] *Thomas Hardy*, 411.

ever dissolved to wan wistlessness or to existlessness.[25] This last is
a word which spectrally shadows forth its own inability to exist—
or which, to put it more routinely, fails to gain admission into even
the 'Second Edition' of the *Oxford English Dictionary*.

Hardy is lapped in lead and he overlaps with Beckett. In
Beckett's early short story 'Yellow', Belacqua awaits what he is
assured is a minor operation. The story opens with a bounce:

> The night-nurse bounced in on the tick of five and turned on the light.
> Belacqua waked feeling greatly refreshed and eager to wrestle with this
> new day. He had underlined, as quite a callow boy, a phrase in Hardy's
> *Tess*, won by dint of cogging in the Synod: *When grief ceases to be
> speculative, sleep sees her opportunity*. He had manipulated that sentence for
> many years now, emending its terms, as joy for grief, to answer his
> occasions, even calling upon it to bear the strain of certain applications
> for which he feared it had not been intended, and still it held good
> through it all. He waked with it now in his mind, as though it had been
> there all the time he slept, holding that fragile place against dreams.[26]

In its weird way this is a great tribute to Hardy, a feat of
manipulation, emendation, and application which amounts to a
form of translation.

Such acts of spiced homage span Beckett's life, from the story
of 1934 to the translation of 1976 in which Beckett rendered
tribute to his like-minded predecessor Sébastien Chamfort.
Beckett's series of renderings claims room for manœuvre with
'After Chamfort', and then gains room for both anachronism and
humility by emending the time-honoured formula to 'Long after
Chamfort'.[27]

Vivre est une maladie dont le sommeil nous soulage toutes les seize
heures. C'est un palliatif; la mort est le remède.

> sleep till death
> healeth
> come ease
> this life disease

---

[25] 'The Voice': 'You being ever dissolved to wan wistlessness' (1923); revised from
'to existlessness' (1919).

[26] Beckett did not translate into French *More Pricks than Kicks* (1934), of which
'Yellow' is the penultimate story.

[27] *Collected Poems 1930–1978* (1984), 167. Translating 'Huit Maximes'.

The line ending suggests that the unit of sense is 'sleep till death', and only after the corner is rounded does there come the consummation devoutly to be wished:

> sleep till death
> healeth

—where 'healeth' has the life in death of archaism, the word entirely understood by the eye and the ear and yet no longer alive on anyone's tongue.

> come ease

—whereupon 'ease' spreads its wings as noun or verb: as summoning ease ('Come, Ease'), or as inciting some shadowed power to come and to ease, 'Come, ease this life' (the syntax would permit of disease's being begged to do so, and the sense might ask death to intervene).

The simple words decline to stay put.

> this life disease

—is this a compound (like life insurance), an apposition (this life which is disease), or a disjunction which implores the last word, disease, to dispatch its cheek-by-jowl enemy, life? As who should say, 'Come, Disease, ease this life, [albeit against your worse nature]'.

> come ease
> this life disease

Just how splendidly 'Long after Chamfort' Beckett's poem is stationed may be judged by contrasting the minimal distance secured by Chamfort's straighter translator, W. S. Merwin:

Living is an ailment which is relieved every sixteen hours by sleep. A palliative. Death is the cure.[28]

It was left to Beckett to turn Chamfort's aphorism into an elegiac prayer, this with the help of wit and poetry and Pope:

---

[28] *Products of the Perfected Civilization: Selected Writings of Chamfort*, trans. W. S. Merwin (1969), 128.

The Muse but serv'd to ease some Friend, not Wife,
To help me thro' this long Disease, my Life,

(*Epistle to Dr. Arbuthnot*, 131–2)

> sleep till death
> healeth
> come ease
> this life disease[29]

POSITIVE ANNIHILATION

There is one thing which all of Beckett's consciousnesses are freely and unremittingly given: pause.

Yes, the confusion of my ideas on the subject of death was such that I sometimes wondered, believe me or not, if it wasn't a state of being even worse than life.[30]

Here 'believe me or not' slyly splices *believe me/believe it or not*, and insinuates more tellingly than had Beckett's franker French: 'je vous dirai franchement'.

In 1937 Beckett planned his play about Dr Johnson:

All this would come in quite naturally in the last act, i.e. his fearing his death, when he was being reproached by his clerical friend, Taylor, for holding the opinion that an eternity of torment was preferable to annihilation. He must have had the vision of *positive* annihilation. Of how many can as much be said.[31]

[29] Dis-ease/Disease: Beckett was elsewhere lured into error (or assisted by misprision) by being a lover of the grave; twice in *Murphy* (33, 75) he has 'Grave's disease' where it should be Graves's or Graves' disease (Dr R. J. Graves, of Dublin be it noted, 'who in 1835 recognized the individuality of the disease', *OED*). The singularizing slip is retained in the (following) French *Murphy* (30, 59), 'La Maladie de Grave'.

[30] *Molloy*, 91. Following *Molloy* in French, 103: 'Mais pour vous faire entrevoir jusqu'où allait la confusion de mes idées sur la mort, je vous dirai franchement que je n'excluais pas la possibilité qu'elle fût encore pire que la vie, en tant que condition.'

[31] Letter to Joseph Hone, 3 July 1937 (Bair, *Samuel Beckett*, 254). Beckett's 'He' (of 'He must have had the vision of *positive* annihilation') floats free rather, but it might fit Taylor better than Johnson (and Boswell better than Taylor?). The exchange in Boswell (15 Apr. 1778) runs:

MISS SEWARD. 'There is one mode of the fear of death, which is certainly absurd; and that is the dread of annihilation, which is only a pleasing sleep without a dream.' JOHNSON. 'It is neither pleasing, nor sleep; it is nothing. Now mere existence is so much better than nothing, that one would rather exist even in pain, than not exist.' BOSWELL. 'If annihilation be

Some such vision of positive annihilation had been glimpsed in
another of Chamfort's maxims:

Quand on soutient que les gens les moins sensibles sont à tout prendre,
les plus heureux, je me rappelle le proverbe indien: 'Il vaut mieux être
assis que debout, couché qu'assis, mort que tout cela.'[32]

Beckett, aware that about even this thought there hangs the
shadow of complaisance, cropped off the preamble, and then disturbed the proverb with meticulous brutality, so that his hobbled
verses are not only 'Long after Chamfort' but Far from Chamfort:[33]

> Better on your arse than on your feet,
> Flat on your back than either, dead than the lot.

There 'feet', at the end of the first line, rounds at once, in sound
and sense, on 'Flat' at the start of the next; 'feet' and 'Flat' find
themselves back to back, corporeally absurd, and compounded by

---

nothing, then existing in pain is not a comparative state, but is a positive evil, which I cannot
think we should choose.'

It ends:

JOHNSON. 'The lady confounds annihilation, which is nothing, with the apprehension of it,
which is dreadful. It is in the apprehension of it that the horrour of annihilation consists.'

Boswell's comment on 'annihilation' that 'existing in pain . . . is a positive evil' may
have coloured Beckett's phrase 'the vision of *positive* annihilation'. (But Beckett may
also have remembered the italicized *positive*, with the adjacent paradox of 'nihil', from
T. S. Eliot: 'Mr. Lewis proposes a Shakespeare who is a *positive* nihilist'; 'Shakespeare
and the Stoicism of Seneca', 1927; *Selected Essays*, 134.)
    The note in Birkbeck Hill and Powell's Boswell describes Taylor's *Letter to Samuel
Johnson on the Subject of a Future State* (1787); in the advertisement, Taylor wrote that
'having heard that his friend Dr. Johnson had said, that he would prefer a state of
torment to that of annihilation, [he] told him that such a declaration, coming from a
person of his weight and character, might be productive of evil consequences' (*Life of
Johnson* (1934), iii. 295–7).
    Beckett was pondering Johnson for a play, *Human Wishes*, of which he wrote only
the opening scene (*Disjecta* (1983), 155–66). Johnson's great title, lopped for the play,
figures in full and in fun within *Watt*, where the names of Vincent and Walter are
tirelessly reiterated, 'and so on, until all trace is lost, on account of the vanity of human
wishes' (p. 60). Preceding *Watt* in French, 61: 'et ainsi de suite, jusqu'à ce que toute
trace se soit perdue, à cause de la vanité des espérances humaines'. On Beckett's
Human Wishes, see Lionel Kelly, in John Pilling and Mary Bryden (eds.), *The Ideal Core
of the Onion* (1992), 21–44.
    [32] Translated by W. S. Merwin (*Products of the Perfected Civilization*, 134): 'When it
is maintained that the insensitive, on the whole, are happiest, I remember the Indian
proverb: "It is better to be sitting than standing; it is better to be lying down than
sitting; it is better to be dead than anything".'
    [33] *Collected Poems*, 159.

the prompt apt 'Flat on your back'. Clinched, finally, with 'dead than the lot', where the upshot is not only the whole kit and boodle but a humbling of the grander sense of the human *lot*. The word had been treated with suspect respect in one of Beckett's translations from the Spanish, where Hope is indicted:

> Who rid thee of the name of homicide?
> For thou art crueler still, if well we mark
> that thou suspendest the deluded soul
>
> between a wretched and a happy lot,
> not to the end that life may be preserved,
> but to inflict a more protracted death.[34]

Not that, in the end, our lot need much matter to us lot. It matters whether the here-and-now is a wretched or a happy lot; the happy lot will be the there-and-then of our quietus. Until which time, there is the killing of time, the pastime.

I was speaking then was I not of my little pastimes and I think about to say that I ought to content myself with them, instead of launching forth on all this ballsaching poppycock about life and death, if that is what it is all about, and I suppose it is, for nothing was ever about anything else to the best of my recollection. But what it is all about exactly I could no more say, at the present moment, than take up my bed and walk. It's vague, life and death. I must have had my little private idea on the subject when I began, otherwise I would not have begun, I would have held my peace, I would have gone on peacefully being bored to howls, having my little fun and games with the cones and cylinders, the millet grains beloved of birds and other panics, until someone was kind enough to come and coffin me. But it is gone clean out of my head, my little private idea. No matter, I have just had another. Perhaps it is the same one back again, ideas are so alike, when you get to know them. Be born, that's the brainwave now, that is to say live long enough to get acquainted with free carbonic gas, then say thanks for the nice time and go.[35]

[34] Juana de Asbaje, in *Anthology of Mexican Poetry*, translated by Beckett (1958), 84.
[35] *Malone Dies*, 51. Following *Malone meurt*, 83–4:

Je parlais donc de mes petites distractions et allais dire je crois que je ferais mieux de m'en contenter au lieu de me lancer dans ces histoires à crever debout de vie et de mort, si c'est bien de cela qu'il est question, et je suppose que oui, car il n'a jamais été question d'autre chose, à mon souvenir. Mais dire de quoi il retourne exactement, j'en serais bien incapable, à présent. C'est vague, la vie et la mort. J'ai dû avoir ma petite idée, quand j'ai commencé, sinon je n'aurais pas commencé, je me serais tenu tranquille, j'aurais continué tranquillement à m'ennuyer ferme, en faisant joujou, avec les cones et cylindres par exemple, avec les grains du millet des oiseaux et autres panics, en attendant qu'on veuille bien venir prendre mes mesures. Mais elle m'est sortie de la tête, ma petite idée. Qu'à cela ne tienne,

Bored, not alas to death, and not quite to tears, but to howls. And with what courteous alliterative deftness the verb *to coffin* is admitted ('kind enough to come and coffin me'). Admitted, not invented: Beckett is miraculously getting the old verb back on its feet ('I could no more say, at the present moment, than take up my bed and walk'), it having seen the light in 1564, and having graced *Coriolanus*, and having been in retirement since 1861. (The author of *Death's Jest-Book* relished it.) Not but what it had darkly suited Beckett's Dantesque undertaker Mr Malacoda in *More Pricks than Kicks*, 'Mr. Malacoda. Keen to coffin'.[36]

Such writing is more than just 'ballsaching poppycock', albeit not for its creator's creature but for the creator and his readers—but only as long as we agree not to consider it *sub specie aeternitatis*. The same goes for 'little pastimes'. Time, unlike eternity, can be passed.

As for 'all this ballsaching poppycock' and 'thanks for the nice time and go': these come together as goodbye, young lover.

Peggy Guggenheim set down her level memories of Beckett the young lover—not that she should have expected an especial bump of amativeness from someone whose attitude to bed had already prompted others to dub him, after Goncharov's anti-hero, *Oblomov*, bed-written:

> He did not make his intentions clear but in an awkward way asked me to lie down on the sofa next to him. We soon found ourselves in bed, where we remained until the next evening at dinner-time. We might be there still, but I had to go to dine with Arp, who unfortunately had no telephone. I don't know why, but I mentioned champagne, and Oblomov rushed out and bought several bottles which we drank in bed. When Oblomov left, he said very simply and fatalistically, as though we were never going to meet again, 'Thank you. It was nice while it lasted.'[37]

'Then say thanks for the nice time and go.'

Swift had understood the conjunction:

Although reason were intended by providence to govern our passions, yet

---

je viens d'en avoir une autre. C'est peut-être la même, les idées se ressemblent tellement, quand on les connaît. Naître, voilà mon idée à présent, c'est-à-dire vivre le temps de savoir ce que c'est que le gaz carbonique libre, plus remercier. Ça a toujours été mon rêve au fond. Toutes les choses qui ont toujours été mon rêve au fond. Tant de cordes et jamais une flèche.

[36] 'Draff', *More Pricks than Kicks*, 268.
[37] Peggy Guggenheim, *Out of this Century* (1946), 194–5.

it seems that, in two points of the greatest moment to the being and continuance of the world, God hath intended our passions to prevail over reason. The first is, the propagation of our species, since no wise man ever married from the dictates of reason. The other is, the love of life, which, from the dictates of reason, every man would despise, and wish it at an end, or that it never had a beginning.[38]

Beckett declined to propagate his species, and he squinnied at the love of life, sharing Byron's surprise:

> While life's strange principle will often lie
> Deepest in those who long the most to die.[39]

Beckett's fictions bodied, and not just bodied forth, Swift's principle:

It is impossible that anything so natural, so necessary, and so universal as death, should ever have been designed by providence as an evil to mankind.[40]

Except only that Beckett did not believe in providence and its designs, he being willing to go no further than to be mildly grateful to it for not existing. For providence could have been counted on to be up to no good, nothing but good intentions paving the way to our living hell:

There is a providence for impotent old men, to the end. And when they cannot swallow any more someone rams a tube down their gullet, or up their rectum, and fills them full of vitaminized pap, so as not to be accused of murder.[41]

No providence, then, but the memory of its having been imagined. Just as Beckett was never able to shake the dust of Ireland off his feet (dust not being shakeable off feet), so he was never able to exorcize the religious convictions which had ceased to convince. He won his way by yielding to the tide, ebb and all. Bishop Ken

[38] 'Thoughts on Religion'.
[39] *Don Juan*, canto IV, st. 11. [40] 'Thoughts on Religion'.
[41] *Malone Dies*, 81. Following *Malone meurt*, 131:

Aux vieillards impotents on donne la pâture, jusqu'au bout. Et quand ils ne peuvent plus ingurgiter on leur enfile un tuyau dans l'œsophage, ou dans le rectum, et on leur entonne de la bouillie vitaminée, histoire de ne pas avoir un meurtre sur les bras.

Where 'on donne la pâture' was silkily pastoral (verging on being put out to grass?), 'There is a providence for impotent old men' is a potent blasphemy. 'There's a speciall Providence in the fall of a sparrow' (*Hamlet*, v. ii).

no doubt played his part in teaching this Oblomov to dread the grave as little as his bed. Instead of Taylor's Christian *Holy Dying*, Beckett wrote and rewrote his secular *Wholly Dying*, aware that Holy and Wholly are cognate, and praying, nonsensically though reasonably enough, not that we should all be saved, but that we should all be wholly lost, 'to Death devote'.

But he did not stare at death, he contemplated it.

Books about death are too prone to concur supinely with the cliché that we should be the better for fronting death more than we do. But it was a good and sane man who found himself remonstrating about his friend's confrontation with skulls and with charnel knowledge: ''Twere to consider too curiously to consider so.'

For the thanatologists too little ponder some of their dearest citations. Take, for instance, La Rochefoucauld's famous apophthegm:

Comme le soleil, la mort ne peut être regardée fixement.

But it is not enough to quote La Rochefoucauld if you have no intention of attending to the implications of his profound saying, which are two. First, that it would be an act of hubris to stare steadfastly upon death, as upon the sun; not only is there no need to do it, there is a need not to do it. Second, the apophthegm asks us to see death as a benign force, a counterpart to the great source of life, the sun, from which likewise we benefit provided that we don't crassly fix our eyes upon it. The thanatologists slight both these implications.

In this they are unlike Nietzsche, who understands art as the smoked glass through which we may contemplate the eclipse of our hopes—but also of our fears: 'We have art that we may not perish of the truth.'

So that although it makes sense to read Beckett, as many do, as a writer who is oddly criss-crossed, a writer who manages to be excruciatingly funny despite his possessing a deeply dispiriting apprehension of life, the opposite makes sense too: the conviction that Beckett's apprehension of death is not dispiriting, but is wise and fortifying, and therefore is unsurprisingly the lens of his translucent comedy.

In his first book, *Proust*, when 'future time' was mostly in his hour-glass, he wrote of future time:

Lazily considered in anticipation and in the haze of our smug will to live, of our pernicious and incurable optimism, it seems exempt from the bitterness of fatality: in store for us, not in store in us.[42]

There 'pernicious' must strike sparks off 'incurable'. Nothing is incurable, or rather *nothing* will cure everything, just as death (the sentiment was Proust's before it became Beckett) will cure many of the desire for immortality.[43]

'Pernicious and incurable': like one of his characters, Beckett had what he drily called a strong weakness for oxymoron. And for oxymoron's unlikely twin, tautology (unidentical twin but liking to twin): alive in such a cry as 'Blessed be the dead that die!' This imagines a conclusive liberty by taking liberties with *Revelation* 14: 13: 'Blessed are the dead which die'—ah, but not stopping there: 'Blessed are the dead which die in the Lord from henceforth.'

The tautology of death[44] creates at last its gratifying click not only in such a cry as

Blessed be the dead that die![45]

but also in the old nursery rhyme:

> Happy are the wed that the sun shines on,
> Blessed are the dead that the rain rains on.

This comfortingly accommodates the very different things which it might mean (good omens, or good states of being, or degrees of

---

[42] *Proust*, 5.
[43] *Proust*, 14. *A la recherche du temps perdu, Albertine disparue*:

Notre amour de la vie n'est qu'une vieille liaison dont nous ne savons pas nous débarrasser. Sa force est dans sa permanence. Mais la mort qui la rompt nous guérira du désir de l'immortalité.

[44] Steven Connor elucidates the energies of 'entropic tautology' in *Samuel Beckett: Repetition, Theory and Text* (1988), 104–5.
[45] But the cry is sardonically set, even more so in the English than in the French because of what becomes of 's'écriera'. *Mercier and Camier* (1974), 115:

His loss is so recent. Tomorrow, before his porridge, he will redden at the recollection.
He will wipe his lips, said Mercier, slip his napkin back into its ring, clasp his hands and ejaculate, Blessed be the dead that die!

Following *Mercier et Camier* (1970), 201:

Son deuil est si récent! Demain, devant son porridge, il en aura honte.
Il s'essuiera la bouche, dit Mercier, il glissera la serviette dans le rond, il joindra les deux mains et il s'écriera, Heureux les morts qui meurent!

felicity), this kindly multiplicity then working against the tautology,
'rain rains on', of meaning the *one* thing *twice*.

The tautology, 'rain rains', seeps deep. As in Edward Thomas's
'Rain':

> Rain, midnight rain, nothing but the wild rain
> On this bleak hut, and solitude, and me
> Remembering again that I shall die
> And neither hear the rain nor give it thanks
> For washing me cleaner than I have been
> Since I was born into this solitude.
> Blessed are the dead that the rain rains upon:
> But here I pray that none whom once I loved
> Is dying tonight or lying still awake
> Solitary, listening to the rain,
> Either in pain or thus in sympathy
> Helpless among the living and the dead,
> Like a cold water among broken reeds,
> Myriads of broken reeds all still and stiff,
> Like me who have no love which this wild rain
> Has not dissolved except the love of death,
> If love it be towards what is perfect and
> Cannot, the tempest tells me, disappoint.

The greatness of Edward Thomas's poem, audible in its
achieving so much more than either acquiescence or repining, is
the more evident in contrast with the interminably flowing and
even flattering prose in which Thomas had earlier failed to convince his nerves. There are nearly a thousand words of this,
beginning

I lay awake listening to the rain, and at first it was as pleasant to my ear
and my mind as it had long been desired; but before I fell asleep it had
become a majestic and finally a terrible thing, instead of a sweet sound
and symbol. It was accusing and trying me and passing judgment. Long I
lay still under the sentence, listening to the rain, and then at last listening
to words which seemed to be spoken by a ghostly double beside me.

And ending:

Now there is neither life nor death, but only the rain. Sleep as all things,
past, present, and future, lie still and sleep, except the rain, the heavy,
black rain falling straight through the air that was once a sea of life. That
was a dream only. The truth is that the rain falls for ever and I am

melting into it. Black and monotonously sounding is the midnight and
solitude of the rain. In a little while or in an age—for it is all one—I
shall know the full truth of the words I used to love, I knew not why, in
my days of nature, in the days before the rain: 'Blessed are the dead that
the rain rains on'.[46]

No, Thomas knew the full truth of those words only when he was
less full of words; that is, in the inspired economy of his tautly
tautological poem.

Beckett, too, in his poems too, is half in love with death-dealing
tautology, its lavish perfect fit, whether momentarily replacing
death by life:

> the summer rain rains on my life[47]

—or whether surrendering itself to death's obduracy and its
elements:

> I would like my love to die
> and the rain to be raining on the graveyard
> and on me walking the streets
> mourning her who thought she loved me[48]

When Jack MacGowran gave a BBC reading of the poems in
1966, he was privileged with changes by Beckett at the studio
rehearsals, including the change from 'and the rain to be falling
on the graveyard' to 'and the rain to be raining on the graveyard'.
The earlier reading (still in *Poems in English*, 1961) had not
arrived at such 'entropic tautology'.

Nineteenth-century hopefulness set itself to accept the universe,
including, reluctantly, its entropy. Twentieth-century hopefulness,
to accept death? But acceptance could never be quite it. If our

[46] *The Icknield Way* (written 1911), 280–3; given by R. George Thomas in *The
Collected Poems of Edward Thomas* (1978), 407–8, with the wise words: 'For an earlier,
and deceptively similar, prose account of Thomas's response to the rain, see . . .'

[47] The French cannot exact such a fit: 'la pluie d'été pleut sur ma vie'. *Collected
Poems*, 59: 'my way is in the sand flowing'. Following 'je suis ce cours de sable qui
glisse'. On a relation of tautology to the short circuit (likewise preoccupying Beckett),
see ch. 3 n. 27 below.

[48] *Collected Poems*, 63. Following the French (p. 62), which denies itself the
tautology of rain raining:

> je voudrais que mon amour meure
> qu'il pleuve sur le cimetière
> et les ruelles où je vais
> pleurant celle qui crut m'aimer

own imminent death is the issue, acceptance asks too much of us; if the fact of general mortality is the issue, acceptance is too grudging. For life would be unimaginably worse if we had to imagine it without death.

It was Robert Lowell, a conscientious objector and not a pacifist, who appreciated that 'the one thing worse than war is massacre'.[49]

The one thing worse than not living for ever would be living for ever.

NEVER DYING

William Blake knew, whether or not torment may hereafter prove eternal, that eternity may itself be a torment to contemplate:

> Time is the mercy of Eternity; without Times swiftness
> Which is the swiftest of all things: all were eternal torment[50]

True, Blake elsewhere assured us that 'Eternity is in love with the productions of time', but the elsewhere is the 'Proverbs of Hell', and in any case no assurance is given that time is in love with the productions of eternity.

Time is the mercy of eternity. Death is, among other things, the mercy of time; but there is very little literature that does justice to this mercy.

Death has not been given a fair crack of the whip.

Socially conscious death-studiers, thanatologists, speak unmisgivingly of 'the human aspiration to live for ever'.[51] As if no counter-aspiration were ever felt.

One surreptitious way, in the old days, for Christians and other afterlifers to acknowledge this half of the truth, and bring home the thought, incompatible with their system of rewards and punishments, that an eternity of consciousness would inherently be torture, was duly to imagine an eternity of torture. To the point at

---

[49] 'Struggle of Non-Existence', *History* (1973), 155:

> since Eden when the funk of Abel proved
> the one thing worse than war is massacre...

(Lowell's ellipsis.)

[50] *Milton* (1804–?8), plate 23: 72–3; *William Blake's Writings*, ed. G. E. Bentley, Jr. (1978), i. 369.

[51] Robert Jay Lifton and Eric Olson, *Living and Dying* (1974), 69.

which some part, at least, of even the most devout conscience might on occasion feel the force incarnate in the Miltonic words 'and now to Death devote'.[52]

Of Beckett's forerunners in embodying this direction in which desire of oblivion may run, the greatest are famously Swift, Milton, and Dante.

Swift, because of the Struldbruggs.

When they came to Fourscore Years, which is reckoned the Extremity of living in this Country, they had not only all the Follies and Infirmities of other old Men, but many more which arose from the dreadful Prospect of never dying. They were not only opinionative, peevish, covetous, morose, vain, talkative; but uncapable of Friendship, and dead to all natural Affection, which never descended below their Grand-children. Envy and impotent Desires, are their prevailing Passions. But those Objects against which their Envy seems principally directed, are the Vices of the younger Sort, and the Deaths of the old. By reflecting on the former, they find themselves cut off from all Possibility of Pleasure; and whenever they see a Funeral, they lament and repine that others are gone to an Harbour of Rest, to which they themselves never can hope to arrive.

At Ninety they lose their Teeth and Hair; they have at that Age no Distinction of Taste, but eat and drink whatever they can get, without Relish or Appetite. The Diseases they were subject to, still continue without encreasing or diminishing. In talking they forget the common Appellation of Things, and the Names of Persons, even of those who are their nearest Friends and Relations. For the same Reason they never can amuse themselves with reading, because their Memory will not serve to carry them from the Beginning of a Sentence to the End; and by this Defect they are deprived of the only Entertainment whereof they might otherwise be capable.[53]

It should be with a wrung understanding that we read the sentence about the fact that if we live long enough, we shall no longer be in any condition to read a sentence; and it is a grim stroke which does *not* place this thought, 'to the End', at the end of the sentence, but grants it only the pause which is still in its prime:

they never can amuse themselves with reading, because their Memory will not serve to carry them from the Beginning of a Sentence to the End; and by this Defect . . .

---

[52] *Paradise Lost*, ix. 901.   [53] *Gulliver's Travels: A Voyage to Laputa*, ch. X.

If unable even to read, then *a fortiori* (a strong phrase from a dead language, a phrase which Beckett particularly relishes when he is speaking of intensities of *weakness*), how much the more true of speaking or of writing.

Beckett is the master of these unmasterable Struldbruggian sentences.

Molloy compares one damaged leg with the other damaged one:

For it was shortening, don't forget, whereas the other, though stiffening, was not yet shortening, or so far behind its fellow that to all intents and purposes, intents and purposes, I'm lost, no matter.[54]

'Their Memory will not serve to carry them': any more than their legs. The solicitous admonition 'don't forget' lags far behind those disabled 'intents and purposes'. And on these occasions *no matter* undertakes what is variously done by Beckett's French 'ça ne fait rien' or 'enfin'; 'no matter' being a casualness as well as a casualty, a mind imagining its final triumph over matter, while having to imagine that from one perspective mind *is* matter.[55]

No matter does good by stealth. As with an unbodied love:

Not that I miss Ninette. But she, at least, who knows, in any case, yes, a pity, no matter.[56]

Or for an eager collapsion:

The fact would seem to be, if in my situation one may speak of facts, not only that I shall have to speak of things of which I cannot speak, but also, which is even more interesting, but also that I, which is if possible even more interesting, that I shall have to, I forget, no matter.[57]

---

[54] *Molloy*, 104. Following *Molloy* in French, 118:

Car elle se raccourcissait, ne l'oublions pas, tandis que l'autre, tout en se raidissant, ne se raccourcissait pas encore, ou avec un tel retard sur sa camarade que c'était tout comme, tout comme, je suis perdu, ça ne fait rien.

[55] *Malone Dies*, 51: 'But it is gone clean out of my head, my little private idea. No matter, I have just had another.' Following *Malone meurt*, 84: 'Mais elle m'est sortie de la tête, ma petite idée. Qu'à cela ne tienne, je viens d'en avoir une autre.'

[56] *Molloy*, 238. Following *Molloy* in French, 268: 'Non pas que je regrette Ninette. Mais elle, peut-être, de toute façon, oui, dommage, enfin.'

[57] *The Unnamable* (1958), 4. Following *L'innommable* (1953), 8:

Le fait semble être, si dans la situation où je suis on peut parler de faits, non seulement que je vais avoir à parler de choses dont je ne peux parler, mais encore, ce qui est encore plus

It was the living death of the Struldbruggs which moved Gulliver, alive to *peine forte et dure*, to his *mot juste*: 'They were the most mortifying Sight I ever beheld'. And which moved him to expatiate upon this contracted extorted life, 'without Relish or Appetite', in these glacial accents: 'The Reader will easily believe, that from what I had heard and seen, my keen Appetite for Perpetuity of Life was much abated.'

Beckett when young had already known these abatements. In the story 'What a Misfortune' from *More Pricks than Kicks*, there is an aged man attending the marriage ceremony, 'a kind of moot Struldbrug'.[58] This turn may have its own living death, given the unsettling range within the term 'moot' (*OED*: 'That can be argued; debatable; not decided, doubtful'). Given, too, that *to moot* is not only to raise for debate but (a different verb at the root) to dig up.

And how might Gulliver recognize a Struldbrug?

He told me, that sometimes, although very rarely, a Child happened to be born in a Family with a red circular Spot in the Forehead, directly over the left Eye-brow, which was an infallible Mark that it should never dye.

Which may conduct us to the second of Beckett's great predecessors in imagining the horror of eternity: Dante, where the high-minded vengeance of God declines to furnish that oblivion for which the sufferers cry out.

From first to last Dante was crucial to the author whose final days at the end of 1989 were spent with a copy of *The Divine Comedy*, and whose first story in his first work of fiction, *More Pricks than Kicks*, in 1934, is called 'Dante and the Lobster'.

There we meet the infallible mark of Cain, his 'countenance fallen and branded, seared with the first stigma of God's pity, that an outcast might not die quickly'.[59] For 'the LORD set a mark upon Cain, lest any finding him should kill him'.[60]

The mark has been much mooted. Ruth Mellinkoff, in *The Mark of Cain*, recognizes that it is itself moot:

---

intéressant, que je, ce qui est encore plus intéressant, que je, je ne sais plus, ça ne fait rien. *The Unnamable* has such crumplings: 'parenthesis unfinished' and 'forgotten my apodosis' (pp. 47, 162). Following *L'innommable*, 71, 237: 'parenthèse inachevée', 'j'ai oublié l'apodose'. [58] *More Pricks than Kicks*, 181.
[59] *More Pricks than Kicks*, 5. [60] *Gen.* 4: 15.

It could denote divine forgiveness, thus suggesting that the mark was a positive and protective device. But most often the mark, though protective, also denoted punishment. It functioned simultaneously as condemnation-curse and taboo-protection.[61]

In such a contradiction, the mark of Cain is whetted to the same two-edged and two-handed enginery as is Beckett's word 'stigma': Cain 'fallen and branded, seared with the first stigma of God's pity':

stigma

1. A mark made upon the skin by burning with a hot iron (rarely, by cutting or pricking), as a token of infamy or subjection; a brand.
2. *fig.* A mark of disgrace or infamy.
3. *pl.* Marks resembling the wounds on the crucified body of Christ, said to have been supernaturally impressed on the bodies of certain saints and other devout persons. (*OED*)

The marks of disgrace can become marks of grace.

'... God's pity, that an outcast might not die quickly'. The first outcasts were Adam and Eve, and in our literature it is Milton who most unforgettably gives voice, in the new-fallen Adam's voice, to the longing for oblivion and the fear of not dying quickly, God's cruel lenience, the stigma of God's pity:

> O welcom hour whenever! why delayes
> His hand to execute what his Decree
> Fixd on this day? why do I overlive,
> Why am I mockt with death, and length'nd out
> To deathless pain? how gladly would I meet
> Mortalitie my sentence, and be Earth
> Insensible, how glad would lay me down
> As in my Mothers lap?
>
>   (*Paradise Lost*, x. 771–8)

>   Yet one doubt
> Pursues me still, least all I cannot die,
> Least that pure breath of Life, the Spirit of Man
> Which God inspir'd, cannot together perish
> With this corporeal Clod; then in the Grave,
> Or in some other dismal place, who knows
> But I shall die a living Death?
>
>   (x. 782–8)

[61] *The Mark of Cain* (1981), 101.

'As in my Mothers lap': but best of all, never to have been born;

> how gladly would I meet
> Mortalitie my sentence

—where 'Mortality' is met alliteratively at the turning of the line, the playing of a death-sentence against an ending.

Adam had eyes to see:

> Since this days Death denounc't, if ought I see,
> Will prove no sudden, but a slow-pac't evill,
> A long days dying to augment our paine,
> And to our Seed (O hapless Seed!) deriv'd.
>
> (x. 962–4)

'That an outcast might not die quickly': in due course the last words of 'Dante and the Lobster', a story which has imagined the imminent execution of the murderer McCabe and the eternities of the Inferno, take in all life:

> She lifted the lobster clear of the table. It had about thirty seconds to live.
> Well, thought Belacqua, it's a quick death, God help us all.
> It is not.[62]

That is a clincher of a final paragraph, or rather, that is an unflinching series of conclusive paragraphs.

A grim pun has reaping still to do: 'a quick death'/'that an outcast might not die quickly'. In the bitter play of the quick and the dead there is the most potent realization of what a living death is, including what it might be to be boiled alive.

The archaism of 'quick' as living, which now so lends itself to the bantering or the arch (pedestrians in our cities may be divided into the quick and the dead), is itself an incarnation of a death-principle within the living, for what else could a comprehensible archaism be?

In Beckett's book on *Proust* there is the insistence that 'the dead annex the quick as surely as the Kingdom of France annexes the Duchy of Orléans'.[63]

In the closing couplet of his translation of Paul Eluard's 'Confections',[64] the French 'vivants' is rendered by a word less simply alive in the English language, albeit unmistakable:

---

[62] *More Pricks than Kicks*, 20.   [63] *Proust*, 25.   [64] *Collected Poems*, 123.

Fatal sun of the quick
One cannot keep thy heart.

Or there is the macabre rendering-down in *Murphy*, where the spiritualist is understood to be 'no ordinary hack medium': 'she could make the dead softsoap the quick in seven languages'.[65] The language is horribly alive, and yet alive with death: 'make the dead softsoap the quick' or 'make the dead softsoap'? Such softsoaping is 'no ordinary' flattery. Not least because of what becomes of the dead:

adipocere
A greyish white fatty or saponaceous substance ... spontaneously generated in dead bodies buried in moist places or submerged in water. [e.g.] 1836 Adipocere . . is a soap composed of margaric acid and ammonia. 1877 The conversion of muscle into adipocere after death is a form of fatty degeneration. (*OED*)[66]

Soapy, and soap can be made out of it; or, life in death and death in life. 'She could make the dead softsoap the quick in seven languages': this converts muscle into adipocere, the language itself a form of fatty degeneration.

Such life in the language, spontaneously generated in dead bodies, is itself 'quick with death', to adopt a phrase from 'Text',[67] an early uncollected poem (1931) which turns to Cain and has many filaments to 'Dante and the Lobster':

pity is quick with death

—'quick with death', for pity runneth soon in gentle heart, and because man's pity, unlike 'God's pity', will grant a quick death; but also 'quick with death' as alive with it—and therefore open to corruption.

Well, thought Belacqua, it's a quick death, God help us all.
It is not.

---

[65] *Murphy*, 104. Preceding *Murphy* in French (78–9): 'n'avait rien du médium professionnel ordinaire', 'elle savait faire amadouer en sept langues les vivants par les morts'.

[66] This reproduces the *OED*'s convention of signalling its omission of material with two rather than three points; likewise in subsequent citations.

[67] *The European Caravan*, ed. Samuel Putnam *et al.* (1931), 478–80. There is an invaluably learned exegesis of this obscure and allusive poem in Lawrence E. Harvey, *Samuel Beckett Poet and Critic* (1970), 287–96.

'It is not': the word *it* (with *its* and *it's*) comes thirteen times in the closing half-page of the story; the first eleven times it is the lobster. But in the end ... It is not.

The most basic English, it is the best of worst endings. Or so one would have said. But Beckett entertained the thought that perhaps 'It is not'. And then apparently thought better of that.

The anecdote may be approached through one of Yeats at a rehearsal for a broadcast reading of his poetry. An actor was busy about the first lines of 'Sailing to Byzantium':

> That is no country for old men. The young
> In one another's arms; birds in the trees

Yeats exclaimed 'Stop! That is the worst bit of syntax I ever wrote', and promptly changed it to:

> Old men should quit a country where the young
> In one another's arms; birds in the trees

Donald Davie's heart warmed to this:

This is a change which would have warmed the heart of Ernest Fenollosa. The copula and the negative are replaced by the energetic verb 'quit'. The syntax of the first version was correct enough; but by the revision the poem is given from the first line a backbone, a head and a tail, a drive to carry through the clutter of images that follow.[68]

But are 'drive' and 'the energetic' altogether right in such circumstances? Yeats did well to stand by the initial reluctant acknowledgement 'That is no country for old men'. And only thereafter to sail out to a world of death in life in art.

Enoch Brater, in *why beckett* (1989), tells a similar tale:

In 1986 Beckett told Barry McGovern, who did a dramatic reading of the story for Irish radio, that he would now reconsider this abrupt conclusion. After listening to a tape of McGovern's recitation, he let the young Irish actor know that 'maybe' he would 'change' the last line. It might read, he suggested, more Dantesque as follows:

Well, thought Belacqua, it's a quick death, God help us all.
Like hell it is.[69]

---

[68] *Articulate Energy* (1955), 125. The anecdote, reported by George Barnes, is from Joseph Hone, *W. B. Yeats, 1865–1939* (1942), 456.

[69] *Why beckett* (1989), 32.

Gone would be the bleached inexorable abstraction, so chilling, of 'It is not'. Instead, with gain but loss, a brave sardonic defiance in the face of such abstraction: 'Like hell it is'.

'Better? Worse? Can't decide.'[70] Both. But either way 'a quick death' is a living death, whether in hell or as being hell. Boiled alive to death.

Or burnt alive, through all eternity. Robert Lowell ends 'Mr. Edwards and the Spider':

> But who can plumb the sinking of that soul?
> Josiah Hawley, picture yourself cast
> > Into a brick-kiln where the blast
> > Fans your quick vitals to a coal—
> > > If measured by a glass,
> How long would it seem burning! Let there pass
> A minute, ten, ten trillion; but the blaze
> Is infinite, eternal: this is death,
> > To die and know it. This is the Black Widow, death.

The horror is in the exclamation mark, for 'How long would it seem burning!' is not a question since it permits of no imaginable answer.

CERTIFIED DEATH

No quick death could be quick enough, and no quick death can be contemplated without such suffering as leaves language far behind—and yet which language can evince in the resistance which 'quick' puts up to 'death'. Some deaths may be distinguished from what, even if we don't like the sound of it, we have to prefer: fully certified death.

Blind Mr Rooney, in the radio play *All That Fall*, dreading retirement, dreads yet more 'the horrors of home life', the days of the week. Whereupon he conjures up a benign form of a disconcerting conjunction of life and death, not—this time—being boiled alive, but being buried alive. The emotion, recollected in tranquillity, actually moves him to entertain the thought that even being dead is only the *next best* thing to such a suspended animation:

[70] Beckett, in a letter about the variant ending, quoted by McGovern, *The Independent on Sunday*, 31 Dec. 1989.

And I fell to thinking of my silent, backstreet, basement office, with its obliterated plate, rest-couch and velvet hangings, and what it means to be buried there alive, if only from ten to five, with convenient to the one hand a bottle of light pale ale and to the other a long ice-cold fillet of hake. Nothing, I said, not even fully certified death, can ever take the place of that.[71]

'Fully certified': not only as the death certificate, and as turning insanity on its head (in *More Pricks than Kicks*[72] Belacqua packs for the suicide pact a sign which proclaims TEMPORARILY SANE), but as calling up the Book of Common Prayer and its rendering of Psalm 39:

Lord, let me know mine end, and the number of my days: that I may be certified how long I have to live.

There, *have to* ('how long I have to live') could be seen as having an unwanted glint.

Samuel Butler seized the opportunity furnished by the word 'certified':

Of all prayers this is the insanest . . . The prayer is a silly piece of petulance and it would have served the maker of it right to have had it granted. 'Cancer in about three months after great suffering' or 'Ninety, a burden to yourself and everyone else'—there is not so much to pick and choose between them.[73]

Beckett has an eternal subject, but like all great writers he has as well a profound sensitivity to the ways in which his own era stands differently even to what is eternal. He is the great writer of an age which has created new possibilities and impossibilities even in the matter of death. Of an age which has dilated longevity, until it is as much a nightmare as a blessing. Swift: 'Every Man desires to live long; but no Man would be old'.[74]

---

[71] *All That Fall* (1957), 31. Preceding *Tous ceux qui tombent* (1957), trans. Robert Pinget in collaboration with Beckett, 63:

Et je me suis repris à songer à mon bureau dans l'impasse, à mon sous-sol silencieux, avec sa plaque où le temps a effacé mon nom, son lit de repos et ses tentures de velours, et à tout ce que ça réprésente d'y être enterré vif ne fût-ce que de dix à cinq, mes rafraîchissements à portée de main. Rien, me disais-je, même pas la mort dûment constatée, ne pourra jamais remplacer ça.

[72] 'Love and Lethe', *More Pricks than Kicks*, 134.
[73] *Samuel Butler's Notebooks*, ed. Geoffrey Keynes and Brian Hill (1951), 269.
[74] 'Thoughts on Various Subjects'.

Ours is an age of intense geriatric tending, at one with a persistent medico-professional indignity visited upon the dying, and with a contempt for the uselessness of old age (the parents in the bins).

It is an age of transplants and trunks, of consciousnesses suspended; Dante and cryonics, deepfreezing against the day when death will have lost its sting.

It is an age which now finds one of its most urgent anxieties to be the definition of death—urgent for family and friends, for doctors and nurses, for courts of law, for philosophers and theologians and even for the Pope.

There has been the Karen Quinlan case, when the parents fought through the courts of the United States of America for the right to turn off what is tendentiously called the 'life support system'—only to find that she did not then die.

There has been the first ruling that an assailant may be charged with murder if death occurs when the support system is turned off, or rather when death is essentially understood as having preceded the being placed upon the support system at all.

There is the Hemlock Society; there is Exit; there is Doctor Jack Kevorkian who assists at suicides.

There has been the six hour film *Near Death* (1989), by the great documentary film-maker of our day, Frederick Wiseman, from the Intensive Care Unit at the Beth Israel Hospital in Boston.

There has been, as reported in *The New York Times* (18 March 1990), the suit brought by an octogenarian named Winter: 'In recent years, right-to-die lawsuits have proliferated . . . But the case brought by Mr Winter . . . is apparently the first "wrongful life" case filed by a patient.'

The New York Times of 7 January 1992 reported, as two distinct items:

Woman, 25, Wins Right to Die

('the Quebec case is said to be the first in which the case for the ending of a life has been taken to a court by the patient') and

A Ruling to Allow a Death

('Boston, Jan. 6 (AP)—The state's highest court ruled today that feeding tubes should be removed from a woman who is in a persistent vegetative state and suffers from a degenerative disease').

There has even been *The Oxford Book of Death*.

Statecraft has been as much affected as family life: one thinks back to the deaths of Tito and Franco, mighty opposites both kept alive in extremity for political ends. Charles Juliet[75] reports a conversation with Beckett in 1975:

> We talk about Spain and he explains why they are trying so hard to keep Franco alive. If he lives until November 25, a member of Franco's party would be able to name the head of the government, which would then continue pro-Franco; but if he dies before then, someone from the other side might be named.
>
> SB: Even Goya did not imagine such things.

Beckett's Murphy, a novice in these matters, makes the rounds of the lunatic asylum: 'when a patient died suddenly and flagrantly', Murphy might be tempted to be confident of the matter; but he is sternly admonished ('let him assume nothing of the kind'): 'No patient was dead till the doctor had seen him'.[76] In its play upon the thought 'Have you seen the doctor?', this has something of Swift's lancing of the profession.

Beckett's art is perfectly continuous with the world of newspaper items, of for instance this letter to *The Times* (8 March 1978, sent from Birmingham—Birmingham has its fatal attractions as a later instance will show):

Defining death
From Professor Brodie Hughes
Sir, Dr Hopkins (March 6) whose arguments concerning the terminology of death were justified by the circumstances, nevertheless tends to perpetuate our difficulties by using the term 'death'. This has been a stumbling block in all the discussions on this matter and the matter is not helped by the use of the qualified term 'brain death'.

What we require is some phrase that indicates that a person, as a person, has ceased to exist.

This, for all its professionalized confidence, suffers from mind death. Set a committee to coin some malleable phrase; speak

---

[75] 'Meeting Beckett', *TriQuarterly*, 77 (1989–90), 23; trans. Suzanne Chamier.
[76] *Murphy*, 159. Preceding *Murphy* in French (117): 'lorsque un malade viendrait inopinément à mourir'; 'qu'il ne se permette aucune supposition dans ce sens'; 'Nul malade n'était mort avant d'être vu par le médecin'.

unruffledly of how the alternative is that we will *perpetuate* our difficulties; and let us have no more of the vexatious term 'death'.

Beckett would in a way, his own way, sympathize with the exasperated yearner for a 'death'-free zone; he wrote of the painting of Bram van Velde that it was 'premièrement une peinture de la chose en suspens, je dirais volontiers de la chose morte, idéalement morte, si ce terme n'avait pas de si fâcheuses associations'.[77]

Cryonics, and let slip the dogs of law. For the law takes its cut:

$1m FINE FOR BODY FREEZE

Los Angeles, June 7 [1981]. Robert Nelson, the former president of a society which froze bodies to await a day when science found a way of restoring life, and Joseph Klockgether, an undertaker, were ordered today to pay nearly $1m (£513,000) in damages.

Relatives of the dead had filed a lawsuit alleging fraud. They claimed that the corpses, which were put in capsules to await a scientific breakthrough, were not kept in a perpetually frozen state.

Perpetually, these things will happen.

'Body' in hearse was still alive, coroner is told

But do not fear, every precaution will henceforth be taken to make sure that you do not come to in a hearse. Placed in a hearse?:

Mr Hugh Chapman, representing W. Yorkshire Regional Health Authority, said that under new instructions that would apply only if a person was obviously dead, decapitated, partly decomposed or certified dead by a doctor.[78]

Decapitated but not obviously dead? (*Sir Gawain and the Green Knight*?) Partly decomposed, not totally?—ah, says the pedantic hearse-man as you seek admission for the corpse, It doesn't say anything about *totally* decomposed . . .

A hearse is not an ambulance, nor an ambulance a hearse, as the W. Yorkshire Regional Health Authority well knows, and as the regulatory power of *Murphy* apprehends when it reports a suicide:

[77] 'La Peinture des van Velde' (1945), Beckett's first publication in French, and not translated by him; *Disjecta*, 126.
[78] *The Times*, 20 Apr. 1978.

The ambulance arrived and the old boy was carried down the stairs, past Celia stuck on the landing, and put into it. This proved that he still lived, for it is a misdemeanour to put a corpse, no matter how fresh, into an ambulance. But to take one out contravenes no law, by-law, section or sub-section, and it was perfectly in order for the old boy to consummate, as he did, his felony on the way to the hospital.[79]

'Consummate' makes its devout bow to Hamlet, and 'felony' brings home that (until the change in the law, within living memory) suicide—*felo de se*—was that contravention of the law which was noteworthy for being beyond the reach of even the longest arm, provided that the felony was more than attempted: consummated.

The style of the W. Yorkshire Regional Health Authority and of the contributors to the public prints is exactly the one of professionalized high-minded insensitivity (enunciating no more than A *Modest* Proposal) which Beckett tempered for himself, all glacial propriety.

As in this article in *The Times* on transplants: 'Perhaps the most deeply-rooted fear in the mind of the public at large is ambiguity over genuine, recognizable death.'[80]

Well, yes, there have been those who have seen *Indiana Jones and the Temple of Doom* as what some would call an encoding of the dangers of the premature heart-transplant, untimely ripped. And this was inscribed all over the film *Coma*.

But Dr Jones of *The Times* perfectly understands:

These fears were not allayed by the example in Birmingham earlier this year when an elderly man, who had been diagnosed as being dead, responded to an incision.

Yes, you *could* say that when this happens, it doesn't exactly *allay* these fears—including the fear of Birmingham.

What is unimaginative in such professionalized prose is imagina-

---

[79] *Murphy*, 135–6. Preceding *Murphy* in French, 101:

L'ambulance arriva, on descendit le vieux, devant Célia figée sur le palier, et on le mit dedans. Ce qui prouvait qu'il vivait toujours, car il est interdit de mettre un cadavre, quelle qu'en soit la fraîcheur, dans une ambulance. Mais en sortir un cadavre n'enfreint nulle loi, ni règlement, ni statut, ni ordonnance, et en consommant son délit sur le chemin de l'hôpital, comme il ne manqua pas de le faire, le vieux était parfaitement dans son droit.

[80] Dr Robert Jones, 19 July 1974.

tively realized in *The Lost Ones*, which attends upon the last dying of our planet:

that here all should die but with so gradual and to put it plainly so fluctuant a death as to escape the notice even of a visitor.[81]

A triumph of mortification, the scourging word 'fluctuant', and it contrives, very oddly since you may very well never have met this exact word before, 'to put it plainly'. If, lying there, you were to overhear that your pulse fluctuated, this might not mean the end; but *fluctuant*. And when nurses and doctors, nearests and dearests, are unnoticing, there may be the more attentive eye of the stranger. What should not escape our notice is Beckett's penchant for locating the word 'escape' in the immediate vicinity of 'death'.

Death is fluctuant as birth is, both necessitating *contractions*.

Edward Young supplies the first entry in *The Oxford Book of Ages*,[82] upon our first entry: 'Our birth is nothing but our death begun'. And our death is nothing, *tout court*?

Coleridge delivered himself of a religious mystery:

Resurrection = Parturition Divae Mortis!—
Mem. A strange but striking instance of the facility in the personifying of General Terms produced by the habits of *Idols* under the ancient polytheism is St Chrysostom's gloss on the text 'having loosed the pangs of Death.'—He at once make a Diva Mors, that suffered the pangs of a Woman in labor till she had been *delivered* of Christ.[83]

The secular thanatologists put the related thought of the birth/death pangs more soothingly:

In a sense, one is ready to give birth to death—and even the birth/death pangs can be tolerated because they are part of a meaningful and necessary act.[84]

This, well meant, is an indignity; it is to be hoped that, propped up on a pillow and told to bear up—'the birth/death pangs can be

[81] *The Lost Ones* (1972), 18. Following *Le dépeupleur* (1970), 16: 'qu'ici tout se meure mais d'une mort si graduelle et pour tout dire si fluctuante qu'elle échapperait même à un visiteur'.

[82] Ed. Anthony and Sally Sampson (1985), 1, from Young's *Night Thoughts*—a title with which Beckett makes play in alluding to 'night's young thoughts' (*Murphy*, 73–4; preceding *Murphy* in French, 58: 'les jeunes pensées de la nuit').

[83] *Notebooks*, ed. Kathleen Coburn and Merton Christensen, iv (1990), entry 4581; June–July 1819.

[84] Robert Kastenbaum and Ruth Aisenberg, *The Psychology of Death* (1972), 107.

tolerated because they are part of a meaningful and necessary act'—a spirited patient would resent the meaninglessness of 'meaningful' and would spit in the consoler's eye.

And yet the same thought, if expressed with a sufficient sense of what is at stake and of how different it will seem when it finally comes upon one's own self, can be stoically precise, comic, and dignified in its own way.

All is ready. Except me. I am being given, if I may venture the expression, birth to into death, such is my impression. The feet are clear already, of the great cunt of existence. Favourable presentation I trust. My head will be the last to die.[85]

'Give birth to' is everyday; 'being given birth to' is already constrained, shouldering; and then Beckett compounds the pressure by venturing an expression between 'given' and 'birth'—'I am being given, if I may venture the expression, birth to into death, such is my impression'. The cautious propriety or docketed etiquette is the more marked in that Malone manifests no such social solicitude in the next sentence when he muses unmisgivingly on 'the great cunt of existence'. As to 'if I may venture the expression': it is brought home that there are in this life two great ventures, both of them expressions: birth and death. We are expressed, once and then once and for all. And 'expression' meets, as if by the pulse of a contraction, its answering 'impression', a reminder that if we were once each of us expressed, it was naturally by the force of impression.

I am being given, if I may venture the expression, birth to into death, such is my impression.

How ungainly—'birth to into'—the whole thing is ('to into': preposition into preposition, and with no liaison of sound from *to* to *into*). It is right too that the death, like the birth, should be the wrong way round: 'The feet are clear already'. And then there is the perfect coinciding within the word 'presentation', by which Malone both admires, with good cause, his own presentation of

---

[85] *Malone Dies*, 114. Following *Malone meurt*, 183:

Tout est prêt. Sauf moi. Je nais dans la mort, si j'ose dire. Telle est mon impression. Drôle de gestation. Les pieds sont sortis déjà, du grand con de l'existence. Présentation favorable j'espère. Ma tête mourra en dernier.

the matter *and* lends his soft obstetric hand, presenting the obstetric term *presentation*:

Obstetr. The presenting of a particular part of the fœtus towards the *os uteri* during labour. 1754–64 SMELLIE *Midwif*. The presentation of the head was always deemed the most natural.

'My head will be the last to die.'

First born by Beckett was his French, and it is much less lethally alive than its English subsequence. 'Je nais dans la mort, si j'ose dire. Telle est mon impression.'

'Je nais dans la mort': this is far more remote from the birth/death pangs than is its English no-equivalent, the French far more equable, smooth; and then, unruffled at the end of its sentence, 'si j'ose dire' can have none of the daring, the intrusive and extrusive venturing that is alive in the placing of 'if I may venture the expression' so that it ruptures 'given' from 'birth':

I am being given, if I may venture the expression, birth to into death, such is my impression.

Moreover the French, in having only *impression* and no pairing with 'expression', cannot enforce the contractions.

Je nais dans la mort, si j'ose dire. Telle est mon impression.

The French language, to which Beckett was not born, was seldom able to do quite as well by him. Yet he and it have their many triumphs. He relished, for instance, its *terminations*, instinct with death *and* with birth. Enoch Brater reports, of the 1984 staging of the fiction *Compagnie*, that

Beckett, who worked closely with Chabert, advised him to pay special attention to words like *terminé* (concluded), for the accent on the last syllable is also heard as *né* (born).[86]

This turns upon *terminé* and how it terminates; and upon the antithetical impulse of this word against its ending, which after all, before all, constitutes our beginning: *né*. The termination *né* (acting as the truly closing suffix while having once been the truly opening prefix) does so again in the French wording of *Watt*, when Beckett imagines what it is, not just for the living to be—as we say—'spared' but for the unborn to be 'spared' (ah, but spared life, not spared death):

If all were spared, the living spared, the unborn spared.[87]

Si tous étaient épargnés, épargnés les vivants, épargnés les pas encore nés.

The sharply fitting contrariety of this is more needling than the too-easily available chime of *womb* and *tomb*. Beckett had entertained this age-old convenience in the early (posthumously published) novel *Dream of Fair to Middling Women* (he re-wrought some of it for *More Pricks than Kicks*).

Many a time had Belacqua, responding to the obscure need to verbalise a wombtombing or suchlike, murmured a syllable or two of incantation.

But in the umbra, the tunnel, when the mind went wombtomb, then it was real thought and real living[88]

It was not. And Beckett came to know so, to know that womb/tomb, though it does well by birth and death, does not do well by the birth/death *pangs*. Geoffrey Hill, writing on Henry Vaughan's 'The Night', cautioned against the ease of the rhyme:

One is impelled, or drawn, to enquire whether that metaphysical rapport felt to exist between certain English rhyme-pairings is the effect of commonplace rumination or the cause of it. Auden, in *New Year Letter*, makes 'womb:tomb' a trick in his 'Devil's' sophistry, implying that the easy availability of the rhyme is complicitous with our trite melancholy and angst.[89]

The dignity and the indignity of death ask more than trite melancholy and angst.

It is now almost impossible to die with dignity in the USA unless one is poverty-stricken. There are too many vested interests; Mammon colludes with the American Medical Association (AMAmmon); and there is such a *technological* fascination with the keeping alive of the all but dead.

Modern technology has managed a last twist of the knife, not

---

[87] *Watt*, 104. Preceding *Watt* in French, 106.

[88] Quoted (from the MS) by Lawrence Harvey, *Samuel Beckett Poet and Critic*, 334, 326. *Dream of Fair to Middling Women* (1992), pp. 148, 45.

[89] 'A Pharisee to Pharisees: Reflections on Vaughan's "The Night"', *English*, 38 (1989), 103.

only the crippling death-duties constituted by the American's dying months, but the new turn given to Arthur Hugh Clough and 'The Latest Decalogue':

> Thou shalt not kill; but needst not strive
> Officiously to keep alive.

Meanwhile there's no use knowing you are gone, you are not, you are writhing yet, the hair is growing, the nails are growing, the entrails emptying, all the morticians are dead. Someone has drawn the blinds, you perhaps.[90]

'Meanwhile there's no use knowing you are gone, you are not': not gone, and therefore not *not*, cruelly. The French offers not a cruel rescinding but a flat brutality: 'inutile de se savoir défunt'. But the French then has its terrifying compensation, for whereas the English offers the bare strange truth: even after death, 'the hair is growing, the nails are growing', the French sets the process before your very eyes:

> les ongles s'allongent

where the movement from 'ongles' to 's'allongent' is a hideous cellular elongation. This, Swiftian, is the anagrammatic method.

And the French *peut-être*—'Quelqu'un a tiré les rideaux, soi-même peut-être'—is able to effect what *perhaps* cannot intimate, an intimation of immortality, that we *may* continue to *be*; the English 'maybe' would carry this sense but would be tonally askew.

Everybody can feel the weirdness of a corpse's hair and nails continuing to grow; but Beckett feels it with special force because of its constituting what may (blessedly) be the only authentic form of life after death, and assuredly is an authentic form of life in death and of death in life. The saint clenched his fists until his nails grew through them, and the nails did not stop when he ceased.

---

[90] *Molloy*, 35. Following *Molloy* in French, 39:

En attendant, inutile de se savoir défunt, on ne l'est pas, on se tortille encore, les cheveux poussent, les ongles s'allongent, les entrailles se vident, tous les croque-morts sont morts. Quelqu'un a tiré les rideaux, soi-même peut-être.

[. . .] clenched his fists all his life thus lived died at last saying to himself latest breath that they'd grow on[91]

(I can't go on, I'll go on; they'll grow on.)

on what the nails that can go on the hand dead a fraction of an inch life a little slow to leave them the hair the head dead [. . .][92]

The syntax of *How It Is* fractionally inches its way forward, like its irreducible consciousness inching through its mud.

> life | a little | slow to leave them

or

> life | a little slow to leave them

—who is to say?

In all these death-dealings, Beckett's ambition is—famously— to fail as no other dare fail. Which is validated by the acknowledgement of the imagination's inevitable failure to imagine its own death.

Philip Larkin asked of 'The Old Fools', as they see imminent death, 'Why aren't they screaming?'

One reason may be that they have made friends with the necessity of dying. Another is quite the contrary: that though the necessity of dying can be imagined, the prospect of dying can never be more than entertained.

For as Freud wrote in his 'Thoughts for the Times on War and Death' in 1915:

Our own death is indeed unimaginable, and whenever we make the attempt to imagine it we can perceive that we really survive as spectators.[93]

There, 'we can perceive' exactly implicates us.

What for Freud is psychologically limitary is for F. H. Bradley philosophically so.

---

[91] *How It Is*, 59. Following *Comment c'est*, 66:

[. . .] serré les poings toute sa vie ainsi vécu mourut enfin en se disant dernier souffle qu'ils allaient pousser encore

[92] *How It Is*, 95. Following *Comment c'est*, 106:

de quoi les ongles qui peuvent continuer la main morte quelques millimètres un peu longue la vie à les quitter la chevelure la tête morte [. . .]

[93] *Collected Papers* (1925), iv. 304–5.

For we can think of our own total surcease, but we cannot imagine it. Against our will, and perhaps unconsciously, there creeps in the idea of a reluctant and struggling self, or of a self disappointed, or wearied, or in some way discontented. And this is certainly not a self completely extinguished.[94]

What we would catch with our own total surcease, would be success. Inevitable failure.

My case, since I am in the dock, is that van Velde is the first to desist from this estheticized automatism, the first to admit that to be an artist is to fail, as no other dare fail, that failure is his world and the shrink from it desertion, art and craft, good housekeeping, living. No, no, allow me to expire.[95]

In his book on Proust, Beckett again conjoins escape and death:

When Albertine was his prisoner, the possibility of her escape did not seriously disturb him, because it was indistinct and abstract, like the possibility of death. Whatever opinion we may be pleased to hold on the subject of death, we may be sure that it is meaningless and valueless. Death has not required us to keep a day free.[96]

Ah, *it*. 'There are times', as Beckett remarks elsewhere, 'when the simplest words are slow to signify. Here "it" was the laggard.'[97]

Whatever opinion we may be pleased to hold on the subject of death, we may be sure that it is meaningless and valueless.

Is 'it' death or the opinion? If we wait long enough for the laggard 'it', the ultimate elision will relieve us of the distinction.

---

[94] *Appearance and Reality* (1893), 502 n.
[95] 'Three Dialogues' (1949), III; *Disjecta*, 145.
[96] *Proust*, 6. Compare p. 15:

He must see his grandmother. He leaves for Paris. He surprises her reading her beloved Mme. de Sévigné. But he is not there because she does not know that he is there. He is present at his own absence.

[97] *Mercier and Camier*, 102:

I hope we have not overstepped it.
Camier did not answer. There are times [etc.]

Following *Mercier et Camier*, 177:

Je dis que j'espère que nous n'avons pas dépassé la mesure, dit Mercier.
    Camier ne répondit pas tout de suite. La vie a de ces occasions où les mots les plus simples et limpides mettent quelque temps à dégager tout leur bouquet. Et mesure prêtait à confusion.

One's own death is unimaginable, since the imagination is itself a principle of life and an exercising of life.

The thanatologists sound as if they are not in the least pain about the matter. 'What it feels like not to feel eludes me.'[98]

But Beckett's accents are more piercing because more pierced.

Imagination Dead Imagine[99]

The syntax of that title has fallen from a great height and its bones pierce its skin and shatter its articulation. Try, just try, to imagine the death of your own imagination, or the death of all imagination on the planet. 'But Watt's imagination had never been a lively one.'[100] Oh yes it had, or it would not have been an imagination, even in Watt's special case.[101]

The same goes for Molloy's:

And I for my part have always preferred slavery to death, I mean being put to death. For death is a condition I have never been able to conceive to my satisfaction and which therefore cannot go down in the ledger of weal and woe.[102]

How much more the birth/death pangs, and the sexual pangs, are alive in 'conceive' (and 'to my *satisfaction*') than in Beckett's less corporeal French:

Et en ce qui me concerne personellement, j'ai toujours préféré l'esclavage à la mort, ou plutôt à la mise à mort. Car la mort est une condition dont je n'ai jamais pu me faire une réprésentation satisfaisante et qui ne peut donc entrer légitimement en ligne de compte, dans le bilan des maux et des biens.

---

[98] Kastenbaum and Aisenberg, *The Psychology of Death*, 9.

[99] (1965). Following *Imagination morte imaginez* (1965).

[100] *Watt*, 83. Preceding *Watt* in French, 83: 'Mais l'imagination de Watt n'avait jamais été des plus vives.'

[101] For a different body of deductions from some of these aspects of Beckett's art, see Daniel Albright, 'Beckett's Recent Acivities [*sic*]: The Liveliness of Dead Imagination', in Susan Dick *et al.* (eds.), *Omnium Gatherum* (1989), 374–83. Albright, who believes that what 'Beckett has done to imagination' is that he has 'killed it', is at once extreme and hedged: '*Perhaps there is some danger that*, if we murder the imaginations of all the great writers of history, we *may* have to murder our own imaginations as well—and *it may turn out that* literary critics need imagination, even if Sophocles, Flaubert, Beckett can dispense with it' (p. 383, my emphases on his bolt-holes).

[102] *Molloy*, 91. Following *Molloy* in French, 103.

But the insistence that your own death is inconceivable is only worth something if a writer will at the same time utter his utmost, his uttermost; do his blessedest or damnedest to conceive it.

How It Is imagines how it might be, this inconceivable imagining of one's own death, perceived by another:

she sits aloof ten yards fifteen yards she looks up looks at me says at last to herself all is well he is working

my head where is my head it rests on the table my hand trembles on the table she sees I am not sleeping the wind blows tempestuous the little clouds drive before it the table glides from light to darkness darkness to light

that's not all she stoops to her work again the needle stops in midstitch she straightens up and looks at me again she has only to call me by my name get up come and feel me but no

I don't move her anxiety grows she suddenly leaves the house and runs to friends[103]

The needle stops in midstitch: but we thread the lines (so strangely stitched or not-stitched), and think of the Fates.

In the last year of his life, Beckett published *Stirrings Still*. It begins with simple finality. 'One night as he sat at his table head on hands he saw himself rise and go.'[104]

He saw himself go out of this life? go out of his body? and go out of his mind?[105]

People imagining 'their own Deaths': an unthinking writer sinks into folly here. *The Art of Sinking in Poetry* (1727) exposed The Infantine:

---

[103] *How It Is*, 11. Following *Comment c'est*, 13–14:

elle est loin dix mètres quinze metres elle lève la tête me regarde se dit enfin c'est bien il travaille

ma tête où est ma tête elle repose sur la table ma main tremble sur la table elle voit bien que je ne dors pas le vent souffle impétueux les petits nuages vont vite la table vogue de la clarté à l'ombre de l'ombre à la clarté

ce n'est pas fini elle reprend les yeux vagues son ouvrage l'aiguille s'arrête au beau milieu du point elle se redresse et me regarde de nouveau elle n'a qu'a m'appeler par mon nom se lever venir me palper mais non

je ne bouge pas son trouble va croissant elle quitte brusquement la maison et court chez des amis

[104] Preceding *Soubresauts* (1989): 'Assis une nuit à sa table la tête sur les mains il se vit se lever et partir.'

[105] Suggested by Jim McCue in an eloquent review, *The Times*, 4 Mar. 1989.

With no less Simplicity does he [Ambrose Philips] suppose that Shepherdesses tear their Hair and beat their Breasts, at their own Deaths:

> *Ye brighter Maids, faint Emblems of my Fair,*
> *With Looks cast down, and with dishevel'd Hair,*
> *In bitter Anguish beat your breasts, and moan*
> *Her Death untimely*, as it were your own.[106]

One knows what Philips means, and only wishes that he had contrived to say it. His is not a true simplicity, but a simpleton's untruth.

A true simplicity, a true art of sinking, knows that a dead dog makes sad dogs of us all.

It was she dug the hole, put in the dog, filled up the hole. On the whole I was a mere spectator, I contributed my presence. As if it had been my own burial. And it was.[107]

'It was she dug the hole', 'filled up the hole. On the whole': here is the totality of vacancy which would imagine one's own burial.

And it was.

It is not.

'Great simplicity', wrote T. S. Eliot, 'is only won by an intense moment or by years of intelligent effort, or by both. It represents one of the most arduous conquests of the human spirit: the triumph of feeling and thought over the natural sin of language.'[108]

For Beckett, great simplicity was a triumph of feeling and thought not over natural sin but over original sin, which for him was the original sin of having been born. And French, the language which was not natural to him but which came naturally to him, afforded him one such triumph of feeling and thought, an inspired simplicity, a glimpse of imagining the unimaginable, through the rotation of simple sounds, not a trope so much as a tropism towards the dark sun of death.

---

[106] Ch. XI; *Selected Prose of Alexander Pope*, ed. Paul Hammond (1987), 195.

[107] *Molloy*, 48. Following *Molloy* in French, 54:

Ce fut elle qui fit le trou, qui mit le chien dedans, qui combla le trou. Je ne faisais en somme qu'y assister. J'y contribuais de ma présence. Comme si ç'avait été mon enterrement à moi. Et il l'était.

[108] *Athenaeum*, 11 Apr. 1919.

The poem is French and French alone.[109] Yet, consummate in its simplicity, it asks us to know so very little of another tongue if we would desire to imagine so much of a foreign world and thereby of a gone world:

> imagine si ceci
> un jour ceci
> un beau jour
> imagine
> si un jour
> un beau jour ceci
> cessait
> imagine

---

[109] (1977); *Collected Poems*, 73. How even more than usually untranslatable the poem is ('even more dead than alive than usual', in the words of *First Love*) can be seen from Kevin Perryman's crack at it (*Babel*, 6 (1990), 31), and particularly from what became of *ceci cessait*:

> just think if all this
> one day all this
> one fine day
> just think
> if one day
> one fine day all this
> stopped
> just think

2. *Words that Went Dead*

There is an entry in *Time Flies* (1885), 'A Reading Diary', by Christina G. Rossetti, where time flies back and returns her from her mid-fifties to her childhood. The mouse and the insect revive, as mortally stark as the groundhog of Richard Eberhart's poem or the hedgehog of Beckett's *Company*. But one would never divine from the scholar's paraphrase in 1987 that such an incident could put the fear of God into anyone:

Rossetti recalls her first experience of death when, in early childhood, she found a dead mouse in the grounds of a cottage. In sympathy she buried the mouse in a mossy spot. Remembering the place, she went back a day or two later, and moving the moss away, discovered a black insect.[1]

This is dead in the telling. Her very words were not dead, they were death:

My first vivid experience of death (if so I may term it) occurred in early childhood in the grounds of a cottage.

This little cottage was my familiar haunt: its grounds were my inexhaustible delight. They then seemed to me spacious, though now I know them to have been narrow and commonplace.

So in these grounds, perhaps in the orchard, I lighted upon a dead mouse. The dead mouse moved my sympathy: I took him up, buried him comfortably in a mossy bed, and bore the spot in mind.

It may have been a day or two afterwards that I returned, removed the moss coverlet and looked . . . a black insect emerged. I fled in horror, and for long years ensuing I never mentioned the ghastly adventure to anyone.

How feelingly she terms it. 'My first vivid experience of death (if so I may term it)': the *caveat* is truly a warning, a *memento* to the fact that none of us will know what *mori* is until it is too late,

---

[1] P. G. Stanwood, in David A. Kent (ed.), *The Achievement of Christina Rossetti* (1987), 244. I draw here on an essay of mine, 'Christina Rossetti and Commonplace Books', *Grand Street*, 9 (1990), 190–8. *Time Flies*, 45: 4 Mar.

and that even then experience will not be quite the word. 'Death is not an event in life: we do not live to experience death' (Wittgenstein).[2] But death sets the term as well as the terms: 'if so I may term it'. 'My first vivid experience of death'? After the first death, there is no other.

'My first vivid experience of death (if so I may term it)': Rossetti taps too the root-incongruity of a *vivid* experience of death. Her transitions constitute an organic tissue of life and death. Three times the innocent word 'grounds' can be heard to toll towards the grave; what might have been the carefree 'haunt' becomes darkened; the sometime-spacious grounds of the cottage resemble not only life in the event, but the grave in its eventuality, in their all being, after all, 'narrow and commonplace'. Ay, Madam, it is common. There is a tremulous play of the light against the heavily dark: 'I lighted upon a dead mouse'. The dead mouse did not, by definition, move, but—even as the words move on—'the dead mouse moved my sympathy'. 'I took him up', tenderly, nursingly ('him', not 'it') and yet as one might take up a cause; and 'buried him comfortably in a mossy bed', where the comfort has come to be understood as for the comforter, not for that which is now beyond comfort. The 'mossy bed', in child-hood's authentic play-acting, is now gentled even further, to 'the moss coverlet'. And then the eruptive harshness: the ellipsis ... which at once buries and reveals the emerging horror of life and death:

It may have been a day or two afterwards that I returned, removed the moss coverlet, and looked ... a black insect emerged.

The sequence 'and looked ... a black insect' is perfect, since what is immediately looked at is something black, something inaudible, the ellipsis ... Shadowing the ultimate ellipsis, death. And *emerged* is the more sinister for being so flat, so prosaic. Emerged from where? From the mossy bed. More darkly, from the bedded mouse. Below all, from the child's lost innocence, from her fears and denials.

Such emergences from the English language, lighted upon by Christina Rossetti, are so corporeal as to resist Beckett's famous

---

[2] *Tractatus logico-philosophicus*, trans. D. F. Pears and B. McGuinness (1961), 147: 6. 4311.

disparagement of (he being an Irishman) his stepmothertongue.

In 1929 he praised James Joyce's *Work in Progress*, the incipient *Finnegans Wake*:

Mr. Joyce has desophisticated language. And it is worth while remarking that no language is so sophisticated as English. It is abstracted to death. Take the word 'doubt': it gives us hardly any sensuous suggestion of hesitancy, of the necessity for choice, of static irresolution. Whereas the German 'Zweifel' does, and, in lesser degree, the Italian 'dubitare'. Mr. Joyce recognises how inadequate 'doubt' is to express a state of extreme uncertainty, and replaces it by 'in twosome twiminds'. Nor is he by any means the first to recognize the importance of treating words as something more than mere polite symbols. Shakespeare uses fat, greasy words to express corruption: 'Duller shouldst thou be than the fat weed that rots itself in death on Lethe wharf'. We hear the ooze squelching all through Dickens's description of the Thames in '*Great Expectations*'. This writing that you find so obscure is a quintessential extraction of language and painting and gesture, with all the inevitable clarity of the old inarticulation. Here is the savage economy of hieroglyphics. Here words are not the polite contortions of 20th century printer's ink. They are alive. They elbow their way on to the page, and glow and blaze and fade and disappear.[3]

This catches a queer certainty endemic to the word 'doubt', its unvacillating clarity, beginning and ending hard and enjoying its long vowel; but these observations by the enthusiastic young Beckett failed to allow for the uses of adversity, of *anti*-onomatopoeia, by which for English-speakers their word for doubt may help to steel them against its temptations.

And there is, come to think of it, that unsounded *b*, to keep alive some small doubt . . .[4]

The unequivocal long vowel in 'doubt' is to be contrasted with the doubt which Joyce builds into his equipollent phrase, 'in twosome twiminds': a long or a short i? twī- as in twilight, or twĭ- under pressure from twosome and from 't w i n'?—twĭm[m]inds. (The word 'twiminds' does carry twins within itself.) Any reader is bound to be in two minds, in twosome twīminds or twĭminds.

---

[3] 'Dante . . . Bruno. Vico . . Joyce', *Our Exagmination Round His Factification for Incamination of Work in Progress* (1929), 15. (*Disjecta*, 28.) Although published a month later than the volume, the version in *transition*, 16–17 (June 1929), is the earlier version, as is clear from the volume's corrections, revisions, and additions. The sentence about Dickens is not in *transition*.

[4] I owe this point to Nancy Patton.

Beckett, though, is single-minded when it comes to his quotation from *Hamlet*.

Shakespeare uses fat, greasy words to express corruption: 'Duller shouldst thou be than the fat weed that rots itself in death on Lethe wharf'.

Or rather, misquotation. Not *death* but *ease*. And this from one of the uneasy uneased dead, returning—all paradox since he returns from 'the Undiscovered Countrey, from whose Borne | No Traveller returns'—with his life in death, and speaking the lines:

> I finde thee apt,
> And duller should'st thou be than the fat weede
> That rots it selfe in ease, on Lethe Wharfe,
> Would'st thou not stirre in this.[5]

'That rots it selfe': itself a phrase which elsewhere in Beckett becomes decomposed, all but imperceptibly, to 'rocks itself' (to death, as in his terminal play *Rockaby*?):

> the livid canal;
> at Parnell Bridge a dying barge
> carrying a cargo of nails and timber
> rocks itself softly in the foaming cloister of the lock;

—where the dying barge hails and hales 'Morte d'Arthur'.[6]

'That rots it selfe in ease' was softsoaped by Beckett, when lauding Joyce, to 'that rots itself in death': but then for Beckett the only ease is death, and he makes so bold as to enquire whether that is not really the case for the rest of us.

> sleep till death
> healeth
> come ease
> this life disease

The misquoting glissade from *ease* to *death* is on the viewless wings of Keats's 'Ode to a Nightingale': 'I have been half in love with easeful death'. His is a line which had rhymed ('seeking the rime, the panting syllable to rime with breath'[7]) with the line

---

[5] *Hamlet*, I. v. 'rots it selfe': Folio. 'roots it selfe': Quartos 2–4.
[6] 'Enueg I' (1935), *Collected Poems*, 10.
[7] *Murphy*, 229:

I have been so busy, so busy, so absorbed, my swan crossword you know, Miss Carridge,

which Beckett unforgettably remembers, breathed out unmarked by quotation-marks, in 'Dante and the Lobster': 'Take into the air my quiet breath'.[8]

The ease/death slide, though, does not square with the disapprobation of death in Beckett's appreciation of Joyce (the English language 'abstracted to death'; Joyce's words 'are alive'). Nor do other things in the appreciation, which therefore anticipates Beckett's profoundest convictions, and his becoming a great writer once he ceased so single-mindedly to use the word *death* as pejorative—and *life* as meliorative. He needed to incarnate a different relation of life to death within his very language. In twosome twiminds about life and death. And his approbation of Joyce's words witnesses that, willy-nilly, already he was after such a thing:

and glow and blaze and fade and disappear

—this, in its flare and flair, is an exultant version of Dr Johnson's disillusioning in *The Vanity of Human Wishes* (75–6):

> Delusive Fortune hears th'incessant Call,
> They mount, they shine, evaporate, and fall.

Beckett never finished his play about Dr Johnson, *Human Wishes*. But he heard the incessant call of those lines, lines which embody life in death and death in life.

His youthful eulogy of Joyce lends, even if it does not quite give, some credit to the death-principle:

This inner elemental vitality and corruption of expression imparts a furious restlessness to the form, which is admirably suited to the

---

seeking the rime, the panting syllable to rime with breath, that I have been dead to the voices of the street, dead and damned, Miss Carridge, the myriad voices.

Preceding *Murphy* in French, 164:

J'ai été si prise, si prise, si absorbée, Mademoiselle, quelque chose est cassé, j'ai été morte aux voix de la rue, morte et damnée, Mademoiselle, les myriades de voix.

[8] *More Pricks than Kicks*, 20:

In the depths of the sea it had crept into the cruel pot. For hours, in the midst of its enemies, it had breathed secretly. It had survived the Frenchwoman's cat and his witless clutch. Now it was going alive into scalding water. It had to. Take into the air my quiet breath.

But in the original printing of the story (*This Quarter*, 5 (1932), 222–36) the allusion to Keats was within quotation-marks. Too heavy breathing; quietened by Beckett thereafter.

purgatorial aspect of the work. There is an endless verbal germination, maturation, putrefaction, the cyclic dynamism of the intermediate.

For Beckett this is 'pure Vico, and Vico, applied to the problem of style'.[9]

And Beckett's own problem of style? That which he insists of Proust, he exacts of himself. 'For Proust, as for the painter, style is more a question of vision than of technique.' 'For Proust the quality of language is more important than any system of ethics or aesthetics.'[10]

In praising Joyce, he came to strain into italics:

His writing is not *about* something; *it is that something itself*[11]

—where in the original version in *transition* he had been more flatly faithful:

He is not writing about something: he is writing something.

But the account he gives of Joyce's linguistic enactments, in their relation of not only form but impulse to content ('Here form *is* content, content *is* form'), was to prove to have its coronary-corollary in the relation of Beckett's death-form to the like impulse and the like content. Of Joyce, he wrote in praise of this particular form of the perfect fit:

When the sense is sleep, the words go to sleep. (See the end of '*Anna Livia*') When the sense is dancing, the words dance.

The language is drunk. The very words are tilted and efferverscent. How can we qualify this general esthetic vigilance wihout which we cannot hope to snare the sense which is for ever rising to the surface of the form and becoming the form itself?

One of the disputes within Beckett studies is whether his art is mimetic. For Daniel Albright, there is simply an assault: 'Beckett's assault on mimesis', his fashioning 'a non-mimetic art'.[12]

Yet what follows from such praise by Beckett as 'When the sense is sleep, the words go to sleep'? The principle is at once

---

[9] *Our Exagmination*, 16. (*Disjecta*, 29.)
[10] *Proust*, 67.
[11] *Our Exagmination*, 14. (*Disjecta*, 27.)
[12] In Susan Dick *et al.* (eds.), *Omnium Gatherum*, 375, 380.

profoundly mimetic and profoundly anti-mimetic. Mimetic, in that nothing could be more imitative than for words to be what they say; anti-mimetic, in that nothing could be *less* compatible with *imitation* than something's actually being that of which it speaks.

'The sense which is for ever rising to the surface': and what is it that for ever rises to the surface for Beckett? Death. The corpse in the garden which begins to sprout. He cultivates his garden, and Eliot's.

In doing what they say, his words are an incarnation. And an incarnation is not an imitation of anything. 'Incarnation' caused the believer T. S. Eliot a twinge but he did not weaken:

I spoke at one point of the culture of a people as an *incarnation* of its religion; and while I am aware of the temerity of employing such an exalted term, I cannot think of any other which would convey so well the intention to avoid *relation* on the one hand and *identification* on the other.[13]

Beckett for his part felt the twinges of the quondam-believer, as in a phantom limb:

We discuss religion, and I ask whether he has been able to free himself from its influence.
SB: Perhaps in my external behavior, but as for the rest . . .[14]

Beckett's English language, then, once he came into possession of his means, is other than that which as a young man he had denigrated; it is not 'abstracted to death', it is an abstract of death. 'When the sense is sleep': and when the sense is sleep's brother, death, or when the sense is its being better to be dead than alive?

We may appreciate the right kind of death in life in language when elsewhere in Beckett we meet the wrong kind: a stately dead march which lacks the authentic fusion of germination and corruption and which does not 'glow and blaze and fade and disappear' but simply never appears. I am thinking of the endlessly pertinent and almost always inert translations from the Spanish which he created for the *Anthology of Mexican Poetry* in 1958.

> Every form eschew and every language
> whose processes with deep life's inner rhythm

[13] *Notes towards the Definition of Culture* (1948, 1962 edn.), 33.
[14] Charles Juliet, 'Meeting Beckett' (here 1977), *TriQuarterly* 77 (1989–90), 27; trans. by Suzanne Chamier. The ellipsis is in Juliet.

> are out of harmony . . . and greatly worship
> life, and let life understand your homage.[15]

On the contrary,

> every form eschew and every language
> whose processes with deep *death*'s inner rhythm
> are out of harmony . . . and *somewhat* worship
> *death*, and let *death* understand your homage.

The processes of death, in their relation to plot, to character, and to language, were exuberantly described in the posthumously published novel *Dream of Fair to Middling Women*. Its hero Belacqua (by courtesy of Dante, but Irished too, in that he is chipped as Bollocky) partakes of the 'furious restlessness' which Beckett had relished in Joyce.

Much of what has been written concerning the reluctance of our refractory constituents to bind together is true equally of Belacqua. Their movement is based on a principle of repulsion, their property not to combine but, like heavenly bodies, to scatter and stampede, astral straws on a time-strom, grit in the mistral. And not only to shrink from all that is not they, from all that is without and that in its turn shrinks from them, but also to strain away from themselves.[16]

This belongs to 1932. But by 1937 Beckett had reluctantly shrunk from, strained away from Joyce. His letter in German, to Axel Kaun, was subsequently dismissed by Beckett as 'German bilge'—but then bilge has its mephitic corruption and germination, its 'principle of repulsion'. Here is part of the letter, in Martin Esslin's translation:

It is indeed becoming more and more difficult, even senseless, for me to write an official English. And more and more my own language appears to me like a veil that must be torn apart in order to get at the things (or the Nothingness) behind it. Grammar and Style. To me they seem to have become as irrelevant as a Victorian bathing suit or the imperturbability of a true gentleman. A mask. Let us hope the time will come, thank God that in certain circles it has already come, when language is most efficiently used where it is being most efficiently misused. As we cannot eliminate language all at once, we should at least leave nothing

---

[15] Enrique González Martínez, in *Anthology of Mexican Poetry*, 160. The ellipsis is in the text.

[16] *Disjecta*, 46–7. *Dream of Fair to Middling Women*, pp. 118–19.

undone that might contribute to its falling into disrepute. To bore one hole after another in it, until what lurks behind it—be it something or nothing—begins to seep through; I cannot imagine a higher goal for a writer today. Or is literature alone to remain behind in the old lazy ways that have been so long ago abandoned by music and painting? Is there something paralysingly holy in the vicious nature of the word that is not found in the elements of the other arts? Is there any reason why that terrible materiality of the word surface should not be capable of being dissolved, like for example the sound surface, torn by enormous pauses, of Beethoven's seventh Symphony, so that through whole pages we can perceive nothing but a path of sounds suspended in giddy heights, linking unfathomable abysses of silence? An answer is requested.[17]

An answer was forthcoming, from Beckett himself. It followed at once, and answered yes and no.

Of course, for the time being we must be satisfied with little. At first it can only be a matter of somehow finding a method by which we can represent this mocking attitude towards the word, through words. In this dissonance between the means and their use it will perhaps become possible to feel a whisper of that final music or that silence that underlies All.

With such a program, in my opinion, the latest work of Joyce has nothing whatever to do. There it seems rather to be a matter of an apotheosis of the word.

Beckett's friend Lawrence Harvey later quoted a sorrowing Beckett: 'Joyce believed in words. All you had to do was rearrange them and they would express what you wanted'.[18] Beckett, however, reposed less confidence in language. Or enjoyed the pleasing paradox of a diffident confidence.

The difference between that valuable thing, a confidence in one's advocacy (the young Beckett lending support to his master Joyce), and that invaluable thing, the confidence of achieved art, may be seen in the juxtaposition of a moment in Beckett's appreciation of Joyce with a moment in *Murphy*.

Pressing Joyce's claims, Beckett scolds his 'Ladies and Gentlemen', as 'You', the middlebrow reader—who would not of course have been caught dead in 1929 reading a book, published in *Paris*,

---

[17] *Disjecta*, 171–3. This and the next quotation are translated by Martin Esslin from Beckett's German.

[18] *Samuel Beckett Poet and Critic*, 249.

called *Our Exagmination Round His Factification for Incamination of Work in Progress*.

You are not satisfied unless form is so strictly divorced from content that you can comprehend the one almost without bothering to read the other. This rapid skimming and absorption of the scant cream of sense is made possible by what I may call a continuous process of copious intellectual salivation.[19]

Getting something for nothing ('almost without bothering to read'), and therefore not really getting anything at all. Skimming, eh. Here now is the milk-of-human-kindness comic counterpart to those gentle readers' sourness: Murphy, in the teashop, bilking and milking the management.

With the fresh cup of tea Murphy adopted quite a new technique. He drank not more than a third of it and then waited till Vera happened to be passing.

'I am most fearfully sorry,' he said, 'Vera, to give you all this trouble, but do you think it would be possible to have this filled with hot?'

Vera showing signs of bridling, Murphy uttered winningly the sesame.

'I know I am a great nuisance, but they have been too generous with the cowjuice.'

Generous and cowjuice were the keywords here. No waitress could hold out against their mingled overtones of gratitude and mammary organs. And Vera was essentially a waitress.

That is the end of how Murphy defrauded a vested interest every day for his lunch, to the honourable extent of paying for one cup of tea and consuming 1.83 cups approximately.

Try it sometime, gentle skimmer.[20]

---

[19] *Our Exagmination*, 13 (*Disjecta*, 26.) The original in *transition* (June 1929) had 'This instinctive skimming'.

[20] *Murphy*, 83–4. Preceding *Murphy* in French, 65:

En présence de la nouvelle tasse de thé, Murphy changeait de technique. Il n'en but qu'un tiers, puis attendit que Véra vînt à passer.

—Je suis navré, dit-il, Véra, de vous donner tant de mal, mais croyez-vous qu'il soit possible de faire ajouter un peu de thé chaud?

Véra prenant l'air de ne vouloir pas se laisser faire, Murphy prononça le sésame, onctueusement:

—Je vous emmerde, je le sais bien, mais que voulez-vous, ils m'ont foutu tout plein de jus de vache.

'Emmerde' et 'vache' furent ici les mots actifs, nulle serveuse ne pouvait résister à leurs harmoniques mélangées d'amour et de maternité.

Et voilà comment Murphy chaque jour, pour le plus grand bien de son déjeuner, fraudait

The last five words are a paragraph in themselves. It works because of its 'mingled overtones' of insult to the gentle reader (and his 'rapid skimming') with the *un*generous—watery, skimmed—form of cowjuice.

When Beckett came to translate this into French, he proffered:

Essayez une fois, ami feuilleteur.

—but this does not have such exquisitely mingled overtones, since Murphy was not wangling millefeuilles. Clearly Beckett despaired of rendering into French the fluid fostering sequence 'generous', 'cowjuice', 'mingled overtones of gratitude and mammary organs'. He reached for something quite other:

—Je vous emmerde, je le sais bien, mais que voulez-vous, ils m'ont foutu tout plein de jus de vache.

'Emmerde' et 'vache' furent ici les mots actifs, nulle serveuse ne pouvait résister à leurs harmoniques mélangées d'amour et de maternité.

More Swiftian, the French, than the English, especially the assurance not just that 'vache' harmonizes with 'maternité' but that 'emmerde' harmonizes with 'amour'. Faced by his untranslatable Irish gallantry or indomitable Irishry, Beckett here is himself somewhat 'emmerde' and 'foutu', but at least he comes out of it with indignity.

Beckett differed from Joyce, and ceased to defer to him. But never ceased to honour him.

He sent in 1980, for the centenary in 1982 of Joyce's birth, this one most telling sentence:

I welcome this occasion to bow once again, before I go, deep down, before his heroic work, heroic being.[21]

This sentence, which has itself become rightly honoured, is alive with the honoured dead, and with the honouring of death; alive in the reiteration of 'before', as both time and stationing, and in the

---

une puissance financière, au point honorable de payer une seule tasse de thé et d'en consommer 1,83 tasse approximativement.
Essayez une fois, ami feuilleteur.

The French, by having merely '1,83 tasse approximativement', lacks the demented scrupulosity of the English: '1.83 cups approximately'. Trust Beckett to acknowledge the infinitely recurring.

[21] S. B. Bushrui and B. Benstock (eds.), *James Joyce: An International Perspective* (1982), p. vii.

upright duplicity which affiliates 'deep down' both with *bowing* and with going where Joyce had gone:

> I welcome this occasion to bow once again, before I go, deep down, before his heroic work, heroic being.

This is the tragic counterpart to Beckett's declining to be celebrated.

A magazine which prides itself on interviewing all the notable writers was mortified to notice that, like everybody else, it had failed to winkle out Samuel Beckett. So the editors suborned a friend of Sam's, who popped the wheedling question, of the 'I know you won't but it would be wonderful if you would be so kind' kind. Back came one of those chaste courteous cards with which the hermit protected himself and his art. 'Not even for you', it said (or so they say), and then it added: 'In any case I have no views to inter'.

Which not only makes 'interview' dead, unseaming it from the nave to the chops, but brings out too that an interview is already a living death. 'Interview' is a word which goes dead.

> She felt, as she felt so often with Murphy, spattered with words that went dead as soon as they sounded; each word obliterated, before it had time to make sense, by the word that came next; so that in the end she did not know what had been said. It was like difficult music heard for the first time.[22]

Deliciously, with a ripe but flat tongue, the paragraph ends so.

But then what words, in the longest of runs, do not go dead, like their speakers? Unless, grim thought, there will be no resting in peace.

> It is a lot to expect of one creature, it's a lot to ask, that he should first behave as if he were not, then as if he were, before being admitted to that peace where he neither is, nor is not, and where the language dies that permits of such expressions.[23]

---

[22] *Murphy*, 40. Preceding *Murphy* in French, 35:

Elle se sentait, comme cela lui était déjà si souvent arrivé en parlant avec lui, éclaboussée de mots qui à peine prononcés tombaient en poussière, chaque mot aboli, avant de pouvoir revêtir un sens, par le mot qui suivait. C'était comme avec une musique difficile entendue pour la première fois.

[23] *The Unnamable*, 65–6. Following *L'innommable*, 97:

C'est beaucoup attendre d'une seule créature, c'est beaucoup en exiger, que d'avoir à faire

What in Beckett's French is both a language and a tongue falls silent ('où se tait la langue'). In his English the language dies. All languages do in the end, *after all*; sometimes the language dies as a result of being killed. Verbal assassination may be both the killing by words and the killing of words:

Ce qui suit ne sera qu'une défiguration verbale, voire un assassinat verbal, d'émotions qui, je le sais bien, ne regardent que moi.[24]

In *Endgame*, Hamm peremptorily demands of Clov the summary justice of one word for the world which the high window gives upon:

HAMM. All is what?
CLOV. What all is? In a word? Is that what you want to know? Just a moment. (*He turns the telescope on the without, looks, lowers the telescope, turns towards Hamm.*) Corpsed.[25]

corpse:
v. slang: 1. *trans*. To make a corpse of, to kill. *vulgar*. 1884.

But also, crucially:

2. *Actors' slang*. To confuse or 'put out' (an actor) in the performance of his part: to spoil (a scene or piece of acting by some blunder).
1873: *Corpse*, to stick fast in the dialogue; to confuse or put out the actors by making a mistake.[26]

Life's a poor player. And death may be not much better.
Meanwhile, 'corpsed' is a stroke, of genius. The word is not a

d'abord comme si elle n'était pas, ensuite comme si elle était, avant d'avoir droit au repos là où ni elle n'est pas, ni elle n'est pas, et où se tait la langue obligeant à de telles expressions.

[24] 'La Peinture des van Velde', *Disjecta*, 124.
[25] *Endgame* (1958), 25. Following *Fin de partie* (1957), 46:

HAMM. Tout est quoi?
CLOV. Ce que tout est? En un mot? C'est ça que tu veux savoir? Une seconde. (*Il braque la lunette sur le dehors, regarde, baisse la lunette, se tourne vers Hamm.*) Mortibus.

Beckett turned to a dead language: 'Mortibus'. The earlier state of the play had 'foutu'. (*Fin de partie*, ed. John Fletcher and Beryl S. Fletcher (1970), 86.)
[26] Kenneth Branagh illustrates another sense of the word (*Beginning* (1990), 61):

'Corpsing'—laughing on stage when you're not supposed to—had already become a hazard. I don't know why it happened to me, but I had been doing it since I'd started acting. People say it's a form of hysterics, which I'm sure is true ... Later in my career, I once corpsed myself in a one-man show, which must be some sort of record ... I then amused myself further by attempting desperately to convert the smiles into 'acting'. Not a chance; once begun, a corpse is a lost cause.

Beckett is the home of such lost causes.

procreant cradle (Beckett is as much the destroyer as the creator of linguistic possibilities) but a mass grave.

CLICHÉS

Here, as elsewhere in art, there must be weighed the relation of a *how* to a *what* to create a *why*: why Beckett writes so and why we should take note.

Beckett's first novel, *Murphy*, begins:

The sun shone, having no alternative, on the nothing new.[27]

Well, actually, *Murphy* does not begin with these words; it begins, after its title, not with a word but with the number 1 at the head of this first chapter, itself in play with 'no alternative'.

But here, at the very beginning of a *novel* (make it new, the novel particularly enjoined), we are presented not just with a cliché but with a meta-cliché, a cliché about the clichéness of everything. I take it that the reader who took Beckett at his word would at once shut the book—you're quite right Sam. Let us not play it again.

Yet Beckett has effected something justly new.

The sun shone, having no alternative, on the nothing new.

It is partly the syntactical alternative in 'having no alternative', swinging as it does on the hinges of its commas. The syntax creates the evanescent grumble that the sun shines only because it has no choice in the matter.

> If the Sun & Moon should doubt,
> Theyd immediately Go out.

Of all Blake's 'Auguries of Innocence', this is the one which it is least imaginable that we could experience.

'The sun shone, having no alternative': but then, the phrase once safely navigated, this proves not to be the case which is being made, which is rather the good old one.

Whereupon the ancient admonition that there is nothing new under the sun, or that there is no new thing under the sun, is fashioned anew:

[27] *Murphy*, 1. Preceding *Murphy* in French, 7: 'Le soleil brillait, n'ayant pas d'alternative, sur le rien de neuf.'

The sun shone, having no alternative, on the nothing new.

This rolls all the globe's strength and all its sweetness—and all its weakness and all its sourness—up into one ball, the noun-clause of 'the nothing new'. And that's new too.

This is a writer laying claim to his territory, not a writer pawing the ground—as even Henry James did when he flexed himself in the opening words of his essay 'Black and White', likewise the start of a book:

If there be nothing new under the sun there are some things a good deal less old than others.[28]

To make friends with the necessity of dying will entail being on friendly terms with another necessity, of not snubbing those dying generations, clichés. Having no alternative but to avail oneself of them.

But having an alternation. *Dream of Fair to Middling Women* gives the grounds for valuing not only figure but ground, not James's 'Black and White' but this:

'Black diamond of pessimism.' Belacqua thought that was a nice example, in the domain of words, of the little sparkle hid in ashes, the precious margaret and hid from many, and the thing that the conversationalist, with his contempt of the tag and ready-made, can't give you, because the lift to the high spot is precisely from the tag and the ready-made. The same with the stylist. You couldn't experience a margarita in d'Annunzio because he denies you the pebbles and flints that reveal it. The uniform, horizontal writing, flowing without accidence, of the man with a style, never gives you the margarita.[29]

Clichés are 'the tag and the ready-made', 'the pebbles and flints'; without them there could be no black diamond or margarita, precious and in danger of preciosity. But 'in the domain of words' there is need not only for a geological metaphor but for a horticultural one too, with its softness played against the stony hardness.

The blown roses of a phrase shall catapult the reader into the tulips of the phrase that follows.[30]

---

[28] (1889); *Picture and Text* (1893), 1.

[29] *Disjecta*, 47. *Disjecta* has, in error, 'and hit from many', corrected here from the typescript at Dartmouth College. *Dream of Fair to Middling Women*, pp. 47–8.

[30] *Disjecta*, 49. *Dream of Fair to Middling Women*, p. 137.

Beckett, who even in his youth was the lean and slippered pantaloon of clichés, puts himself in our shoes. As with that phrase itself.

She caught up the lamp off the mantelpiece where she had set it down, that's the idea every particular, it flung her waving shadow over me, I thought she was off, but no, she came stooping down towards me over the sofa back. All family possessions, she said. I in her shoes would have tiptoed away, but not she, not a stir.[31]

For a split second, you glimpse (through the interstices of 'in her shoes' and 'tiptoed') the puzzled derelict perched in a woman's shoes, the effect teetering upon the absence of any liaison of sound from 'I' to 'in'; not 'In her shoes I would have tiptoed away', but 'I in her shoes'. There is something fetching and childlike about the frozen gait: 'but not she, not a stir'. *A Child's Garden of Verses*: 'Not a stir of child or mouse'. Robert Louis Stevenson shares with Beckett the distinction of having written a work called 'Not I'.

Beckett's original French here is *flat* in comparison, as if Beckett could not quite put himself in its shoes; it offers the more abstract, less corporeal, play of 'à sa place' against 'parti':

A sa place je serais parti, sur la pointe des pieds. Mais elle ne bougea pas.

'Not a stir': but whether one stirs or not, clichés are always crossing one's path. This next is likewise from *First Love*, as the gnarled narrator is taking a room at his surprising crone's:

She lit an oil-lamp. You have no current? I said. No, she said, but I have running water and gas. Ha, I said, you have gas. She began to undress. When at their wit's end they undress, no doubt the wisest course. She took off everything, with a slowness fit to enflame an elephant, except her stockings, calculated presumably to bring my concupiscence to the boil. It was then I noticed the squint. Fortunately she was not the first naked woman to have crossed my path, so I could stay, I knew she would not

---

[31] *First Love* (1973), 50–1. Following *Premier amour* (1970, but written 1945), 45:

Elle prit la lampe sur le dessus de cheminée où elle l'avait déposée, précisons, précisons, au-dessus de moi son ombre gesticulait, je crus qu'elle allait me quitter, mais non, elle vint se pencher sur moi, par-dessus le dossier. Tout ça, c'est des choses de famille, dit-elle. A sa place je serais parti, sur la pointe des pieds. Mais elle ne bougea pas.

explode. I asked to see the other room which I had not yet seen. If I had seen it already I would have asked to see it again.[32]

This comic masterpiece or mistresspiece is in its way a gruesome slower-than-motion striptease. 'She took off everything [comma] with a slowness fit to enflame an elephant [comma] except her stockings [comma] calculated presumably to bring my concupiscence to the boil'. Whereupon he immediately looks her straight in the eye: 'It was then I noticed the squint'. Not quite straight in the eye, then. She is naked. Is he, in concentrating on her face, at heart a gentleman? Or a wincer? Or is it that her face, though leaving much to be desired, has now come to seem the lesser evil?

But of course the phrase which brings my critical concupiscence to the boil is the cliché 'cross my path'. 'Fortunately she was not the first naked woman to have crossed my path, so . . .' One doesn't ordinarily think of naked women as crossing one's path exactly. Not even in the heyday of streaking. And in combination with that elephant, 'crossed my path' takes on disconcerting suggestions of a sexual safari. Even the innocentish 'no doubt the wisest course' plays its traipsing part, unlike the French ('sans doute ce qu'elles ont de mieux à faire').

The French, on a more straightforward course, has: 'Ce n'était heureusement pas la première fois que je voyais une femme nue'—which could have gone perfectly well into English as 'fortunately it wasn't the first time that I had seen a naked woman'. No need of that weird path-crossing at all. But when he came to translate his French, there must have crossed Beckett's mind the happy infelicity of 'not the first naked woman to have crossed my path'. And this is uttered in *First Love* with as entire an equanimity as if this were what Bishop Sprat had meant in his famous praise

---

[32] *First Love*, 45–6. Following *Premier amour*, 40:

Elle alluma une lampe à pétrole. Vous n'avez pas l'électricité? dis-je. Non, dit-elle, mais j'ai l'eau courante et le gaz. Tiens, dis-je, vous avez le gaz. Elle se mit à se déshabiller. Quand elles ne savent plus que faire, elles se déshabillent, et c'est sans doute ce qu'elles ont de mieux à faire. Elle enleva tout, avec une lenteur à agacer un éléphant, sauf les bas, destinés sans doute à porter au comble mon excitation. C'est alors que je vis qu'elle louchait. Ce n'était heureusement pas la première fois que je voyais une femme nue, je pus donc rester, je savais qu'elle n'exploserait pas. Je lui dis que j'avais envie de voir l'autre chambre, car je ne l'avais pas encore vue. Si je l'avais déjà vue je lui aurais dit que j'avais envie de la revoir.

'Tiens, dis-je, vous avez le gaz': even more than the English wording, this keeps a strait fesse.

of the Royal Society for having 'exacted from all their members a close, naked, natural way of speaking'.[33]

In *First Love* there is a spectral double-exposure in 'to have crossed my path'; we narrow our eyes at it, trying to have the cliché be real, and finding it absurdly unreal, really absurd. Or surreal.

The complementary contrast would be with the solidity, the substantiality, of the path, both within the phrase and then following its path, when Beckett traces it in *Company*:

And tossing in your warm bed waiting for sleep to come you were still faintly glowing at the thought of what a fortunate hedgehog it was to have crossed your path as it did. A narrow clay path edged with sere box edging. As you stood there wondering how best to pass the time till bedtime it parted the edging on the one side and was making straight for the edging on the other when you entered its life.[34]

The French does not follow the same path; instead it varies its turn of phrase:

de croiser ton chemin comme il l'avait fait. En l'occurrence un sentier de terre bordé de buis flétri.

Clichés are an opportunity for a writer exactly in being on the face of it nothing to write home about.

The story 'The End' comes on its second page to the old man's discharge from the mercy hospital:

I didn't feel well, but they told me I was well enough. They didn't say in so many words that I was as well as I would ever be, but that was the implication. I lay inert on the bed and it took three women to put on my trousers. They didn't seem to take much interest in my private parts which to tell the truth were nothing to write home about, I didn't take

---

[33] *The History of the Royal Society* (1667), I. xx.

[34] *Company* (1980), 40–1. The English preceded the French but was then itself revised before publication in the light of Beckett's translation of it into French. So, preceding and following *Compagnie* (1980), 40:

Et te tournant et te retournant dans la chaleur des draps en attendant le sommeil tu éprouvais encore un petit chaud au cœur en pensant à la chance qu'avait eue ce hérisson-là de croiser ton chemin comme il l'avait fait. En l'occurrence un sentier de terre bordé de buis flétri. Comme tu te tenais là en t'interrogeant sur la meilleure façon de tuer le temps jusqu'à l'heure du coucher il fendit l'une des bordures et filait tout droit vers l'autre lorsque tu entras dans sa vie.

much interest in them myself. But they might have passed some remark. When they had finished I got up and finished dressing unaided.[35]

The triumph here is the union of the balanced with the unbalanced. Unbalanced, because what would he have had the three women say? 'My my'? 'Dear me'? 'Tsk tsk'? 'Wow'? 'Tiens'? (In so many words.) Balanced, though, because if it is, they say, terrible to be a sexual object, it is scarcely less so to be so totally a non-sexual object.

It is the dignity of 'But they might have passed some remark' which does it, the stoical formality of the formula trembling on the brink. That, and the delicate discriminations within the run of the thought. 'They didn't seem to take much interest in my private parts': he isn't saying they didn't take much interest, only that they didn't *seem* to (you never know with people, and particularly with women?); and then again it is not that 'they didn't seem to take *any* interest', but '*much* interest', a specification which is repeated darkly. ('I didn't take much interest in them myself'—ah.) As so often in comedy, the art is in the timing, the punctuation.

There, and in the bizarrerie of the cliché, 'nothing to write home about':

They didn't seem to take much interest in my private parts which to tell the truth were nothing to write home about, I didn't take much interest in them myself.

In what circumstances does one write home about one's private parts?

Now for the original French, and then for Beckett's first published translation of the story:

Je gisais inerte sur le lit et il fallut trois femmes pour m'enfiler le pantalon. Elles n'avaient pas l'air de s'intéresser beaucoup à mes parties qui à vrai dire n'avaient rien de particulier. Moi-même non plus je ne m'y intéressais pas. Mais elles auraient pu dire un petit quelque chose.

---

[35] 'The End' (1954); *Stories and Texts for Nothing* (1967), 48. Following 'La Fin' (1946), *Nouvelles et textes pour rien* (1955), 79:

Je ne me sentais pas bien, mais ils me dirent que je l'étais assez. Ils ne dirent pas expressément que j'étais aussi bien que je le serais jamais, mais c'était sous-entendu. Je gisais inerte sur le lit et il fallut trois femmes pour m'enfiler le pantalon. Elles n'avaient pas l'air de s'intéresser beaucoup à mes parties qui à vrai dire n'avaient rien de particulier. Moi-même non plus je ne m'y intéressais pas. Mais elles auraient pu dire un petit quelque chose. Quand elles eurent fini je me levai et finis de m'habiller tout seul.

Lovely in its way, 'mes parties qui à vrai dire n'avaient rien de particulier' ('about which there was nothing especial'?), but its way is less intimate with life and death than is the lethal liveliness of the cliché 'nothing to write home about'. Meanwhile *inert* ('I lay inert on the bed and it took three women to put on my trousers') makes him sound as good as dead. Well, not as *good* as dead, if you take the large view, but at any rate already as hard to be-trouser as a corpse apparently is. (They say it takes three people.)

The tremulous indignation of the English idiom, or rather the Irish, 'But they might have passed some remark', biting back the tears of outrage, had been in French the smaller dryer joke: 'Mais elles auraient pu dire un petit quelque chose'. This properly takes improper advantage not only of the fact that the words could have been, whether cutting or sorrowing, *direct* speech, as the three women contemplate his private parts—'un petit quelque chose', that is what they might have said in measured tones—but also of the linguistic quirk, highly germane to the occasion, that whereas *chose* is feminine, *quelque chose* is masculine.

In comparison with either the original French or the final English, the first published translation, in *Merlin* (1954), by Richard Seaver in collaboration with the author (as is the final translation), went off at half-cock:

I didn't feel very strong, but they told me I was strong enough. They did not expressly say I was as strong as I would ever be, but that was implied. I lay inert on the bed, and it took three of the women to put on my new trousers. They did not seem to take much interest in my private parts. I didn't take much interest in them myself any more. But I felt they might have said something. When they had finished I got up and put on the other clothes all alone.

The punctuation had not arrived at its delicious misplaced resilience; very stiff and segregated here, inert at the full stops:

They did not seem to take much interest in my private parts. I didn't take much interest in them myself any more. But I felt they might have said something.

For 'any more' offered an inappropriate wistfulness, as did the incipient pathos of 'all alone', 'I got up and put on the other clothes all alone', unlike the due independent pride, slightly cracked, of 'unaided': 'I got up and finished dressing unaided'.

As for 'But I felt they might have said something', which trails away rather, it lacks indignation's unexpected comic dignity.

Such a translation is better than you or I could do, but it is as nothing to the account finally rendered:

I lay inert on the bed and it took three women to put on my trousers. They didn't seem to take much interest in my private parts which to tell the truth were nothing to write home about, I didn't take much interest in them myself. But they might have passed some remark.

What makes this remarkable is the way in which it introduces into dead phrases an unexpected mingling of life and death.

For death is the supreme nothing to write about. As John Jay Chapman lay dying, two days before the end, he reshaped Caroline Norton's poem 'A soldier of the Legion lay dying in Algiers', with its melancholy 'There was lack of woman's nursing', as 'But there is lack of nothing here'—an exquisite paradox.[36] In 1817 Jane Austen lay dying:

and on being asked by her attendants whether there was anything that she wanted, her reply was, '*Nothing but death.*' These were her last words.[37]

'Wanted': desired and lacked, akin to Philip Larkin's 'Wants'.

Jane Austen foresaw her death. The over-zealous constable in *Mercier and Camier* does not know what he is letting himself in for. (Death, in fact.) Who could have foreseen it?

Camier gave a scream of pain. For the constable, holding fast his arm with one hand the size of two, with the other had dealt him a violent smack. His interest was awakening. It was not every night a diversion of this quality broke the monotony of his beat. The profession had its silver lining, he had always said so. He unsheathed his truncheon. Come on with you now, he said, and no nonsense. With the hand that held the truncheon he drew a whistle from his pocket, for he was no less dexterous than powerful. But he had reckoned without Mercier (who can blame him?) and to his undoing, for Mercier raised his right foot (who could

---

[36] *John Jay Chapman and His Letters*, ed. M. A. DeWolfe Howe (1937), 463:

On the early morning of the 2nd [November 1933], I [Chapman's wife] heard him murmuring, 'A soldier lay dying, a soldier lay dying'. I bent over him to catch the words, and he repeated the first four lines of 'A soldier of the Legion lay dying in Algiers', adding, '*But there is lack of nothing here,*' in a voice of deep feeling.

[37] *A Memoir of Jane Austen* by her nephew J. E. Austen Leigh (1869), ch. xi.

have foreseen it?) and launched it clumsily but with force among the
testicles (to call a spade a spade) of the adversary (impossible to miss
them).[38]

The voice cannot render the parenthesis-markings (the sort of
thing for which a lecturer twitters his hands, as when quoting with
crooked fingers). But the eye can see these central asides, can see,
snugly tucked-up, the clucked '(who could have foreseen it?)'
Four times there are these cuppings:

But he had reckoned without Mercier (who can blame him?) and to his
undoing, for Mercier raised his right foot (who could have foreseen it?)
and launched it clumsily but with force among the testicles (to call a
spade a spade) of the adversary (impossible to miss them).

Not to beat about the bush, these suspensions ( ) are notably
scrotal.

In a learned brilliant book, John Lennard recently gave the
world not only his imaginative understanding of 'the exploitation
of parentheses in English printed verse'[39] but a word for the
simple marks themselves: 'lunulae', by courtesy of Erasmus.
Lennard is acutely persuasive on the graphic possibilities of these
little moons, lunulae, for instance their Jacobean mounting to
suggest both a vagina and bandy legs: a vivid nothing between the
lunulae ( ), there where life itself emanates.[40]

The body of this thought, Lennard might have added, can
be confirmed elsewhere, not only in the suggestive seventeenth-
century postures but in the decorous nineteenth-century stance of
a prim primer of 1824, *Punctuation Personified*:

---

[38] *Mercier and Camier*, 92–3. Following *Mercier et Camier*, 157:

Aïe! dit Mercier.
    Maintenant d'une seule main, grande comme deux mains ordinaires, rouge vif et couverte
de poils, le bras de Camier, l'agent lui appliqua de l'autre une gifle violente. Cela
commençait à l'intéresser. Ce n'était pas tous les jours qu'un divertissement de cette qualité
venait rompre la monotonie de sa faction. Le métier avait du bon, il l'avait toujours dit. Il
sortit son bâton. Allez hop, dit-il, et pas d'histoires. De la main qui tenait le bâton il prit un
sifflet dans sa poche et se le mit aux lèvres, car il n'était pas moins adroit que vigoureux.
Mais il ne prenait pas Mercier suffisamment au sérieux (qui l'en blâmera?), et ce fut sa
perte, car Mercier leva son pied droit (qui aurait pu s'y attendre?) et l'envoya maladroitement
mais avec sécheresse dans les testicules (appelons les choses par leur nom) de l'adversaire
(pas moyen de les rater).

[39] The subtitle of *But I Digress* (1991).
[40] *But I Digress*, 40, on Marston.

> The arms are the ACCENTS, both GRAVE & ACUTE,
> And for legs the PARENTHESIS nicely may suit.

Beckett has an eye to these graphic exploits, as when Murphy offers to stand in for Ticklepenny as a mental nurse:

> When Ticklepenny had quite done commiserating himself, in a snivelling antiphony between the cruel necessity of going mad if he stayed and the cruel impossibility of leaving without his wages, Murphy said:
>
> 'Supposing you were to produce a substitute of my intelligence' (corrugating his brow) 'and physique' (squaring the circle of his shoulders), 'what then?'[41]

This is, and is meant to be, too much. It is sturdy (unlike the delectably mincing parentheses of *Mercier and Camier*); it is physical and physique-al (the brow turned on its side, and the shoulders too, and yet with the lunulae suggesting first the shape of a face and then that of the upper body). It is a happy cliché. It is an enactment and at the same time an embodiment (mimetic and not so). And it is the resolution of an ancient impossibility. To create an art which both is and is not mimetic: this is squaring the circle. Or shaping curved parallels. All of which intelligently square up to a 'cruel impossibility'.

Then there are the lunulae of ancient decompositions, as when Beckett in his book on Proust writes of Habit:

> The periods of transition that separate consecutive adaptations (because by no expedient of macabre transubstantiation can the grave-sheets serve as swaddling-clothes) represent the perilous zones in the life of the individual.[42]

The lunulae are themselves a form of perilous zoning, and they effect a macabre transubstantiation which is pure Beckett: by some expedient of macabre transubstantiation the grave-sheets *can* serve as swaddling-clothes. The lunulae, which are themselves effecters of 'transition', swaddle the thought, grave-sheet it

---

[41] *Murphy*, 92. Preceding *Murphy* in French, 70:

Quand Ticklepenny eut tout a fait fini de se lamenter, oscillant dans une antienne nerveuse entre la cruelle nécessité de devenir fou s'il restait et la cruelle impossibilité de s'en aller sans ses gages, Murphy dit:

—Et si vous leur ameniez un substitut de mon intelligence (il triséqua l'angle de son front) et de mon physique (il carra le cercle de ses épaules), alors?

[42] *Proust*, 8.

on the page, transubstantiate it. And those readers sceptical of
Beckett, or of this devotion to his zones of punctuation, should at
least remark how and where Beckett chose to move here in his
own 'periods of transition', his own 'consecutive adaptations':

The periods of transition that separate consecutive adaptations (because
by no expedient of macabre transubstantiation can the grave-sheets serve
as swaddling-clothes) represent the perilous zones in the life of the
individual, dangerous, precarious, painful, mysterious and fertile, when
for a moment the boredom of living is replaced by the suffering of being.
(At this point, and with a heavy heart and for the satisfaction or dis-
gruntlement of Gideans, semi and integral, I am inspired to concede a
brief parenthesis to all the analogivorous, who are capable of interpreting
the 'Live dangerously,' that victorious hiccough in vacuo, as the national
anthem of the true ego exiled in habit. The Gideans advocate a habit of
living—and look for an epithet. A nonsensical bastard phrase. They
imply a hierarchy of habits, as though it were valid to speak of good
habits and bad habits. An automatic adjustment of the human organism
to the conditions of its existence has as little moral significance as the
casting of a clout when May is or is not out; and the exhortation to
cultivate a habit as little sense as an exhortation to cultivate a coryza.)
The suffering of being: that is, the free play of every faculty.[43]

A *brief* parenthesis? One would like to see young Beckett's idea of
a lengthy one. But the gambit is that of a writer who knows a
parenthesis when he sees one—and who is able, preposterously,
to give an air of meaning it when he says 'a brief parenthesis' by
taking up his thought exactly where he had left it, confident that it
would not go away, fifteen lines earlier:

when for a moment the boredom of living is replaced by the suffering of
being. [. . .] The suffering of being: that is, the free play of every faculty.

But let me take a leaf out of Beckett's book, and after this
parenthesis about parentheses, return to where I left off, the
episode in *Mercier and Camier*, the constable's fate: '(who could
have foreseen it?)'. I should not myself ever have foreseen the
force of 'launched it clumsily but with force *among* the testicles'. It
is a most disconcerting preposition, and proposition come to that.
(The French had simply 'dans les testicules'.) And yet what would
be the right preposition exactly? For the male genitals are a

---

[43] *Proust*, 8–9. A 'coryza', for those not in the know, is a running at the nose; it is
caught from the nearby thought about not casting a clout till May is out.

metaphysical union of the one and the many, so it is by no means clear just how to put it. 'Launched it clumsily but with force *at* the testicles'? But that's not it. In? Into? Upon? Within? Between? But '*Between* relates the position of an object to a definite or exclusive set of discrete objects, whereas *among* relates to nondiscrete objects'.[44] Few objects could be more non-discrete than testicles. Mmm, perhaps 'among the testicles' is right—though admittedly lumpish, what with its suggestion that the constable may be more than usually endowed.

There follow two laconic parenthetical clichés:

launched it clumsily but with force among the testicles (to call a spade a spade) of the adversary (impossible to miss them).

The first cliché here is openly (though parenthetically) a specious disclaimer, since 'testicles' is exactly *not* calling a spade a spade on such an occasion. The constable, not to put too fine a point on it, gets kicked in the balls. But then the cliché is brought to a mortal liveliness by the sudden flashing of *spade*, a eunuch (odd that *spayed* takes in the female eunuch). A character in *Murphy* is drily described as a 'spado of long standing'.[45] If you kick a man with enough force, you will be able to call a spade a spade.[46]

And a *spade* is naturally, in Beckett and outside him, the means

---

[44] Randolph Quirk, Sidney Greenbaum, Geoffrey Leech, and Jan Svartvik, *A Comprehensive Grammar of the English Language* (1985), 680.

[45] *Murphy*, 99, where the medium Rosie Dew rattles on:

Lord Gall of Wormwood, perhaps you know him, a charming man, he sends me objects, he is in a painful position, spado of long standing in tail male special he seeks testamentary pentimenti from the *au-delà*.

Preceding *Murphy* in French, 75:

Baron Fiel d'Absinthe, vous le connaissez peut-être, un homme charmant, il m'envoie des objets, il est dans les choux, héritier en substitution mâle spéciale sans espoir d'enfants, pas même d'une petite fille figurez-vous, il cherche dans l'au-delà des appendices testic—que dis-je—testamentaires.

The English left to the imagination the relation of 'spado' to 'testamentary', but the French felt obliged to spell it out, or half out: 'testic—que dis-je—testamentaires'. Nor could the French come up with an equivalent to the expansive 'spado of long standing'. There is more fun, too, in 'from the *au-delà*' than in 'dans l'au-delà', since in the English the French words are themselves *au-delà*.

[46] Perhaps Beckett remembered the odd bodily passage in Swift's *Polite Conversation* (Fourth Dialogue), that obsessive garnering of clichés:

—O Miss, 'tis nothing what we say among ourselves.

—Ay, Madam, but they say, Hedges have Eyes, and Walls have Ears.

—Well, Miss, I can't help it, you know I am old Tell-truth, I love to call a Spade a Spade.

for the end, the instrument with which the living bury their dead.

The dog had ticks in his ears, I have an eye for such things, they were buried with him. When she had finished her grave she handed me the spade and began to muse, or brood.[47]

So 'to call a spade a spade' is worth musing or brooding over, a cliché so diversely bearing witness to the encompassing cliché that in the midst of life we are in death.

'To call a spade a spade': once again the French, although it is the original, is in comparison incorporeal, less in touch with these fecund matters of life and death: 'dans les testicules (appelons les choses par leur nom)'.

It is a further injustice that these little witnesses (for such, at the root, are testicles) are not of a sort that the constable would ever have been able to call. Beckett toys with such a thought in *Watt*, where a policeman is summoned because of a putative act of indecency:

> Officer, he cried, as God is my witness, he had his hand upon it.
> God is a witness that cannot be sworn.[48]

Not that the resisted constable would have been in any position to summon witnesses. Mercier and Camier, picked-upon unjustly as they were, proceed to kill him in their injured exuberance.

Mercier launched his right foot 'clumsily but with force among the testicles (to call a spade a spade) of the adversary (impossible to miss them)'. The closing parenthesis, of which it is impossible to misunderstand the thrust, must not have its reticence missed. Impossible to miss them because such is the male anatomy? Or because the constable is well hung? ('holding fast his arm with one hand the size of two'). Or because 'among'—'among the

---

[47] *Molloy*, 48. Following *Molloy* in French, 54:

Le chien avait des tiques aux oreilles, j'ai l'œil pour ces choses-là, elles furent enterrées avec lui. Quand elle eut fini de fossoyer elle me passa la bêche et se recueillit.

[48] *Watt*, 9. Preceding *Watt* in French, 8:

Sergent, s'écria-t-il, Dieu m'est témoin qu'il avait la main dessus.
Dieu est un témoin inassermentable.

The big witness is acknowledged elsewhere in Beckett too: *Molloy*, 198–9: 'I took advantage of being alone at last, with no other witness than God, to masturbate'. No, since this is a man, there were little witnesses. Following *Molloy* in French, 224: 'Je profitai de ce que j'étais seul enfin, sans autre témoin que Dieu, pour me masturber'.

testicles'—suggests that perhaps we should move beyond binary thinking?

> I had so to speak only one leg at my disposal, I was virtually onelegged, and I would have been happier, livelier, amputated at the groin. And if they had removed a few testicles into the bargain I wouldn't have objected.[49]

Beckett enjoys the oddities of number hereabouts, while proceeding to prosecute this etymology and what it bears witness to:

> I longed to see them gone, from the old stand where they bore false witness, for and against, in the lifelong charge against me. For if they accused me of having made a balls of it, of me, of them, they thanked me for it too, from the depths of their rotten bag, the right lower than the left, or inversely, I forget, decaying circus clowns.[50]

'The old stand': now there is a witness-stand for you.

'A balls of it': odd, when you think about it, especially when uttered so evenly. There is a moment in an Anthony Burgess novel when the man in danger, fascinated as any good Burgessman is by *language*, watches someone advancing on him with a pair of scissors, and can only marvel at such intersections of the singular and the plural as the three which comprise his imminent fate: scissors/trousers/bollocks.

Beckett, too, is drawn to these singular plurals. Including that very trinity.

At the birth of Larry, in *Watt*: 'She severed the cord with her teeth, said Goff, not having a scissors to her hand'.[51] How meticulously spoken, not just the syntax ('not having') but 'not having a scissors'.

---

[49] *Molloy*, 47. Following *Molloy* in French, 52:

Je ne disposais pour ainsi dire que d'une jambe, j'étais moralement unijambiste, et j'aurais été plus heureux, plus léger, amputé au niveau de l'aîne. Et ils m'auraient enlevé quelques testicules à la même occasion que je ne leur aurais rien dit.

[50] *Molloy*, 47. Following *Molloy* in French, 52:

j'avais plutôt envie de les voir disparaître, ces témoins à charge à décharge de ma longue mise en accusation. Car s'ils m'accusaient de les avoir couillonnés, ils m'en congratulaient aussi, du fond de leur sacoche crevée, le droit plus bas que le gauche, ou inversement, je ne sais plus, frères de cirque.

[51] *Watt*, 14. Preceding *Watt* in French, 14:

Elle a sectionné le cordon avec les dents, dit Goff, n'ayant pas de ciseaux sous la main.

Ensconced within a three-hundred-word sentence in *Watt* there appear

the castoff clothes, of which Mr Knott, who was a great caster-off of clothes, had a large store, being handed over, now a coat, now a waistcoat, now a greatcoat, now a raincoat, now a trousers, now a knickerbockers, now a shirt, now a vest, now a pant, now a combination, now a braces, now a belt[52]

The oddity has it both ways: the singularity of saying 'a trousers', 'a knickerbockers', and 'a braces', cheek by jowl with the singularity of doing the opposite and postulating as items of clothing (oh the *words* exist in the singular all right, but) 'a pant' and 'a combination'.

In Beckett, clichés are seen from inside as well as from outside:

Seen from outside it was a house like any other. Seen from inside too.

This is a fitting rebuke to the journalistic drum-roll which is heralded by 'Seen from outside'. Yet Beckett does not leave it at the externality of the flip.

Seen from outside it was a house like any other. Seen from inside too. And yet it emitted Camier. He still took the air in a small way, when the weather was fine.[53]

'Emitted' is decorously embarrassing, bent to vent the pent. I should prefer not to think that a house 'emitted' me, especially if I 'took the air'. ('Smell? His own? Long since dulled. And a barrier to others if any. Such as might have once emitted a rat long dead'.[54])

[52] *Watt*, 100. Preceding *Watt* in French, 102:

les vannes des vêtements de rebut dont Monsieur Knott, grand rebuteur de vêtements, avait d'immenses réserves, tantôt une veste, tantôt un gilet, tantôt un manteau, tantôt un imperméable, tantôt un pantalon, tantôt un knickerbocker, tantôt une chemise, tantôt un tricot, tantôt un caleçon, tantôt une combinaison, tantôt une bretelle, tantôt une ceinture

Handsome of French to hand the self-translator something so comically elegant as 'tantôt un manteau'.

[53] *Mercier and Camier*, 109. Following *Mercier et Camier*, 190:

Vue de l'extérieur c'était une maison comme tant d'autres. Vue de l'intérieur aussi. Camier en sortit. Il se promenait encore, un peu, quand il faisait beau.

[54] *Company*, 72. Preceding and following *Compagnie*, 71:

L'odorat? Son odeur à lui? Depuis longtemps assumée. Et barrage à d'autres s'il y en a. Par exemple à un moment donné d'un rat depuis longtemps mort.

The English 'emitted' purses its nostrils; the French 'donné' opens them in quasi-

Mercier et Camier is less mephitic, and thereby less physical, less an inspired relation of an inside to an outside, less a mingling of fresh air and dead wind:

Camier en sortit. Il se promenait encore, un peu, quand il faisait beau.

Neither 'en sortit' nor 'se promenait' is to be nosed, and there is no current from the one to the other, unlike 'emitted' with 'took the air'. Beckett's English is not abstracted to death, albeit it hovers above dead and standing pools of air; it has bodily functions.

Clichés are a way in which we all keep body and soul together. Habited.

Camier has inscribed on his card:

> F. X. CAMIER
> Private Investigator
> Soul of Discretion[55]

Less insinuatingly assured, the French had:

> FRANCIS XAVIER CAMIER
> Enquêtes et Filatures
> Discrétion assurée

Delicious, and so discreet, the announcement of oneself professionally as (without the article 'the'): 'Soul of Discretion'. And the English is in another way more discreet than the French (for all its 'Discrétion assurée'), in that when Beckett rethought the card he muted Xavier to X. Discreet, and yet not difficult privately to investigate. What but Xavier could lurk behind X.? Especially given the given name Francis.[56]

The insinuating power of Beckett's unofficial English is often a

---

gratitude. But then the French was given the chance to scent the rat in the smell, as if 'L'odorat' emanated from 'un rat'.

[55] *Mercier and Camier*, 54. Following *Mercier et Camier*, 84.

[56] *Mercier and Camier* does not leave the name for ever tacit; on p. 100,

Hell, said Mercier, who the devil are you, Camier?
Me? said Camier. I am Camier, Francis Xavier.

Following *Mercier et Camier*, 171:

Enfin, qui es-tu, Camier? dit Mercier.
Moi? dit Camier. Je suis Camier, Francis Xavier.

matter of the decorous meeting the freakish. Discretion is a
natural location for these studied coincidings. In the French, the
cliché can be left for dead, flatly horizontal: 'Je suis la discrétion
même. Un tombeau'.[57] But when this is resurrected as English, it
becomes Irish, at once extravagant and proverbial: 'I'm discretion
itself. The wild horse's despair'.

A constable, a private investigator: cliché is the dead letter of
the law. Also its dead hand, at the end of its long arm. Beckett's
characters have their own, not unreasonable, judgement of the
relation of the police to the law:

Were they of the opinion that it was useless to prosecute me? To apply
the letter of the law to a creature like me is not an easy matter. It can be
done, but reason is against it. It is better to leave things to the police.[58]

Take the penal pen into your own hands? It may be better to leave
things to clichés, provided that they are policed.

RESURRECTION

One truth about cliché allies it with death. A cliché is a dead piece
of language, of which one cliché might be that it is dead but won't
lie down.

Though no language could survive without such deaths,
languages stand differently to cliché. William Empson maintained
this ground:

All languages are composed of dead metaphors as the soil of corpses, but
English is perhaps uniquely full of metaphors of this sort, which are not
dead but sleeping, and, while making a direct statement, colour it with an
implied comparison.[59]

The following year, 1931, Beckett wrote in his *Proust*:

---

[57] *Mercier et Camier*, 194. Preceding *Mercier and Camier*, 111.
[58] *Molloy*, 31. Following *Molloy* in French, 34:

Estimait-on que ce n'était pas la peine de me poursuivre en correctionnelle? Châtier de
façon systématique un être comme moi, ce n'est pas commode. Ça arrive, mais la sagesse le
déconseille. Il est préférable de s'en remettre aux agents.

[59] *Seven Types of Ambiguity* (1930, rev. 1947), 25. On metaphor and dead metaphor,
the most revelatory critic since Empson is Donald Davie, *Purity of Diction in English
Verse* (1952). For clichés seen under other aspects, see an essay of mine in *The Force of
Poetry* (1984), 356–68.

But less drastic circumstances may produce this tense and provisional lucidity in the nervous system. Habit may not be dead (or as good as dead, doomed to die) but sleeping.[60]

The lunulae are as good as swaddling-bands. Clichés are themselves a force of habit: the bad habit of living, the good habit of dying. 'Breathing is habit. Life is habit.'

Dead metaphors? Sleeping ones? Sometimes there are other suspended animations. Such as a rogue element: a drowned man, perhaps, neither living nor dead, who might be brought back—but would it be a mercy? There is Rogue Riderhood, in *Our Mutual Friend*:

He is struggling to come back. Now he is almost here, now he is far away again. Now he is struggling harder to get back. And yet—like us all, when we swoon—like us all, every day of our lives when we wake—he is instinctively unwilling to be restored to the consciousness of this existence, and would be left dormant, if he could.[61]

Or a cliché may be possessed of a resurrected or galvanized or zombie life, each of which has an eerier effect than that of awakening a sleeper or of bringing back one who hovers between death and life.

> From their graves resuscitate the dead,
> that I may see them, touch them, shuddering . . .[62]

That corpse in the garden, which begins to sprout: the poet who imagined such a corpse is also the poet who imagined, in 'Little Gidding',

> Dead water and dead sand
> Contending for the upper hand

—where the evacuated deadness is a matter of the grisly unimaginable life in that cliché, the upper hand. What would the hands of water and sand look like, and how could they sufficiently meet to contend?

How It Is inflicts its own wound on being left for dead:

---

[60] *Proust*, 9.
[61] Book the Third, ch. 3.
[62] Ignacio Rodríguez Galván, in *Anthology of Mexican Poetry*, 97, translated by Beckett. The ellipsis is in the text.

bright dark that family for every hundred times they come three laughs
four laughs brought off the kind that convulse an instant resurrect an
instant then leave for deader than before[63]

Time is for Beckett 'a condition of resurrection because an
instrument of death'. Which brings in its wake the phrase 'as
happy as Larry'.

It comes in *Murphy*, where it is instinct with a solicitude for the
melancholic, the manic, and the paranoid:

Left in peace they would have been as happy as Larry, short for Lazarus,
whose raising seemed to Murphy perhaps the one occasion on which the
Messiah had overstepped the mark.[64]

End of paragraph: no overstepping here.

When on a previous occasion he attended to the raising of
Lazarus, Beckett had limited himself to mimicking a camp
ostentation about the matter. The plump speaker twits Christ:

He is the first great self-contained playboy. The cryptic abasement
before the woman taken red-handed is as great a piece of megalomaniacal
impertinence as his interference in the affairs of his boy-friend Lazarus.[65]

But in the unburlesque art of *Murphy*, the judgement delivered as
'perhaps the one occasion on which the Messiah had overstepped
the mark' is shockingly temperate, redolent with its own determination not to overstep the mark (that phrase itself, and the
scrupulous delicacy of 'perhaps'). But then this particular intervention by the Messiah had indeed overstepped the Mark; it is
not to be found in his gospel, but in that of St John.

The cliché's modest miracle of resurrection comes with 'as
happy as Larry, short for Lazarus', Beckett possessing a faith
denied to the uncertain *OED*:

[Etym. uncertain.] *happy as Larry*, extremely happy. 1905.

The second edition of the *OED* includes this crux in Beckett,
1938, and makes no effort to explode its etymologizing; but the
Dictionary also proffers, from 1966, Baker, *Australian Language*:

---

[63] *How It Is*, 119. Following *Comment c'est*, 134:

clair noir cette famille-là sur cent fois qu'ils arrivent trois quatre rires réussis de ceux qui
secouent un instant ressuscitent un instant plus laissent pour plus mort qu'avant

[64] *Murphy*, 180. Preceding *Murphy* in French, 131.

[65] 'A Wet Night', *More Pricks than Kicks*, 74.

'Possibly but not certainly commemorating the noted Australian pugilist Larry Foley (1847–1917)'.[66]

One can see why Beckett would not want to be bilked by a boxer, fobbed off with a Foley. Only as happy as Foley? That falls far short of 'as happy as Larry, short for Lazarus'.

The subsequent French, lacking 'as happy as Larry', was unable to raise Lazarus, and settled for raising its Catholic eyebrows:

Laissés en paix, ils auraient été heureux comme Dieu en France.

What Beckett catches with the catchphrase is the raising of Lazarus from Larry, only then to leave Lazarus to die down again. 'Etym. uncertain', after all. Meanwhile Beckett casts a powerful shaft of dark on the phrase itself. 'As happy as Larry'? If Lazarus, happy to have been brought back to life? Ah, but perhaps happy (prior to Christ's 'interference') to have died? Call no man happy till then.

You look like Lazarus frantic in the daylight[67]

Or, in the next round of the life and death cycle, happy to have been allowed thereafter to die? At last. Twice and for all.

When with obsessive care Swift assembled clichés (in *Polite Conversation*, a phrase which figures in Beckett's story 'The End'), it was with that sense of life and death which animates, if that is the word, his fiercest foray, *A Modest Proposal*.[68] What will your

---

[66] Eric Partridge says only 'Very happy: Australian coll.: late C. 19–20', *A Dictionary of Slang and Unconventional English* (5th edn., 1961).

[67] *Collected Poems*, 147, translating Apollinaire, 'Zone', 'Tu ressembles au Lazare affolé par le jour'. John Berryman ends a sequence, 'Op. posth. no. 14' (Dream Song number 91), with a latterday Lazarus frantic in the dark:

> A fortnight later, sense a single man
> upon the trampled scene at 2 a.m.
> insomnia-plagued, with a shovel
> digging like mad, Lazarus with a plan
> to get his own back, a plan, a stratagem
> no newsman will unravel.

There is a Larry in *Watt* (p. 13 in English and French), whose birth has been linked with his author's and with the Lazarus Larry, unearthed by Lawrence [Larry?] Harvey, *Samuel Beckett Poet and Critic*, 352.

[68] The imaginary proposer is careful not to claim too much for his bright dark idea; self-deprecatingly, this is a *modest* proposal merely. Or, to give it the full obsequious title, *A Modest Proposal for preventing the Children of Poor People from being a Burthen to their Parents, or the Country, and for making them Beneficial to the Publick*.

ingenious solution (not enough food in Ireland, and too many babies—eat the babies!) do about the nuisance that is the aged population?

Some Persons of a desponding Spirit are in great concern about that vast Number of poor People, who are aged, diseased, or maimed, and I have been desired to imploy my thoughts what Course may be taken, to ease the Nation of so grievous an Incumbrance. But I am not in the least pain about the matter, because it is very well known, that they are every Day *dying*, and *rotting*, by *cold*, and *famine*, and *filth*, and *vermin*, as fast as can be reasonably expected.

How glacially a phrase like 'not in the least pain' or 'as fast as can be reasonably expected' preserves its antiseptic political rectitude. It was from Swift that Beckett learned such iciness, witnessing such deaths of the imagination, bureaucratic and other.

Clichés gravitate naturally to death and to resurrections of a sort. So it is that Murphy asks to be handed his horoscope: 'My life-warrant. Thank you.'[69] Or there is Belacqua fretting as he awaits his operation:

But he will make up for it later on, there is a good time coming for him later on, when the doctors have given him a new lease of apathy.[70]

Another of those measured irresistible paragraph-endings.

The good time coming is the best of times, it is the worst of times. The new lease (Belacqua dies under the knife) has all too short a date, but it brings him the supreme apathy: death. Yet 'a new lease of apathy' is a turn which gives to the cliché 'a new lease of life' a new lease of—well, not exactly life.

In Beckett, such leases of death are seconded by what he calls a 'syntax of weakness'.[71] As in the scattered fraying of dear dead Belacqua's women:

---

[69] *Murphy*, 31. Preceding *Murphy* in French, 28: 'Mon arrêt de vie. Merci'.

[70] 'Yellow', *More Pricks than Kicks*, 234. There is a reprise (no reprieve) in the funeral story 'Draff', following the death of our hero in 'Yellow', which concludes the book (pp. 272–3):

Belacqua dead and buried, Hairy seemed to have taken on a new lease of life. He spoke well, with commendable assurance; he looked better, less obese cretin and spado than ever before; and he felt better, which was a great thing. Perhaps the explanation of this was that while Belacqua was alive Hairy could not be himself, or, if you prefer, could be nothing else.

[71] Lawrence Harvey reports ('according to Beckett'): 'Someday somebody will find an adequate form, a "syntax of weakness"'. *Samuel Beckett Poet and Critic*, 249.

Then shortly after that they suddenly seemed to be all dead, Lucy of course long since, Ruby duly, Winnie to decency, Alba Perdue in the natural course of being seen home.[72]

But Beckett's syntax of weakness, in the vicinity of clichés and other forms of life in death, asks a larger sequence than a single sentence however singular. It is not that such syntax is weak; rather, that it is a 'syntax of weakness', pressing on, unable to relinquish its perseverance and to arrive at severance.

Here is the opening of *First Love*:

I associate, rightly or wrongly, my marriage with the death of my father, in time. That other links exist, on other levels, between these two affairs, is not impossible. I have enough trouble as it is in trying to say what I think I know.

I visited, not so long ago, my father's grave, that I do know, and noted the date of his death, of his death alone, for that of his birth had no interest for me, on that particular day. I set out in the morning and was back by night, having lunched lightly in the graveyard. But some days later, wishing to know his age at death, I had to return to the grave, to note the date of his birth. These two limiting dates I then jotted down on a piece of paper, which I now carry about with me. I am thus in a position to affirm that I must have been about twenty-five at the time of my marriage. For the date of my own birth, I repeat, my own birth, I have never forgotten, I never had to note it down, it remains graven in my memory, the year at least, in figures that life will not easily erase. The day itself comes back to me, when I put my mind to it, and I often celebrate it, after my fashion, I don't say each time it comes back, for it comes back too often, but often.

Personally I have no bone to pick with graveyards, I take the air there willingly, perhaps more willingly than elsewhere, when take the air I must. The smell of corpses, distinctly perceptible under those of grass and humus mingled, I do not find unpleasant, a trifle on the sweet side perhaps, a trifle heady, but how infinitely preferable to what the living emit[73]

---

[72] 'Draff', *More Pricks than Kicks*, 255–6.
[73] Following *Premier amour*:

J'associe, à tort ou à raison, mon mariage avec la mort de mon père, dans le temps. Qu'il existe d'autres liens, sur d'autres plans, entre ces deux affaires, c'est possible. Il m'est déjà difficile de dire ce que je crois savoir.

Je suis allé, il n'y a pas très longtemps, sur la tombe de mon père, cela je le sais, et j'ai relevé la date de son décès, de son décès seulement, car celle de sa naissance m'était indifférente, ce jour-là. Je suis parti le matin et je suis rentré le soir, ayant cassé la croûte au cimetière. Mais quelques jours plus tard, désirant savoir à quel âge il est mort, j'ai dû

'Personally I have no bone to pick with graveyards': so in the English edition (1973 and subsequently), though in the US edition (1974) it was: 'Personally I have nothing against graveyards', a faithful but insufficiently mordant swallowing of the original French: 'Personellement je n'ai rien contre les cimetières'.[74]

Add the *petit guignol* of 'having lunched lightly in the grave-yard'[75]—disconcerting and yet ordinary enough, graveyards being among the few pastoral locations which survive. Add, too, the gastronomy which custards the thought that the smell is 'a trifle on the sweet side'; and the obduracy which incisively moves from 'the grave' to 'it remains graven in my memory'. Most cunningly composed and decomposed is the scrupulous sequence:

Personally I have no bone to pick with graveyards, I take the air there willingly, perhaps more willingly than elsewhere, when take the air I must. The smell of corpses, distinctly perceptible under those of grass and humus mingled, I do not find unpleasant,

—where 'when take the air I must' makes *must* decay before your very nose, from a verb to a noun. It is the dried-out counterpart to the hideous moistness of 'she could make the dead softsoap the quick in seven languages'.[76]

Beckett moulds as wormy circumstance what in Thomas Hood's punnery was never a true disgust—rather, a pot-pourri:[77]

> Even the bright extremes of joy
> Bring on conclusions of disgust,

retourner sur sa tombe, pour relever la date de sa naissance. Ces deux dates limites, je les ai notées sur un morceau de papier, que je garde par-devers moi. C'est ainsi que je suis en mesure d'affirmer que je devais avoir à peu près ving-cinq ans lors de mon mariage. Car la date de ma naissance à moi, je dis bien, de ma naissance à moi, je ne l'ai jamais oubliée, je n'ai jamais été obligé de la prendre par écrit, elle reste gravée dans ma mémoire, le millésime tout au moins, en chiffres que la vie aura du mal à effacer. Le jour aussi, quand je fais un effort je le retrouve, et je le célèbre souvent, à ma façon, je ne dirai pas chaque fois qu'il revient, non, car il revient trop souvent, mais souvent.

Personellement je n'ai rien contre les cimetières, je m'y promène assez volontiers qu'ailleurs, je crois, quand je suis obligé de sortir. L'odeur des cadavres, que je perçois nettement sous celle de l'herbe et de l'humus, ne m'est pas désagréable. Un peu trop sucrée peut-être, un peu entêtante, mais combien préférable à celle des vivants

[74] By 1976 Grove Press came to follow the English text ('no bone to pick'), in Richard Seaver's anthology from Beckett, *I can't go on, I'll go on*.

[75] The French 'ayant cassé la croûte au cimetière' is not without its necrophagous gusto.

[76] *Murphy*; see p. 30 above.

[77] I owe my knowledge of the Hood poem to Walter Redfern, *Puns* (1984), 63.

> Like the sweet blossoms of the May,
> Whose fragrance ends in must.

But the original French is not abstracted to death, rather it is abstracted from death, in comparison with the corpse-light corporeality of Beckett's English, formal-sounding and formality-sounding.

> Personally I have no bone to pick with graveyards, I take the air there willingly, perhaps more willingly than elsewhere, when take the air I must. The smell of corpses

> Personellement je n'ai rien contre les cimetières, je m'y promène assez volontiers qu'ailleurs, je crois, quand je suis obligé de sortir. L'odeur des cadavres

The shabby-genteel formality of 'take the air', taken up subsequently with the mild flourish of the old-world syntactical inversion, 'when take the air I must': these old mortalities were originally in French no more than the daily life of 'je m'y promène' and 'quand je suis obligé de sortir'.

It is the timing which most matters, *sub specie aeternitatis*. Beckett's engagement is not with life's little ironies, but with death's large ones, and ironies not sarcasms, as being true to some degree in both senses.

> I met her on a bench, on the bank of the canal, one of the canals, for our town boasts two, though I never knew which was which. It was a well situated bench, backed by a mound of solid earth and garbage, so that my rear was covered. My flanks too, partially, thanks to a pair of venerable trees, more than venerable, dead, at either end of the bench. It was no doubt these trees one fine day, aripple with all their foliage, that had sown the idea of a bench, in someone's fancy.[78]

The relation of the venerable to the dead is quizzed here with scepticism, not cynicism (did Bede manage to enter the grave as The Venerable?); and the final exfoliating flourish of the trees

[78] *First Love*, 19–20. Following *Premier amour*, 18:

Je fis sa connaissance sur un banc, sur les bords du canal, de l'un des canaux, car notre ville en a deux, mais je n'ai jamais su les distinguer. C'était un banc très bien situé, adossé à un monceau de terre et de detritus durcis, de sorte que mes arrières étaient couverts. Mes flancs aussi, partiellement, grâce à deux arbres vénérables, et même morts, qui flanquaient le banc de part et d'autre. C'est sans doute ces arbres qui avaient suggéré, un jour qu'ils ondayaient de toutes leurs feuilles, l'idée du banc, à quelqu'un.

does comic, not satiric, wonders with what in the original French
had been the unsuggestive word *suggéré*:

C'est sans doute ces arbres qui avaient suggéré, un jour qu'ils ondayaient
de toutes leurs feuilles, l'idée du banc, à quelqu'un.

It was no doubt these trees one fine day, aripple with all their foliage,
that had sown the idea of a bench, in someone's fancy.

Trees not only sow the idea of a bench, they constitute the reality
of a bench; the trees are more than venerable, dead, and they
furnish in their death some repose for the living. They go on. As
does this creature, this creation, of Beckett's.

I turned on my heel and went, for good, full of doubt. But some weeks
later, even more dead than alive than usual, I returned to the bench, for
the fourth or fifth time since I had abandoned it, at roughly the same
hour, I mean roughly the same sky, no, I don't mean that either, for it's
always the same sky and never the same sky, what words are there for
that, none I know, period.[79]

   'But some weeks later, even more dead than alive than usual':
the French had no such pertinacious continuance, this 'syntax of
weakness' (such weakness being indomitable): simply 'plus mort
que vif'. Nor, at the close, does the French 'voilà' effect the
finality of 'period', partly because the English word is allowed at
once to make its mark, its punctuation mark. How equivocal the
close is, all the same, despite that indubitable *period*.

what words are there for that, none I know, period.

—'none (that) I know'? or 'none, I know'? The French expressed
it less aptly, less indecisively: 'comment exprimer cette chose, je
ne l'exprimerai pas, voilà'.

   Such punctuation-words, especially 'period', suit Beckett down
to the ground, down to what will be the final full stop. He played
PERIOD against the cabled STOP and (mindful of the body of the
sentence) against COLON in his telegram to *The Times* when asked
his resolutions and hopes for the New Year 1984:

---

[79] *First Love*, 41. Following *Premier amour*, 36:

je fis demi-tour et m'en allai, pour de bon, plein d'incertitude. Mais quelques semaines plus
tard, plus mort que vif, je retournai encore au banc, cela faisait la quatrième ou cinquième
fois depuis que je l'avais abandonné, à la même heure à peu près, je veux dire à peu près
sous le même ciel, non, ce n'est pas cela non plus, car c'est toujours le même ciel and ce
n'est jamais le même ciel, comment exprimer cette chose, je ne l'exprimerai pas, voilà.

RESOLUTIONS COLON ZERO STOP PERIOD HOPES COLON ZERO STOP

BECKETT

This has its wan smile; for something in the vicinity but broader, one would return nearly half a century to the cruelly successive telegrams in *Murphy* when Cooper is sending word to Neary about the search for Murphy:

FOUND STOP LOOK SLIPPY STOP COOPER.[80]

But no.

LOST STOP STOP WHERE YOU ARE STOP COOPER.

Just as Beckett's convictions are his own but not only his own, so these acknowledgements of death within the very life of his language are not something of which he holds the franchise. Since they are acknowledgements of one half of the truth, such intimations of mortality will always betray themselves. The great writer is someone who does not betray *them*—by obliviousness to their desire for oblivion, their subterranean energies. Beckett said in conversation: 'I am like a mole in a tunnel'.[81] 'Well said old Mole, can'st worke i' th' ground so fast?'

In the commonplace writer, these eruptions are no more than mole-hills. Consider two zones: funerary art-history and the philosophy of death.

First, ponder some of James Stevens Curl's ways of putting things, in his admirably informative book on funerary architecture, *A Celebration of Death*.

The main bone of contention seems to have been the fee payable to the incumbent of the parish from which any corpse derived.

Perhaps the London Borough of Southwark will give Nunhead a new lease of life as a cemetery.

Golders Green . . . is one of the most architecturally successful of all crematoria in Britain . . . built of a warm red brick.

A tradition of Baroque ironwork to mark graves is still very much alive.

---

[80] *Murphy*, 57. Preceding *Murphy* in French, 46:

TROUVE STOP VENEZ STOP COOPER.

PERDU STOP STOP STOP COOPER.

[81] Charles Juliet, 'Meeting Beckett' (here 1968), *TriQuarterly*, 77 (1989–90), 13; trans. Suzanne Chamier.

Forest Lawn . . . was originally an older cemetery of 1906 that had gone to seed.

Monumental funerary architecture became common, usually in the form of ambitious chamber-tombs. From this period, belief in the immortality of the individual gained ground.

Deep common graves were to be sunk. According to the approving Loudon, Buxton took 'a deep interest in the Nunhead Cemetery, and in the subject of cemeteries generally'. This is an understatement.

Many other professionals attempted to scramble on to the cemetery bandwagon.[82]

Beckett, though, actively relishes, and sees that we relish, that which unmisgiving cliché reduces to the callous, such as this real-life advertisement:

Recreation Department: Assistant Cemeteries Superintendent.

I was once at a funeral occasion and heard someone being asked, merely socially, how he was. 'Surviving'. As a witticism, it would be cruelly pertinent; as a blankness, impertinent.

Second, there is Karen Grandstrand Gervais, whose book *Redefining Death* (1986) is one of the most thorough and cogent of such philosophical efforts; it is a keen study of the Harvard criteria for death, and it elucidates the confusions and falterings in the discussion of brain-death; of brain-stem; and of the higher brain. And yet it betrays itself with its own inadvertent deathlines. For instances:

Thus, the analysis forms the backbone of my entire argument.

The redefinition of death is such a dilemma, and I hope that this book may help lay it to rest.

For instance, the significance upon which the traditional criteria rest might be fleshed out something like this.

In deference to entrenched human sensibilities, the remaining spontaneous functions should be stopped prior to burial or cremation.

According to the higher-brain formulations, the use of the traditional criteria is now overkill.[83]

In the abstract ('abstracted to death'), such inattentions incite a

---

[82] *A Celebration of Death* (1980), 287, 238, 310, 366, 275, 25, 234, 223.
[83] *Redefining Death* (1986), pp. ix, xi, 4, 193, 194.

rictus; when a particular person is in range, one does not know whether to laugh or to cry.

On 7 February 1990 the *New York Times* told the story of Mr McAfee, a quadriplegic, who had changed his mind about dying. 'Turning off the ventilator still remains a very viable option for me.' Viable: capable of living; able to maintain a separate existence. In Beckett, the life of language is, among much else, a life-support system. It is no less a death-supporting system.

THE OBITUARY

Are obituaries still viable? Well, viduity still exists. As *More Pricks than Kicks* nears its end, Beckett subtracts Belacqua's quondam women, leaving his relict:

She and no other therefore is the Mrs Shuah who now, after less than a year in the ultra-violet intimacy of the compound of ephebe and old woman that he was, reads in the paper that she had begun to survive him.[84]

An obituary will enjoy its day of being hot off the press, but the ink may long have been dry. The witty Geoffrey Madan characterized the paper's need to be prepared:

The Times obituary department: emotion anticipated in tranquillity.

But what was witty in Madan (especially as the poet who is twisted and twitted at the end was the author of three 'Essays on Epitaphs') is often unwitting in the obituary-writer. Yet the obituary will manifest a co-operative subconscious, precipitating a turn of phrase at once very like and very unlike the co-operations of art and intention.[85]

From *The Times*:

Sandy Watney was born at a time when he was able to absorb the skills of a dying generation of horsemen and thus was able to pass on the tradition as he remembered it. His gentle charm, dry wit, unfailing good manners and approachability set him apart.

---

[84] 'Draff', *More Pricks than Kicks*, 256.

[85] A separate case is the Joycean misprint or typo, as when someone was praised in a *Times* obituary for his 'joie de vivrex'. Unintended? Who knows. Clearly not quite the real thing, 'joie de vivrex' combines a suggestion of toiletry with the old story ('Death is king, and Vivat Rex!', Tennyson).

How discreetly 'approachability set him apart' passes on the halitosis of bonhomie.

Of the philosopher G. S. W. Melhuish, the entire final paragraph was devoted to the last twist:

> At his death he was at work on his final thesis, on the metaphysical significance of death.

On the death of G. S. Fraser, the penultimate paragraph gave a further spin to such self-enfolding:

> He was a valued contributor to *The Times Literary Supplement* of which he had been poetry editor, and he had a long and fruitful connexion with the obituary department of *The Times*.

It is the word 'fruitful', flatly savoured, which makes this so much more than one of your common or garden obituaries. Connexion? Only connect.

Or there may be the tempting self-attention which a dangling participle may effect, as in the closing paragraph of Sir John Gielgud's appreciation of Elisabeth Bergner:

> An amazingly original and enigmatic personality of enormous fascination, I am very proud to have known her.

And, always lurking, there is all the gratuitous anonymous aggression, the knackering of a dead horse.

The Times obituary usually offers one of two turns: that the late-lamented was pleasant though often not seeming so, or that though often not seeming so, the late-lamented was pleasant. One such obituary spoke of the man's central goodness, and then executed its turn: 'but woe to those who crossed'—at which point one expected the word 'him', only to find the words 'his path'.

To have woe visited on you, you didn't have to cross him, all you had to do was cross his path. How much less called-for than the straight threats of a Beckett character:

> Woe betide the meddler who crossed him when his mind was really set on this meal.[86]

Confronted by 'but woe to those who crossed his path', one knows

---

[86] 'Dante and the Lobster', *More Pricks and Kicks*, 7. For 'cross my path' in Beckett, see pp. 64–6 above.

what it might well mean, but was this what the obituarist meant? Perhaps not. For as Housman said of an unthinking editor:

This of course is not what he was trying to say, but the pen is mightier than the wrist.[87]

Housman's wrist is a reminder of the corporeality of cliché, of how the body of the words can be wise with bodily decrepitude. Or with lacerations.

[...] he resists I claw his left hand to the bone it's not far he cries but won't let go [...]

Who but Beckett would have seized 'to the bone' and then clawed even it?[88]

to the bone it's not far

That is a vision of death unforthcoming. Elsewhere there is cliché incarnate in imminent death, as when Molloy meets a version of pastoral:

So I knew at once it was a shepherd and his dog I had before me, above me rather, for they had not left the path. And I identified the bleating too, without any trouble, the anxious bleating of the sheep, missing the dog at their heels. It is then too that the meaning of words is least obscure to me, so that I said, with tranquil assurance, where are you taking them, to the fields or to the shambles? I must have completely lost my sense of direction, as if direction had anything to do with the matter. For even if he was going towards the town, what prevented him from skirting it, or from leaving it again by another gate, on his way to new pastures, and if he was going away from it that meant nothing either, for slaughter-houses are not confined to towns, no, they are everywhere, the country is full of them, every butcher has his slaughter-house and the right to slaughter, according to his lights.[89]

---

[87] *The Classical Papers of A. E. Housman*, ed. J. Diggle and F. R. D. Goodyear (1972), iii. 1012.

[88] *How It Is*, 72. Following *Comment c'est*, 80:

[...] il résiste je lui griffe la main gauche jusqu'à l'os ce n'est pas loin il crie mais ne lâche pas [...]

[89] *Molloy*, 37. Following *Molloy* in French, 41:

Je sus donc aussitôt que c'était un berger et son chien que j'avais devant moi, au-dessus de moi plutôt, car ils n'avaient pas quitté le chemin. Et le bêlement du troupeau aussi, inquiet de ne plus se sentir talonné, je l'identifiai sans peine. C'est à ce moment aussi que le sens des paroles m'est le moins obscur, de sorte que je dis, avec une tranquille assurance, Où les

'It is then too that the meaning of words is least obscure to me':
the meaning of the word 'lights' is not obscure at all.

The opinions, information, and capacities, natural or acquired, of an
individual intellect. Often in phr., *according to (one's) lights*.

Yet a grim light is cast on it in the vicinity of the slaughter-house
(and of the dog at the sheep's heels).

The lungs. Now only applied to the lungs of beasts (sheep, pigs,
bullocks), used as food (chiefly for cats and dogs).

'According to his lights'—the French was much less inward,
less visceral: 'selon ses besoins'.

Beckett illuminates things according to his lights when there is
a phosphorescence or even a putrescence active in his very words.
When he translates others, he sometimes offers little more than a
description of a plight; he reserves to his own art his truest
plighted cunning for what is not a description but an enactment of
the longing that all should be done with.

His subject matter is all there in the Spanish poem by Manuel
Gutiérrez Nájera[90] which Beckett translated as 'To Be' (aware
presumably that for the English reader there would be pressure
from the unuttered 'or not to be'). But subject matter is very
different from matter, matter with its germination and corruption,
maggoty-headed. This translation remains an idea of the thing,
not the thing itself.

To Be

A fathomless abyss is human pain.
Whose eye has ever pierced to its black depths?
To the shadowy gulf of times that are
no more incline your ear. . . .

Within there falls

the eternal tear!

---

amenez-vous, aux champs ou à l'abattoir? J'avais dû perdre complètement le sens de la
direction, comme si cela avait quelque chose à voir avec la question, la direction. Car même
s'il se dirigeait vers la ville, qu'est-ce qui l'empêchait de la contourner, ou d'en sortir par une
autre porte, pour gagner des pâturages reposés, et s'il s'en éloignait cela ne signifiait rien
non plus, car ce n'est pas seulement dans les villes qu'il y a des abattoirs, mais il y en a
partout, dans les campagnes aussi, chaque boucher a son abattoir et le droit d'abattre, selon
ses besoins.

[90] *Anthology of Mexican Poetry*, 135–7. The ellipses are in the text.

> To the defenceless mouths
that in another age life such as ours
inspired, curious draw nigh. . . .
>> A groan
arises trembling from the whitened bones!

Life is pain. And life persists, obscure,
but life for all that, even in the tomb.
Matter disingegrates and is dispersed;
the eternal spirit, the underlying
essence suffers without pause. It were
in vain to wield the suicidal steel.
Suicide is unavailing. The form
is changed, the indestructible being endures.

In thee, Pain, we live and have our being!
The supreme yearning of all existing things
is to be lost in nothingness, annulled,
deep in dreamless sleep. . . . And life continues
beyond the frozen confines of the tomb.

There is no death. In vain you clamour for death,
souls destitute of hope. And the implacable
purveyor of suffering creatures ravishes
us to another world. There is no pause.
We crave a single instant of respite
and a voice in the darkness urges: 'On!'

Yes, life is an evil and an evil
that never ends. The creating God
is the creature of another terrible God
whose name is Pain. And the immortal
Saturn is insatiate. And space,
the nursery of suns, the infinite,
are the mighty prison, issueless,
of souls that suffer and that cannot die.

Oh implacable Saturn, make an end
at last, devour created things and then,
since we are immortal, ruminate our lives!
We are thine, Pain, thine for evermore,
but pity for the beings that are not yet,
save in thy mind that hunger stimulates. . . .
Pity, oh God, have pity on nothingness!
At last be sated, that the eternal womb,
begetter of the seed of humankind,
turn barren and that life come to an end. . . .

And let the world like a dead planet whirl
amid the waveless oceans of the void!

But the unignorable 'vision of positive annihilation', of a dead planet, is truly realized, incarnate, not in that translation from the Spanish, but in the closing words of *Ill Seen Ill Said* (1981), imagining the fullness of time which will assuredly come when here on this planet all will be said and done.

Farewell to farewell. Then in that perfect dark foreknell darling sound pip for end begun. First last moment. Grant only enough remain to devour all. Moment by glutton moment. Sky earth the whole kit and boodle. Not another crumb of carrion left. Lick chops and basta. No. One moment more. One last. Grace to breathe that void. Know happiness.[91]

The French, unusually, is likewise distinctly right, not equivalent but equipollent. Instead of 'Know happiness':

Connaître le bonheur.

The birth/death pangs are there in this last knowledge, with *con/naître* ready to split into the two obscene inescapabilities from which we misguidedly escaped at birth and from which we will truly escape only at death. Escape 'from the world that parts at last its labia and lets me go'.[92]

---

[91] Following *Mal vu mal dit* (1981):

Adieu adieux. Puis noir parfait avant-glas tout bas adorable son top départ de l'arrivée. Première dernière seconde. Pourvu qu'il en reste encore assez pour tout dévorer. Goulûment seconde par seconde. Ciel terre et tout le bataclan. Plus miette de charogne nulle part. Léchées babines baste. Non. Encore une seconde. Rien qu'une. Le temps d'aspirer ce vide. Connaître le bonheur.

Beckett is likely to have admired the apocalyptic vision at the end of Italo Svevo's *Confessions of Zeno*; he explicitly admired the planetary heights gained by Svevo's admirer, Joyce. Richard Ellmann reports, in a note added to the revised edition of his *James Joyce* (1982), 709:

In later life Beckett thought this ability to contemplate with telescopic eye Joyce's most impressive characteristic, and quoted four lines from Pope's *Essay on Man* to illustrate:

> Who sees with equal eye, as God of all,
> A hero perish, or a sparrow fall,
> Atoms of systems into ruin hurled,
> And now a bubble burst, and now a world.

[92] *Malone Dies*, 12. Following *Malone meurt*, 24: 'du monde qui se dilate enfin et me laisse passer'.

Decorous but open, the French word *connaître* carnally acknowledges its invisible stitches.

But the English has instead its own nobility, as it moves through its negations, 'No but slowly', 'No', to its last words: 'Know happiness'. Not, indeed not, 'No happiness'. Rather the reverse. The negation is positive, the vision of positive annihilation, effected through a perfect identity of sound. Such happiness is a stylistic, though not only a stylistic, felicity. 'Know happiness'. Even happier than Larry.

3. *Languages, Both Dead and Living*

A language is a matter of life and love, as well as of life and death.

Yes, I loved her, it's the name I gave, still give alas, to what I was doing then. I had nothing to go by, having never loved before, but of course had heard of the thing, at home, in school, in brothel and at church, and read romances, in prose and verse, under the guidance of my tutor, in six or seven languages, both dead and living, in which it was handled at length.[1]

Coming at length to 'handled at length', this ends in both a climax and a detumescence. It is at once dead-limp (a cliché, within a flaccid syntax—eleven commas before the full stop) and disconcertingly erectile in its tissue. Consummately manipulated.

These 'six or seven languages, both dead and living'? Does this simply distinguish dead ones (Latin and Greek) from living ones (English and French)? Or does it insinuate that all languages are 'both dead and living'? So-called dead languages are alive in that to know them, even to know of their existence, is to acknowledge that they must still have *some* kind of life. Living languages are dead in that every language, like every species, goes towards death. 'At length'.

dead
fig. Of things (practices, feelings, etc.): No longer in existence, or in use; extinct, obsolete, perished, past; *esp.* of languages, no longer spoken.

---

[1] *First Love*, 31. Following *Premier amour*, 27–8:

Oui, je l'aimais, c'est le nom que je donnais, que je donne hélas toujours, à ce que je faisais, à cette époque. Je n'avais pas de données là-dessus, n'ayant jamais aimé auparavant, mais j'avais entendu parler de la chose, naturellement, à la maison, à l'école, au bordel, à l'église, et j'avais lu des romans, en prose et en vers, sous la direction de mon tuteur, en anglais, en français, en italien, en allemand, où il en était fortement question.

The term 'dead languages' had found itself unseamed ('dead [. . .] languages') in the gruesome praise of the medium Rosa Dew in *Murphy*: 'she could make the dead softsoap the quick in seven languages' (see p. 30 above); this earlier turn has its affinity with 'six or seven languages, both dead and living'.

This is ill-fitting. It is not the case that Latin is no longer *in existence* or *in use*, though its existence and its use are not what they were. Or that Latin is exactly *extinct* and *perished*, though it is *obsolete* (is it?) and *past* (but). As to the equating, for a language, of being dead with being 'no longer spoken': it is not simply or altogether true that Latin is no longer spoken, and there are other ways, even for a language, of being alive than being spoken.

The Dictionary entry valuably brings out the rich muddle of all this, and it offers what was—at least to me—a pat surprise, in that the first citation for 'dead languages' is much later than might have been expected: Addison, *Spectator* No. 285 (1712), 'The Works of Ancient Authors, which are written in dead Languages'. That it should have been Augustan England which gave to the English language this characterization of Latin and Greek is a paradox of power.

Beckett set down the gist of this love-reminiscence, in *First Love* and in *Premier amour*, in two languages, both living languages—and both necessarily both dead and living. But the original French had not entered upon this particular combination of a distinction between groups of languages and an insistence that in the end, and even in the meantime, it is all one:

sous la direction de mon tuteur, en anglais, en français, en italien, en allemand, où il en était fortement question.

Not a dead language among them. But there is a taunting weakly abstraction in the French—'où il en était fortement question'—where in the English there is the oddly bodily: 'in which it was handled at length'.

Not but what the French language enjoys one bodily advantage hereabouts. English, though it can speak formally of languages as 'tongues', finds awkward in the mouth the phrase 'dead tongues'. Even Walter Redfern was unable to effect a fitting translation of Roland Topor, 'who offers as number 55 of his "cent bonnes raisons pour me suicider tout de suite: parce que j'ai toujours eu envie de posséder une langue morte" ("a hundred good reasons for committing suicide straight off: because I've always wanted to have a dead tongue/know a dead language")'.[2]

It was the act of translating, under the guidance of his supreme tutor (a tutor being at once a master and a servant), language itself, which prompted Beckett anew to the antithesis of dead languages and living languages, an antithesis which upon reflection is at once true and false. The syntax keeps its cards close to its chest. 'Languages, both dead and living.'

As so often with this great bilingual writer, the antithesis of the one language and the other (French and English) is intimate with other antitheses: of the *what* and the *how* in art's realizing, for one, and, for another, of recycling and minting.

There is an important sense in which it is true that Beckett wrote, for instance, two distinct works called *Molloy*. Yet Beckett did, after all, specifically characterize one as a translation of the other. Nevertheless, it would be simple-minded to deny, all the same, that the two works called *Molloy* are, when considered under one aspect, not at all the same. The antithesis of translation and creation is both indispensable and inadequate, and the same goes for texture and context in the very writing. In all of these cases, we shall need, not to settle for, but not to be unsettled by, the conviction that the terms antithesized are distinguishable even though they are not distinct.

Within Beckett, it will often be a dead language which will strike the right note and a chill. And, by the same token, will be available for a heated rebuff.

> 'What did they say at the inquest?' said Celia.
> '*Felo-de-se*,' said Miss Carridge, with scorn and anger, 'and got the room a bad name all over Islington. God knows now when I'll get it off. *Felo-de-se*! Felo-de my rump.'[3]

Suicide may be weirdly a *modus vivendi*. The death of Murphy—suicide? accidental death? indifference to any such distinction? ah, 'A classical case of misadventure'—allows Dr Killiecrankie

---

[3] *Murphy*, 145. Preceding *Murphy* in French, 107:

—Qu'est-ce qu'ils ont dit à l'enquête? demanda-t-elle.
—Suicide! dit Mademoiselle Carridge, sur un ton méprisant et courroucé. Me voilà fichue de réputation dans tout Islington. Trouver à louer après ça, je vous le demande. Suicide! Eh ben, nom de Dieu!

The French has 'Eh ben', which may be a misprint or may be Eh bien when all is not well. The English has its homonymic cross-linguistic move: 'What did they say [...] *Felo-de-se*'. A cross-flanker of 'felo-de my rump' had figured in 'Love and Lethe': 'that she should connive at his felo de se, which he much regretted he could not commit on his own bottom' (*More Pricks than Kicks*, 123).

the frigid decorum of a dead language: 'severe burns let it be, followed by severe shock. So much for the *modus morendi*, the *modus morendi*.'[4]

When Beckett invokes a dead language, this is often to catch a compacting of its having lived on with its speaking of dying. When a dead language, dead but refusing to lie down, speaks of death, the interest is compounded, as it is by other forms of the self-referential or the ingrown.

> 'What ails you?' asked Winnie.
> He had allowed himself to get run down, but he scoffed at the idea of a sequitur from his body to his mind.[5]

The reader's mind has no difficulty in taking the meaning of the word 'sequitur' there, but the word proves an apt obstacle to any smooth following, whether in the mind or from body to mind. For 'sequitur' remains obstinately a word from elsewhere, from a dead language, altogether the odd man out in the sentence in which it occurs. Added to which, the positive 'sequitur' is even less at home in English than is the negative 'non-sequitur'. Non-sequiturs, though not ten a penny, do turn up in intellectual circles; sequiturs, seldom. With the help of 'the idea of a sequitur', the scoff vindicates itself.

As does scoffing at lapidary institutional boasts of durability. Beckett, a Trinity College Dublin man, has Belacqua recognize

> implicit behind the whole length of its southern frontage the College. Perpetuis futuris temporibus duraturum. It was to be hoped so, indeed.[6]

Any such vaunt has its own failure-safety, since either it will be there to be read, in its Latinate dignity, or it will not be there in which case it will not be open to the discomfiture of disconfirmation.

---

[4] *Murphy*, 262. Preceding *Murphy* in French, 187–8:

Des brûlures sévères, ainsi soit-il, suivies d'un sévère choc. Je crois que c'est une fleur de rhétorique, par dessus le marché. Tant mieux. Tant mieux. Et nous voilà fixés sur le *modus moriendi*, le *modus moriendi*. [. . .] Un cas classique de mésaventure.

The French, unlike the English, has the Latin correct. But the English solecism permits of a closer assimilation to *modus vivendi*.

[5] 'Fingal', *More Pricks than Kicks*, 32. The French language was to offer Beckett a different kind of sequitur, in a passing conjunction of *suivre* and *être*. Je suis, ergo je suis.

[6] 'Ding-Dong', *More Pricks than Kicks*, 49.

Latin lasts, and, a dead language, it lives through mutation. Virgil's *Quantum mutatus ab illo!* has done sterling work when mutated into English:

> If thou beest he; But O how fall'n! how chang'd
> From him, who in the happy Realms of Light
> Cloth'd with transcendent brightness didst outshine
> Myriads though bright:

> *(Paradise Lost,* i. 84–7)

It was for Beckett to make the mutation, slily and self-enactingly enfolded within *quantum mutatus,* into a matter of a beady glance at *ab illo,* 'how chang'd | From him'. For Ticklepenny, though 'a male nurse', has his effeminate side. He assures Murphy, well met,

> 'It is the same Ticklepenny, but God bless my soul *quantum mutatus.*'
> '*Ab illa,*' said Murphy.[7]

This is bantering a darling. In the early poem 'Enueg I' the darling is more savagely disowned:[8]

> Exeo in a spasm
> tired of my darling's red sputum
> from the Portobello Private Nursing Home

Lawrence Harvey has attended to this:

The word *exeo,* left in Latin for the sake of the ambiguity, denotes not only departure (after a visit to the sick) but also the final departure of death; and from a nursing home one is perhaps as frequent as the other.[9]

Tellingly put, but 'Exeo' was left in Latin not only 'for the sake of the ambiguity', but for other sakes: its foreign chill, the alienation, the living death incarnate in a word from a dead language which lives on. Exeo (Roman and in romans not italics) has not altogether departed, whatever it may say. And it constitutes its own 'spasm', being the first word of the poem but its first and last word in a dead language. For 'sputum', one line later, is a word which has been antiseptically accommodated.

A discrete item within the Addenda at the end of *Watt* intones

---

[7] *Murphy,* 87. Preceding *Murphy* in French, 67:

C'est le même Ticklepenny, mais, Seigneur, *quantum mutatus.*
—Ab illa, dit Murphy.

[8] *Collected Poems,* 10.

[9] *Samuel Beckett Poet and Critic,* 98.

this mingled blessing and curse, though which is which is always strongly in question.

pereant qui ante nos nostra dixerunt[10]

This, since it is neither in English nor in French, is one of the few things in *Watt* that did not have to be translated when Beckett turned *Watt* from an English novel to a French one.[11] And what, in our words, would the Latin say? 'Let those who used our words before us perish.'

Does that include those who used those very words? The *mise-en-page* is then a *mise-en-abyme*. Then again to whom do we owe this invoking in Latin of 'our words'? The words are 'variously attributed': St Jerome, Aelius Donatus, even Anon.[12]

Beckett's book on Proust ends with an extraordinary panoply of a sentence, stretched across a dozen lines before it reaches its conclusive revelation of a language both dead and living, the word to end words.

The narrator—unlike Swann who identifies the 'little phrase' of the Sonata with Odette, spatialises what is extraspatial, establishes it as the national anthem of his love—sees in the red phrase of the Septuor, trumpeting its victory in the last movement like a Mantegna archangel clothed in scarlet, the ideal and immaterial statement of the essence of a unique beauty, a unique world, the invariable world and beauty of Vinteuil, expressed timidly, as a prayer, in the Sonata, imploringly, as an inspiration, in the Septuor, the 'invisible reality' that damns the life of the

---

[10] *Watt*, 250. Preceding *Watt* in French, 263.

[11] Did not have to be, but Beckett was not above the supererogatory. His Latin comes and goes. *Mercier et Camier*, 109:

Que notre devise soit donc, dit Mercier.
Ah oui, dit Camier. Que notre devise soit donc lenteur et circonspection

Preceding *Mercier and Camier*, 67:

Let our watchword be, said Mercier.
Ah yes, said Camier, lente, lente, and circumspection

In *Murphy*: 'our *bonam fidem*' (p. 231) becomes in French 'notre bonne foi' (p. 166); but 'one of Nature's jokes' (p. 248) becomes '*lusus naturae*' (p. 178); and 'even in some cases *a priori*' (p. 206) is a case where the Latin goes unrepresented, *a posteriori* and preposterously enough, in the later French (p. 148).

[12] There is a very informative note in Rubin Rabinovitz, *The Development of Samuel Beckett's Fiction* (1984), 173–4. John Pilling has noted that this Latin tag is in Beckett's notebook of *Murphy*-time, where it 'appears twice, on its first appearance fully glossed as St. Jerome's preceptor Donatus's extension of an adage of Terence' (Pilling and Bryden (eds.), *The Ideal Core of the Onion*, 5).

body on earth as a pensum and reveals the meaning of the word: 'defunctus'.

The closing word 'defunctus' might implore, in the words of the late poem of Beckett's, 'come ease'. Yet this defunctus-sentence has a manner so grand as to invite rather the urchin-retorts, 'Come off it', or, 'Come again?'

But then such scarlet criticism asks to be heard as opera—and anyway 'defunctus' insists that no one will actually say Come again. Defunctus: from 'to discharge, to have done with'. And what would be the past of 'to have done with'?

Flights of Mantegna-archangels hymn this to its rest. The older Beckett, less trumpeting, is more laconic when it comes to the relation of 'the life of the body on earth' to the dead language Latin. He says of a painting by Geer van Velde:[13]

C'est un drôle de *memento mori*, la peinture radieuse de G. van Velde. Je le note en passant.

'En passant' is perfect, perfected in death. For the Latin tag is in the process of passing, and so are we all. Stealthily 'en passant' is itself a *memento mori*. Yet droll the while, 'un drôle de *memento mori*.'

GAELIC

An Irishman may be especially sensitive to dead languages, to mother tongues, and to stepmother tongues.

The famous story is of Beckett's being asked whether he was an Englishman, and replying: 'Au contraire'. What is the opposite, the contrary, of an Englishman? Not just an Irishman, but a Protestant from the Republic of Ireland.

¡UPTHEREPUBLIC!

Such was the entire contribution made by Author Beckett to a Spanish Civil War effort.[14] It was a serious joke, urging the

---

[13] 'La peinture des van Velde', *Disjecta*, 129.
[14] *Authors take sides on the Spanish War* (1937). The question asked was:

Are you for, or against, the legal Government and the People of Republican Spain?
Are you for, or against, Franco and Fascism?

Insofar as ¡UPTHEREPUBLIC! is a one-word answer, Beckett's was the shortest of

Republic on, while genially goosing these Republican resisters of the goose-step, and turning the battle-cry arsy-versy just like that introductory Spanish exclamation-mark—all while being down on, and in exile from, the Irish Republic. ¡UPTHEREPUBLIC! No time to waste, no time to breathe: a one-word burst, three in one, a trinity.[15]

'Au contraire': Beckett needed French to express the contrariety. 'On the contrary' would not have been the same reply at all, since as English it would have belied itself. 'Rather the reverse'?

Gaelic would have saved him, but Beckett would not have been the man to dig up the Gaelic, or as some would say the Irish, for 'Au contraire'. Rather the reverse here too, where the novels quip:

These were sounds that at first, though we walked glued together, were so much Irish to me.

Tears and laughter, they are so much Gaelic to me.[16]

---

the contributions. The only answer of such brevity was Rose Macaulay's AGAINST FRANCO. Beckett's name was not in 1937 one to be reckoned with; he is not listed among the forty names on the cover of the sixpenny pamphlet (which include Ruby M. Ayres and E. Ibbotson James) but tarries among the 'over 100 others'.

[15] Some such sentiment turns up later in *Malone Dies*, 62–3:

Yes, that's what I like about me, at least one of the things, that I can say, Up the Republic!, for example, or, Sweetheart!, for example, without having to wonder if I should not rather have cut my tongue out, or said something else.

Following *Malone meurt*, 102, which had respected the phrase as foreign, as English or Irish:

Oui, c'est ce que j'aime en moi, enfin une des choses que j'aime, le don de pouvoir dire *Up the Republic!* par exemple, ou Chérie! sans avoir à me demander si je n'aurais pas mieux fait de me taire ou de dire autre chose

[16] *Watt*, 169. Preceding *Watt* in French, 174:

C'était là des sons qui d'abord, malgré notre marche agglutinante, étaient du gaélique pour moi.

'Irish' or 'gaélique' here stands as the bathetic climax to a series of descriptions of Watt's incomprehensibility:

These were sounds that at first, though we walked face to face, were devoid of significance for me.

Then: 'made little or no sense to me'; 'were not perfectly clear to me'; 'were so much wind to me'; 'seemed so much balls to me'; and grandly, climactically, 'were so much Irish to me' (*Watt*, 164–9). *Watt* in French, 170–4:

C'étaient là des sons qui d' abord, malgré notre marche vis-à-vis, étaient vides de sens pour moi.

'ne me disaient pas grand'chose'; 'n'étaient que du vent pour moi'; 'laissaient plutôt à

How much Irish or Gaelic is so much Greek?

The French, whether later or earlier (later in the first case, and earlier in the second), cannot call upon so much, and has to be content with one or the other flatness, of saying merely 'du gaélique' or merely 'je ne m'y connais guère'.

Mercier and Camier has a good ear for the false throb:

he sometimes felt it would have been wiser on his part, during the great upheaval, to devote his energies to the domestic skirmish, the Gaelic dialect, the fortification of his faith and the treasures of a folklore beyond compare. The bodily danger would have been less and the benefits more certain.[17]

But Beckett's attitude to these indomitable Irishries is not always that clear-cut. In *More Pricks than Kicks*, there is some intricate crediting and debiting in the exchange after the funeral:

'Now in Gaelic' said Hairy on the way home 'they could not say that.'

'What could they not say?' said the parson. He would not rest until he knew.

'O Death where is thy sting?' replied Hairy. 'They have no words for these big ideas.'

This was more than enough for the parson, a canon of the Church of Ireland.[18]

A tilt at Gaelic, no doubt; but Hairy has his limitations, and anything which wins the endorsement of that parson cannot be all good. As for the relation of the all-but-dead language Gaelic to the question 'O Death where is thy sting?', this keeps its sting at the ready for each and every nearby complacency. Beckett was

---

désirer pour moi'; 'me les brisaient plutôt qu'autre chose'; 'étaient du gaélique pour moi'.

Also *Molloy*, 49. Following *Molloy* in French, 54: 'Les pleurs et les ris, je ne m'y connais guère.'

There is a flavoured precision about 'so much Greek to me' as against 'Greek—or, All Greek—to me'. *OED* under *Greek* 8 ('Unintelligible speech or language, gibberish') runs from Dekker in 1600.

[17] *Mercier and Camier*, 14. Following *Mercier et Camier*, 18–19:

il lui semblait parfois qu'il aurait mieux fait, pendant la grande tourmente, de se consacrer aux escarmouches domestiques, à la langue gaélique, au raffermissement de sa foi et aux trésors d'un folklore unique au monde. Le danger corporel eût été moindre et les bénéfices plus certains.

[18] 'Draff', *More Pricks than Kicks*, 272.

always one to give his own particular timbre to that question, so that instead of the reassurance of eternal life, it might promise rather the reassurance of no such thing, of nothing. O Death where is thy sting?

There is something suspect about the thought of pleading that one has *two* second languages. But such in a way was Beckett's privilege. It went with his coming to have two first languages too. Katharine Worth has observed that during the war, in occupied France, Beckett's life may have depended 'on his being able to act the Frenchman; a harrowing way of having one's second language become the "natural" one'.[19]

As an Irishman Beckett had too, though it was out of the running, a third language, not quite a dead language but more and more seeming as good as dead.

'Irish as a living language is dying out year by year', Synge wrote, Irishly. 'Can we go back into our mother's womb?', he asked (it is a question of which not only the sense but the tone is very elusive) in a letter to the Gaelic League.[20]

No wonder Mrs Rooney, in *All That Fall*, is self-conscious. She asks Christy:

Do you find anything ... bizarre about my way of speaking? (*Pause.*) I do not mean the voice. (*Pause.*) No, I mean the words. (*Pause. More to herself.*) I use none but the simplest words, I hope, and yet I sometimes find my way of speaking very ... bizarre.[21]

There 'bizarre' loiteringly enacts its own bizarrerie. 'None but the simplest words'? Who uses 'bizarre' without slightly wondering whether to do so is bizarre? Who among us knows its etymology? By what bizarre route did it journey from Italian 'angry, choleric',

[19] Alec Reid's point, adapted by Katharine Worth in *Beckett the Shape Changer* (1975), 7.

[20] *Collected Works*, ii. 399. I owe my adducing Synge to Katharine Worth, *Beckett the Shape Changer*, 4. P. J. Murphy has quoted from Beckett's unpublished work, 'The Voice', a stage towards *Company*: 'No mention of accent. Indefinable. Of one whose mother tongue as foreign as the others' (Pilling and Bryden (eds.), *The Ideal Core of the Onion*, 77–8).

[21] *All That Fall*, 8; Beckett's ellipses. Preceding *Tous ceux qui tombent*, trans. Pinget, 10:

Vous ne trouvez pas ma façon de parler un peu ... bizarre? (*Un temps.*) Je ne parle pas de la voix. (*Un temps.*) Non, je parle des mots. (*Un temps. Presqu'à elle-même.*) Je n'emploie que les mots les plus simples, j'espère, et cependant quelquefois je trouve ma façon de parler très ... bizarre.

and Spanish 'handsome, brave', to French 'odd, fantastic'? The *OED* hears Littré out, but then shows Littré the door: 'the history of the sense has not been satisfactorily made out'.

In the manuscript it had not been 'bizarre' at all, but 'anything strange or unusual [...] my way of speaking very strange'.[22] Nothing very strange or unusual about that.

Mr Rooney marvels at Mrs Rooney's elegant yesterwords.

MR. ROONEY. Never pause ... safe to haven ... Do you know, Maddy, sometimes one would think you were struggling with a dead language.
MRS. ROONEY. Yes indeed, Dan, I know full well what you mean, I often have that feeling, it is unspeakably excruciating.
MR. ROONEY. I confess I have it sometimes myself, when I happen to overhear what I am saying.
MRS. ROONEY. Well, you know, it will be dead in time, just like our own poor dear Gaelic, there is that to be said.[23]

There are double dealings here. Immediately upon the radio-play's performance and publication, Donald Davie brilliantly pinpointed both the socio-linguistics and the sweep of this sorrowing over Gaelic:

'Our own poor dear Gaelic'—if it was ever anybody's own, it certainly wasn't the shabby-genteel Maddy Rooney's; but to get this you need to know very exactly the significance, to the Catholic majority in present-day Ireland, of Mrs. Rooney's allegiance to the Church of Ireland.[24]

[Mrs. Rooney] speaks by formula, but she does not live and feel by formula—or she strives not to, though her language continually traps her

---

[22] Clas Zilliacus, *Beckett and Broadcasting* (1976), 49, quoting the MS now at the University of Texas.

[23] *All That Fall*, 31–2; Beckett's ellipses. Preceding *Tous ceux qui tombent*, trans. Pinget, 64:

MONSIEUR ROONEY.—Sans halte ni trêve! ... Jusqu'au havre! ... Tu sais, Maddy, on dirait quelquefois que tu te bats avec une langue morte.
  MADAME ROONEY.—C'est vrai, Dan, je ne sais que trop bien de ce que tu veux dire, j'ai souvent cette impression, c'est indiciblement pénible.
  MONSIEUR ROONEY.—J'avoue que moi-même je l'ai par moments. Quand il m'arrive de surprendre ce que je suis en train de dire.
  MADAME ROONEY.—Eh bien, tu sais, elle finira bien par mourir, tout comme notre pauvre vieux gaélique, après tout.

[24] *Spectrum* (Winter 1958). Reprinted in Lawrence Graver and Raymond Federman (eds.), *Samuel Beckett: The Critical Heritage* (1979), 153–6. When Davie incorporated this point within his obituary-article on Beckett in *The Independent* in 1989, the revision changed his expression: 'the Catholic majority in present-day Ireland' became 'the Roman Catholic majority in Eire'.

into it. From this point of view there is more hope for her, and it may be quite true that the hope will indeed be consummated when her language is as dead as 'our own poor dear Gaelic', that is to say, without the sort of zombie life it now has, which suffices to thwart her feelings while good for nothing else.

DE RIGUEUR

So-called dead languages do not have a monopoly of zombie life. The antithesis of dead languages and living ones, then, is at once true and false, like the antithesis of life and death. It is all very well, better than very well, for Bob Dylan to sing that he not busy being born is busy dying, but then he busy being born is dying too.

Art is—among so much else—a mediation between life and death, a means by which both individually and collectively human beings can be brought to contemplate with honesty the thought of their no longer being. Art can live on after the life that gave it existence. It is natural for artists, and lovers of art, to entertain the thought that art is immortal; natural, too, for us to find strange but true comfort in the counter-acknowledgement that, in the long run, art is no more immortal than we are. To Swinburne's claim that 'All men born are mortal but not man', Tennyson retorted within a longer perspective: 'Man is as mortal as men'. Art is as mortal as men, but it is a stay, though not triumphantly against mortality, yet enduringly against confusion or consternation about mortality.

Steven Connor, in his study of Beckett and repetition, cites Gilles Deleuze, 'criticizing the simple opposition of life and death which he finds at work in Freud'.[25] 'Which he finds' prudently distances itself from the judgement on Freud, who might be judged to be well aware that the simple opposition will not do. There is, for instance, Freud's thinking, germane to Beckett's short-circuiting language, about the death-impulse:

What we are left with is the fact that the organism wishes to die only in its own fashion. Thus these guardians of life, too, were originally the myrmidons of death. Hence arises the paradoxical situation that the living organism struggles most energetically against events (dangers, in fact) which might help it to attain its life's goal rapidly—by a kind of short-circuit.[26]

---

[25] *Samuel Beckett: Repetition, Theory and Text*, 11.

[26] *Beyond the Pleasure Principle* (1950 edn.), trans. James Strachey, 51.

This neither rests upon nor rests content with a simple opposition of life and death.

Many a 'kind of short-circuit' fascinated Beckett, and each of them evokes a death-dealing energy.

Of such was Neary's love for Miss Dwyer, who loved a Flight-Lieutenant Elliman, who loved a Miss Farren of Ringsakiddy, who loved a Father Fitt of Ballinclashet, who in all sincerity was bound to acknowledge a certain vocation for a Mrs. West of Passage, who loved Neary.

'Love requited,' said Neary, 'is a short circuit,' a ball that gave rise to a sparkling rally.[27]

Such is the case for the long circuit, love's vistas having a counterpart these days in criticism's exquisite distentions.[28] But it is not long before love's requital arrives in *Murphy*:

He closed his eyes and opened his arms. She sank down athwart his breast, their heads were side by side on the pillow but facing opposite ways, his fingers strayed through her yellow hair. It was the short circuit so earnestly desired by Neary, the glare of pursuit and flight extinguished.[29]

---

[27] *Murphy*, 5. Preceding *Murphy* in French, 10:

Tel était l'amour de Neary pour Mademoiselle Dwyer, qui aimait un certain lieutenant-navigateur-mécanicien Elliman, qui aimait une certaine demoiselle Farren de Ringsakiddy, qui admirait passionément de loin un certain Révérend Père Fitt de Ballinclashet, qui en toute sincérité ne pouvait se dissimuler une certaine vocation pour une certaine Madame West de Passage, qui aimait Neary.
—L'amour partagé, dit Neary, est un court circuit.

The French cuts short the circuit of the English, and does not give rise to any counterpart to 'a ball that gave rise to a sparkling rally'.

[28] Brian T. Fitch, *Beckett and Babel: An Investigation into the Status of the Bilingual Work* (1988), 183 n.

Here, the form of my own text (as was also the case in ch. 8) can, in fact, be seen to problematize its own subject matter since when I am citing Derrida's essay in its English version, I am providing my reading of Graham's reading of Derrida's reading of Gandillac's reading of Benjamin!

It is the closing exclamation-mark which is so endearing!

[29] *Murphy*, 29. Preceding *Murphy* in French, 27:

Il ferma les yeux et ouvrit les bras. Elle s'affaissa sur la poitrine ainsi dégagée, les têtes étaient sur l'oreiller à côté l'une de l'autre mais opposées quant à l'orientation. Ses doigts (à lui) erraient dans les cheveux jaunes. C'était le court circuit si ardemment désiré par Neary, une fin de fuite et de poursuite, comme une lumière crue éteinte.

Sighle Kennedy sets these short circuits within Surrealism (*Murphy's Bed* (1971), 218–19):

Living organisms, in Freud's account, struggle against the premature death which would be 'a kind of short-circuit'. Making love, a kind of dying, is also a short circuit, extinguished to extinction. Beckett finds in the very language a criss-cross to effect this, perversely raising the word 'athwart'—'athwart his breast'—to help constitute a scene not of thwarted but of consummated love. The word 'athwart', while making perfect sense, can be felt to run athwart its own solicitations here.

Deleuze could not be accused of reducing things to the unproblematic, his being a world in which no one ever exclaims, But things aren't that unsimple.

Death is reducible neither to the negation of opposition nor the negation of limitation. It is neither limitation of mortal life by matter, nor the opposition between immortal life and matter, which gives death its nature. Rather, death is the last form of the problematic, the source of problems and questions, the mark of their persistence underneath every answer, the Where? and When? which designates this (non)being where every affirmation grows.[30]

It has not been pure gain, the move from conceiving of death as the entrance upon Le Grand Peut-Être, to conceiving of it as 'the last form of the problematic'; but it does bring some aspects of the truth into view.

The consciousness in *How It Is* thinks—or says—to itself:

[. . .] that's not said any more it must have ceased to be of interest [. . .][31]

The interest of the thought, in the unpunctuated though spaced murmuring which is *How It Is*, is in the slicing and the splicing:

Murphy makes frequent reference to another well-known Surrealist theory described in *The Second Manifesto*: that of the psychological 'short circuit'. This phrase seems to be taken from Freud's essay, *Wit of the Unconscious* . . . Breton uses the term to describe the psychic shock experienced in the mind as a result of its sudden perception of contraries . . . One of the major aims of Surreal art, Breton declares, is 'to increase the number of artistic short circuits'.

On the extinguished, see p. 119 below. Shira Wolosky writes, of the sounds of crawling and falling in *Company*: 'they signify crawling and falling only, almost in a short circuit of signification akin to tautology—one figure Beckett retains in all its emptiness'. There 'almost' is akin to evasion, within 'Samuel Beckett's Figural Evasions' (S. Budick and W. Iser (eds.), *Language of the Unsayable* (1989), 168).

[30] *Différence et Répétition* (1968), trans. Connor, in *Samuel Beckett: Repetition, Theory and Text*, 11.

[31] p. 23. Following *Comment c'est*, 25:

[. . .] ça ne se dit plus ça doit être sans intérêt [. . .]

it must have ceased-to-be-of-interest

or

it-must-have-ceased   to-be-of-interest

—Beckett feels, and inflicts, the agonizing pincer-jaws of both those *musts*.

At least, he does so in English; the French is single-minded:

ça doit être sans intérêt

Elsewhere in *How It Is*, the same goes for the single prong of

plus qu'à recommencer ne pas perdre courage

as against the pincers or forceps, the antithetical pressure, of the English

simply try again not yet say die[32]

The English says 'simply' but proceeds to the duplicity of 'not yet say die'.

Beckett will have had a sneaking sympathy with the Grand Academy of Lagado, and its 'Scheme for entirely abolishing all Words whatsoever':

And this was urged as a great Advantage in Point of Health as well as Brevity. For, it is plain, that every Word we speak is in some Degree a Diminution of our Lungs by Corrosion; and consequently contributes to the shortning of our Lives.[33]

Balnibarbi Government Warning: Speaking may damage your health.

But then liveliness is itself mortal. 'Malone is there. Of his mortal liveliness little trace remains.'[34] Yet he remains there (there in *The Unnamable*), past his not-strictly-eponymous novel, *Malone Dies*.

---

[32] p. 79. Following *Comment c'est*, 88.

[33] *Gulliver's Travels: A Voyage to Laputa*, ch. V.

[34] *The Unnamable*, 5. Following *L'innommable*, 10:

Malone est là. De sa vivacité mortelle il ne reste que peu de traces.

The French 'vivacité' lacks a particular form of life to be found in the English 'liveliness', and the French does not come to the juddering end, 'remains'.

Malone, nearing death, considers the ultimate diminution of his lungs.

Decidedly it will never have been given to me to finish anything, except perhaps breathing. One must not be greedy. But is this how one chokes? Presumably. And the rattle, what about the rattle? Perhaps it is not de rigueur after all. To have vagitated and not be bloody well able to rattle. How life dulls the power to protest to be sure. I wonder what my last words will be, written, the others do not endure, but vanish, into thin air.[35]

One word there, 'vagitated', has the air of having materialized from thin air. Even today it has not yet materialized—in Beckett's sense—within the *OED*, which still has only 'to roam or travel' (medieval Latin *vagitare*, Latin *vagari*, to wander), obsolete, with the one citation:

1614 RALEIGH *Hist. World* Before the use of the compass was known it was impossible to vagitate athwart the Ocean.

Not that roaming and travelling are beside the point at being born.[36] But what Beckett needed was an Englishing of the French *vagir*: 'pousser un cri faible, semblable à celui des nouveau-nés'. This had been alive in his French in *Malone meurt*: 'Avoir vagi, puis ne pas être foutu de râler.'

After *vagi*, 'foutu' cracks a foul mouth of a joke; after 'To have vagitated', 'and not be bloody well able to rattle' is exasperatedly sleek with the blood of birth.

The English language delivers some words within this family. There is 'vagitus' (from Latin *vagire*, to utter cries of distress, to wail): 'A cry or wail; *spec.* that of a new-born child'.[37] Within

---

[35] *Malone Dies*, 76–7. Following *Malone meurt*, 124:

Décidément il ne m'aura jamais été donné de rien achever, sinon de respirer. Il ne faut pas être gourmand. Mais est-ce ainsi qu'on étouffe? Il faut croire. Et le râle, qu'est-ce qu'on en fait. Peut-être n'est-il pas de rigueur après tout. Avoir vagi, puis ne pas être foutu de râler. Ce que la vie peut faire passer le goût des protestations. Allons, c'est un détail. Je me demande quel sera mon dernier mot, écrit, les autres s'envolent, au lieu de rester.

[36] William Empson: 'A son of my own at about the age of twelve, keen on space travel like the rest of them, saw the goat having kids and was enough impressed to say "It's better than space travel". It is indeed absolutely or metaphysically better, because it is coming out of the nowhere into here; and I was so pleased to see the human mind beginning its work that I felt as much impressed as he had done at seeing the birth of the kids.' 'Donne the Space Man', *Kenyon Review*, 19 (1957), 338.

[37] Beckett has his musical comedy with the vagitus and the rattle in *Murphy*, 71

earshot is *vagient*: 'Of infants, infancy, etc.: Crying, squalling, wailing'; this with the Beckett-like earliest citation of 'nor vagient Youngling, nor decrepit Ageling' (1628).

'To have vagitated': Beckett did not undeviatingly judge this the *mot juste* here (the *mot juste* needing to be surprising as well as just, and therefore seldom on easy terms with cliché). 'To have vagitated' is in both the American edition of *Malone Dies* (1956) and in the English edition (1958), as well as in the American edition of the trilogy (1959), but the 1959 English edition of the trilogy has (temporarily?) something altogether different: *mewled*. 'To have mewled and not be bloody well able to rattle'.[38]

In which case the aged man remembers the ages of man:

> At first the Infant,
> Mewling, and puking in the Nurses armes.[39]

What 'mewl' does, scarcely a word, more like a sound-effect (but then an infant can't fant), is not only transport us to second childhood, but colour the rattle.

'And the rattle, what about the rattle?' Even without 'mewl' ('the Infant, | Mewling') this abbreviation of the death-rattle to the rattle might make us hear the baby's rattle.[40] But 'mewled' increases the likelihood.

(also p. 23 for 'the precise moment of vagitus'); preceding *Murphy* in French, 56–7 (also p. 23, 'le moment précis du vagissement').

His troubles had begun early. To go back no further than the vagitus, it had not been the proper A of international concert pitch, with 435 double vibrations per second, but the double flat of this. How he winced, the honest obstetrician, a devout member of the old Dublin Orchestral Society and an amateur flautist of some merit. With what sorrow he recorded that of all the millions of little larynges cursing in union at that particular moment, the infant Murphy's alone was off the note. To go back no further than the vagitus.
His rattle will make amends.

Beckett lets the forthcoming rattle enjoy a five-word paragraph to itself.

Ses malheurs avaient commencé de bonne heure. Son vagissement, pour ne remonter que jusque là, au lieu du [*sic*] la traditionnel de concert international, à 435 doubles vibrations par seconde, n'avait donné qu'un sol poussif. Quelle déception pour le brave gynécologue, membre ardent de la vieille Société Orchestrale de Dublin et flûtiste amateur d'un certain mérite! Quelle douleur de devoir constater que, parmi tous les millions de petits larynx en train de blasphémer à l'unisson, seul celui de l'enfant Murphy ne donnait pas la note! Pour ne remonter qu'au vagissement.
Son râle compensera.

[38] 1956, p. 77. American trilogy, 1959, p. 341; 1965, p. 249. English trilogy, 1959, p. 250.
[39] *As You Like It*, II. vii.
[40] I am indebted to Shawn Smith.

As does *An Essay on Man*:

> Behold the child, by Nature's kindly law,
> Pleas'd with a rattle, tickled with a straw.

What for Beckett is Nature's kindly law? Mankind's dying.

Pope had set his couplet within a sequence which is even more apt to Beckett and would be amenable to his good offices:

> See some strange comfort ev'ry state attend,
> And Pride bestow'd on all, a common friend;
> See some fit Passion ev'ry age supply,
> Hope travels thro', nor quits us when we die.
>   Behold the child, by Nature's kindly law,
> Pleas'd with a rattle, tickled with a straw:
> Some livelier play-thing gives his youth delight,
> A little louder, but as empty quite:
> Scarfs, garters, gold, amuse his riper stage;
> And beads and pray'r-books are the toys of age:
> Pleas'd with this bauble still, as that before;
> 'Till tir'd he sleeps, and Life's poor play is o'er!
>   (ii. 271–82)[41]

Pope could himself have been making play with the death-rattle (his immediately preceding sentence ended with 'when we die').[42] But anyway Beckett may, on his own initiative, have been moved by Pope's setting the rattle within a sequence of death, of strange comfort, and of Nature's kindly law.

And the rattle, what about the rattle? Perhaps it is not de rigueur after all.

The original French ('Et le râle') did not glance towards the child's rattle, since in French the toy is not *le râle* but *le hochet*. Beckett's French thought is transformed as it passes into English. But then so is his French thought even when it passes, on the face

---

[41] 'Some livelier play-thing' is succeeded by 'his riper stage' and by 'Life's poor play'.

> Life's but a walking Shadow, a poore Player,
> That struts and frets his houre upon the Stage.

>   (*Macbeth*, v. v)

[42] The first citation for 'death-rattle' in the *OED* is not till Lytton in 1829, but the earlier form had been simply 'rattle', as in Berkeley (1752): 'Persons have been recovered by tar-water after they had rattles in the throat'.

of it untransformed, into English: 'Perhaps it is not de rigueur after all'.

There is a touch of class about 'de rigueur', a formal stoical resilience: at such a moment to be so solicitous of social propriety, so concerned not to incommode others. A death rattle is deeply considerate. How else will the stander-by know when it is all over, leave alone know to rise and twitch his mantle blue? 'De rigueur' effects so much—in English, particularly. In the original French it is more limited, less supple: 'Peut-être n'est-il pas de rigueur après tout.'

French like the very word *etiquette*, 'de rigueur' is itself de rigueur as the term to formalize mourning. Is death a black tie occasion? Think of the early 1880s:

Linen collars and cuffs cannot be worn with crape; crêpe lisse frills are *de rigueur*. Sable or any coloured fur must be left off; sealskin is admissible, but it never looks well in really deep mourning.[43]

But the great thing about 'de rigueur' is that it stiffens, death in the joints of life and life in the jaws of death.

Beckett was helped to think well of the painter Jack B. Yeats by thinking ill of life's stiffening:

There is at least this to be said for mind, that it can dispel mind. And at least this for art-criticism, that it can lift from the eyes, before *rigor vitae* sets in, some of the weight of congenital prejudice.[44]

Wary of rigor vitae, Beckett has a soft spot for rigor mortis—and a healthy respect for vigor mortis.

Malone, unexpectedly the gentleman, is not so crass as to mention rigor mortis, though he acknowledges its existence and its imminence in that passing 'de rigueur'. He and his creator are more sensible of these things than is the thanatologist who deplores both 'la conception populaire (séparation de l'âme et du corps)' and 'la dimension impressionniste (rigidité cadavérique)'

---

[43] Quoted by John Morley, *Death, Heaven and the Victorians* (1971); *The Oxford Book of Death*, 118.

[44] 'MacGreevy on Yeats' (1945), *Disjecta*, 95. As to stiffening: *Molloy*, 83: 'My two legs are as stiff as a life-sentence and yet I sometimes get up'. Following *Molloy* in French, 93: 'Mes deux jambes sont raides comme la justice et cependant je me lève de temps en temps'.

and then wanly urges us to distinguish 'plus rigoureusement ce que spécifie la mort'.[45]

'Perhaps it is not de rigueur *after all*'. My italics, his tacitness.

Elsewhere in Beckett the indurated French phrase finds itself in the vicinity of something tactilely so different, so soft—only to have the corporeal comfort pushed away by the soul and the mind. Of all living things, an alpaca llama in the infernal landscape.

she would not come to me I would go to her huddle in her fleece but they add no a beast here no the soul is de rigueur the mind too a minimum of each otherwise too great an honour[46]

Hell is reserved for soul-bearers: 'the soul is de rigueur'.

ARCHAISM AND THE MORIBUND

What mortals are up against is 'the crass tenacity of life and its diligent pains', where both the deeply internal rhyme (crass tenacity) and the pun on 'pains' are tenacious. All the trouble we take to go on being in trouble.

She stood a moment irresolute, bowed forward with her hands on the table, before she sat down again. Her day of toil over, day dawned on other toils within her, on the crass tenacity of life and its diligent pains. Sitting, moving about, she bore them better than in bed.[47]

Malone Dies: does he? In a first person narrative, you can never know for sure.

Malone Dies: does Arthur mort in the *Morte d'Arthur*? The one thing we anciently know for sure is that 'King Arthur is not dead'.

[45] Louis-Vincent Thomas, *Anthropologie de la Mort* (1975), 29.

[46] *How It Is*, 15. Following *Comment c'est*, 17:

il ne viendrait pas à moi j'irais à lui me blottir dans sa toison mais on ajoute qu'une bête ici non l'âme est de rigueur l'intelligence aussi un minimum de chaque sinon trop d'honneur

[47] *Malone Dies*, 42. Following *Malone meurt*, 70:

Elle resta un instant irrésolue, les mains appuyées sur la table, avant de se rasseoir. Sa journée finie le jour se levait sur d'autres labeurs, en dedans d'elle, ceux de la vie sottement tenace, aux douleurs diligentes. Assise, allant et venant, elle les endurait mieux qu'allongée.

For 'pains', compare *Company*, 69: 'Till again with no dead end for his pains he renounces and embarks on yet another course'. Preceding and following *Compagnie*, 68: 'Et là encore sans le moindre terminus pour sa peine il finit par renoncer et par changer encore de cap'.

W. H. Mallock offered a recipe for successful surcease, 'How to Make an Epic Poem like Mr Tennyson's':

Take, then, one blameless prig. Set him upright in the middle of a round table, and place beside him a beautiful wife, who cannot abide prigs . . . Then wound slightly the head of the blameless prig; remove him suddenly from the table, and keep in a cool barge for future use.[48]

Malone muses:

There is naturally another possibility that does not escape me, though it would be a great disappointment to have it confirmed, and that is that I am dead already and that all continues more or less as when I was not. Perhaps I expired in the forest, or even earlier.[49]

The usually-vacant drawled idiom, of possibilities that escape one, is charged with what it really would be to escape. More, what it would be to escape *me*, the being me: 'another possibility that does not escape *me*', to italicize where the original is a roman thought.[50]

By the time we meet it in *Malone Dies*, the phrase 'dead already' is one which we know already. From the previous volume in the trilogy, *Molloy*.

It was a simple Latin cross, white. I wanted to have my name put on it, with the here lies and the date of my birth. Then all it would have

---

[48] *Every Man his own Poet* (1872), 10–11.
[49] *Malone Dies*, 45. Following *Malone meurt*, 74–5:

La possibilité ne m'échappe pas non plus bien sûr, quelque décevante qu'elle soit, que je sois d'ores et déjà mort et que tout continue à peu près comme par le passé. Peut-être ai-je expiré dans la forêt, même avant.

[50] *How It Is*, 39:

[. . .] my life that day will not escape me that life not yet

Following *Comment c'est*, 43:

[. . .] ma vie ce jour-là ne m'échappera pas cette vie-là pas encore

In his own tombstone inscription in *Premier amour* (10), the narrator's escape is much in view:

> Ci-gît qui y échappa tant
> Qu'il n'en échappe que maintenant

Preceding *First Love* (11), where the inscription, far from reaching escape, is trapped in the toils of paradox:

> Hereunder lies the above who up below
> So hourly died that he lived on till now.

wanted was the date of my death. They would not let me. Sometimes I smiled, as if I were dead already.[51]

'All it would have wanted was the date of my death', not only as lacked but as desired. 'Beneath it all, desire of oblivion runs.'

Beckett's vision of desired negation needs its knotted *nots*, rather as Milton needed such a nexus for his different Paradise ('which not nice Art | In Beds and curious Knots, but Nature boon'[52]):

that does not escape me [...] that I am dead already and that all continues more or less as when I was not.

That conclusive 'not' has to mean not *dead*: a turn which is peacefully at odds with the impulse of the words themselves, which sound as if they already mean unexisting. No: not *not*.

The French for 'as when I was not' had been bleachedly impersonal: 'comme par le passé'. The English, though, usually means, within and without Beckett, the days before one first saw the light:

Oh I know I too shall cease and be as when I was not yet, only all over instead of in store, that makes me happy[53]

(Again the French is impersonal, no 'I' but instead, a perfect fit in its different way, 'être comme avant d'être'.)

Hazlitt thought that the traditional variant of this might make you, though not as happy as Larry, less fearful:

Perhaps the best cure for the fear of death is to reflect that life has a beginning as well as an end. There was a time when we were not: that gives us no concern—why then should it trouble us that a time will come

---

[51] p. 185. Following *Molloy* in French, 209:

C'était une simple croix latine, blanche. J'avais voulu faire mettre mon nom dessus, avec le ci-gît et ma date de naissance. On n'aurait plus eu qu'à ajouter celle de ma mort. On ne me l'avait pas permis. Quelquefois je souriais, comme si j'étais mort déjà.

[52] *Paradise Lost*, iv. 241–2.
[53] *From an Abandoned Work* (1958), 17. Preceding 'D'un ouvrage abandonné' (1967), trans. Ludovic and Agnès Janvier in collaboration with Beckett; *Têtes-mortes* (1967), 21:

Oh je sais que moi aussi je vais finir et être comme avant d'être, sauf que tout bu au lieu d'à boire, ça fait mon bonheur

when we shall cease to be? . . . To die is only to be as we were before we were born.[54]

The grimmer accents of Schopenhauer attempt the same con-solation: 'After your death you will be what you were before your birth.'[55] But in 'The Old Fools', Larkin scotched this, at least for the likes of him:

> At death, you break up: the bits that were you
> Start speeding away from each other for ever
> With no one to see. It's only oblivion, true:
> We had it before, but then it was going to end,
> And was all the time merging with a unique endeavour
> To bring to bloom the million-petalled flower
> Of being here. Next time you can't pretend
> There'll be anything else.

How piercing the rhyming: *endeavour* flowering as the union of two previous rhyme-words, *end* and *ever*; and then 'can't pretend' taking them both to task.[56]

> Next time you can't pretend
> There'll be anything else.

Beckett knew very well what he thought about the notion of a next time:

To be buried in lava and not turn a hair, it is then a man shows what stuff he is made of. To know you can do better next time, unrecognizably better, and that there is no next time, and that it is a blessing there is not, there is a thought to be going on with.[57]

---

[54] 'On the Fear of Death'; *The Oxford Book of Death*, 31.

[55] 'On the Doctrine of the Indestructibility of Our True Nature', *Parerga and Paralipomena* (1851).

[56] Larkin's rhyming breaks up Hopkins's compacted moment, and makes the bits speed away from each other:

> Why do sinners' ways prosper? and why must
> Disappointment all I endeavour end?

The answering rhyme in Hopkins had not been Larkin's dour 'can't pretend' but the agonistic 'contend': 'Thou art indeed just, Lord, if I contend | With thee; but, sir, so what I plead is just'.

[57] *Malone Dies*, 83. Following *Malone meurt*, 134:

Sous la lave rester froid comme marbre, c'est là où l'on voit de quel bois on se chauffe. Savoir pouvoir faire mieux, à s'y méconnaître, la prochaine fois, et qu'il n'y a pas de prochaine fois, et que c'est une chance qu'il n'y en ait pas, il y a là de quoi se régaler pendant un moment.

'Look thy last on all things lovely, | Every hour'? Rather, look lively; and concede that there are occasions on which life is glimpsed for the first time only as it is going.

In September 1932, *This Quarter* published a translation of René Crevel, 'Rendered into English by Samuel Beckett'. It looks into the eyes of a dog hit by a car:

> As long as I live I shall never be able to visualize death otherwise than as a heavy ball of wool growing cold, on a road, at the fall of evening. They came to life and to light in my dreams, the eyes of Madame Hebdomeros, they came to life only to be extinguished.[58]

Nomen est omen: the name Crevel must have come to life and to light in Beckett's dreams. *Crever* was to be one of his words:

le bon vieux temps où on crevait d'envie d'être mort

(in English, 'the good old days when we wished we were dead').

ces histoires à crever debout de vie et de mort

('all this ballsaching poppycock about life and death').

à bout de vœux d'appeler la crève

('dumb with howling to be put out of my misery').[59]

Those eyes of the dog, 'they came to life only to be extinguished'. Such last-minute life, on the verge of extinction or extinguishing, is a recurrent current in Beckett, often an apocalyptic chronographia which splits the second of time; not

> And now the Sun had stretch'd out all the hills,
> And now was dropt into the Western bay;[60]

but:

and the sun, already down, was manifest in the livid tongues of fire darting towards the zenith, falling and darting again, ever more pale and languid, and doomed no sooner lit to be extinguished.[61]

---

[58] 'Every One Thinks Himself Phoenix . . .', *This Quarter*, 5 (1932), 163.

[59] (i) *Cendres*, trans. Robert Pinget and Beckett, in *La dernière bande* suivi de *Cendres* (1959), 47; following *Embers* (1959), *Krapp's Last Tape* and *Embers* (1959), 23. (ii) *Malone meurt*, 83; preceding *Malone Dies*, 51. (iii) *L'innommable*, 41; preceding *The Unnamable*, 58.

[60] 'Lycidas', 190–1.

[61] *Molloy*, 87–8. Following *Molloy* in French, 98–9:

Et le soleil, sans être exactement visible comme disque, se signalait par des flammèches

The sun is the source of life, and is itself dying, and itself dies and rises day after day. Beckett preserves the death in this solar energy when he translates from the Spanish a line about the sun:

Then, by her very downfall vivified[62]

'Vivifying', antiseptic, at arm's length and in rubber gloves, recurs more brutally when a dead mule is buried to its owner's satisfaction: 'He felt better. The end of a life is always vivifying.'[63] What kind of life is there now in the word 'vivifying' or 'vivified'? Now, as against a century ago, when Christina Rossetti was still able to speak without deathliness of light and heat, 'the great vivifiers of the material world'.[64]

Beckett brought to an end his tribute to Proust with the word 'defunctus': Proust saw the 'invisible reality' that 'reveals the meaning of the word "defunctus"'.[65] How then did Beckett in his turn give palpable visible reality to the meaning of the word 'defunctus'? 'Languages, both dead and living': we should not put it past the English language to muster a verb hereabouts, a verb at once dead and living.

But let us leave these morbid matters and get on with that of my demise, in two or three days if I remember rightly. Then it will be all over with the Murphys, Merciers, Molloys, Morans and Malones, unless it goes on beyond the grave. But sufficient unto the day, let us first defunge, then we'll see.[66]

Let us first consider what Beckett first wrote: his French original here, 'défungeons', has been deprecated. Beckett 'tends to

jaunes et roses, s'élançant vers le zénith, retombant, s'élançant à nouveau, toujours plus faibles et plus claires, et vouées à s'éteindre à peine allumées.

[62] Juana de Asbaje, in *Anthology of Mexican Poetry*, 92.

[63] *Malone Dies*, 37. Following *Malone meurt*, 62: 'Ça allait mieux. La fin d'une vie, ça ravigote.' The end of a life is, under one aspect, the kind of failure which amounts to a final success. For Beckett it may be failure that vivifies: 'Success and failure on the public level never mattered much to me, in fact I feel much more at home with the latter, having breathed deep of its vivifying air all my writing life up to the last couple of years' (11 Jan. 1956, letter to Alan Schneider, about *Endgame*; *Disjecta*, 106).

[64] *Seek and Find* (1879), 26.

[65] See pp. 101–2 above.

[66] *Malone Dies*, 63. Following *Malone meurt*, 103:

Mais laissons là ces questions morbides et revenons à celle de mon décès, d'ici deux ou trois jours si j'ai bonne mémoire. A ce moment-là c'en sera fait des Murphy, Mercier, Molloy, Moran et autres Malone, à moins que ça ne continue dans l'outre-tombe. Mais pas de midi à moins vingt-trois heures, défungeons d'abord, après nous aviserons.

indulge in neologisms that are not always very successful, such as *défunger* for "to die" (concocted from *défunt*)'.[67] But 'defunge' has in its marrow an incorporation of death and life. It is perfectly clear what 'defunge' means; perfectly clear too that there is no such verb in English—it is not even that 'defunge' has become defunct (not that 'defunct' has). Though a dead language once had *defungi* (from 'to discharge, to have done with'), the English 'defunge' was never really born.

Beckett said in conversation in 1968 (not the very words, because translated from the French):

I have always sensed that there was within me an assassinated being. Assassinated before my birth. I needed to find this assassinated person again. And try to give him new life.[68]

New life? Though dead before birth? A paradox—let it pass. For Beckett went on directly:

I once attended a lecture by Jung in which he spoke about one of his patients, a very young girl. After the lecture, as everyone was leaving, Jung stood by silently. And then, as if speaking to himself, astonished by the discovery that he was making, he added: In the most fundamental way, she had never been really born. I, too, have always had the sense of never having been born.[69]

This encounter famously went to the making of *All That Fall*:

When he had done with the little girl he stood there motionless for some time, quite two minutes I should say, looking down at his table. Then he suddenly raised his head and exclaimed, as if he had had a revelation, The trouble with her was she had never been really born! (*Pause.*) He spoke throughout without notes. (*Pause.*) I left before the end.[70]

---

[67] John Fletcher, *The Novels of Samuel Beckett* (1964), 164.

[68] Charles Juliet, 'Meeting Beckett', *TriQuarterly*, 77 (1989–90), 10.

[69] There may have been for Beckett a further personal pain in this. For the lecture of Jung's which Beckett heard was in 1935 (Bair, *Samuel Beckett*, 208–10), and the previous year Jung had become the twentieth doctor called in to help Joyce's daughter Lucia in her madness, Lucia Joyce whose love Beckett was unable to return.

[70] *All That Fall*, 33–4. (*Collected Shorter Plays* (1984), 36, has—presumably in error—'never really been born'.) Preceding *Tous ceux qui tombent*, trans. Pinget, 68–9:

Quand il en a eu fini avec la petite fille il est resté courbé sur sa table un bon moment, deux minutes au moins, puis brusquement il a relevé la tête et s'est écrié, comme s'il venait d'avoir une révélation, Elle n'était jamais née réellement, voilà ce qu'elle avait! (*Un temps.*) Il a parlé sans notes d'un bout à l'autre. (*Un temps.*) Je suis partie avant la fin.

Like his Mrs Rooney, Beckett took note. And none of us will leave before the end. An act of new linguistic life, life in death and death in life, such as 'defunge', is astonished by the discovery that it is making, a revelation.

'But sufficient unto the day, let us first defunge, then we'll see.' An Irish bull, 'then we'll see', since it pretended to have every intention of meaning, Then (it is to be hoped) we'll be blessedly in no position to see. For if we'll see, then it will be the case that we have failed to defunge.[71]

All over?—'unless it goes on beyond the grave': this is the possibility which haunts Beckett.

Ada too, conversation with her, that was something, that's what hell will be like, small chat to the babbling of Lethe about the good old days when we wished we were dead.[72]

It is often intimated that Beckett is not a disinterested inquirer into the human condition but has something wrong with him. His declining to marry Peggy Guggenheim is sometimes cited, though this might rather be deemed evidence that there was a great deal right with him. But it is true that the reasons which he gave to her for not being able to return the love of Joyce's daughter Lucia do strike a chill. As does Peggy Guggenheim's bright young prose, but differently:

My passion for Oblomov was inspired by the fact that I really believed he was capable of great intensity, and that I could bring it out. He, on the other hand, always denied it, saying he was dead and had no feelings that were human and that was why he had not been able to fall in love with Joyce's daughter.[73]

'Dead and had no feelings that were human': this does go beyond the called-for. Most of us manage something less intense by way of unrequital.

But Beckett, a great writer, has two spurs, one private and the

---

[71] The Irish bull occupies Chapter 4 below.

[72] *Embers*, *Krapp's Last Tape* and *Embers*, 24. Preceding *Cendres* (*La derniere bande suivi de Cendres*), trans. Pinget and Beckett, 47:

Et Ada, causer avec elle, ça c'était quelque chose, ce sera ça l'enfer, des bavardages au murmure du Léthé sur le bon vieux temps où on crevait d'envie d'être mort.

[73] Peggy Guggenheim, *Out of this Century*, 205.

other public, as he sets forth what is called in *The Unnamable* 'a ponderous chronicle of moribunds in their courses'.

For if I could hear such a music at such a time, I mean while floundering through a ponderous chronicle of moribunds in their courses, moving, clashing, writhing or fallen in short-lived swoons, with how much more reason should I not hear it now, when supposedly I am burdened with myself alone.[74]

The adjective 'moribund' is infrequent but not unusual; what stiffens it with a further touch of death is the offering of the word as a noun, and in the plural to boot. 'Moribunds': it is like what passes for compassion in the social sciences. I once heard a talk on penal reform in which we were urged not to think of people in prison as criminals necessarily: 'Many of them are not criminals; they are "inadequates".' This, flat-tongued.

It is bad enough being inadequate; worse to be an inadequate; worst to be one of a slew of inadequates. Who would not rather be a criminal?

Yet it matters that the noun, a moribund, is not a coinage; though Beckett has his unforgettable coinages (*Worstward Ho* for one, 'niobaloo' for another[75]), his convictions require him rather to act inspiredly upon the paradox of giving *new* life to something in the language which had never been really born. Such as the noun 'a moribund' which has been enjoying its long days' dying, there in the *OED*:

A person in a dying state. 1835 Every day the moribund's door was besieged by crowds of anxious inquirers. 1852 more medicos than moribunds.[76]

---

[74] *The Unnamable*, 28. Following *L'innommable*, 43:

Car si une telle musique a pu me parvenir alors que je me débattais dans une lourde histoire de moribonds se déplaçant, s'entre-choquant, s'agitant sur place et tombés en brèves syncopes, ne devrait-elle pas à plus forte raison se faire entendre à présent, où soi-disant je ne suis encombré que de moi?

[75] *Murphy*, 138–9, Murphy being hard on Celia's soft heart towards the suicide: 'A decayed valet severs the connexion and you set up a niobaloo as though he were your fourteen children.' Preceding *Murphy* in French, 103: 'Un valet de chambre décati lâche la rampe et tu commences à gueuler comme s'il était tes quatorze enfants.' No Niobe-hullabaloo there.

[76] As to moribunds elsewhere in Beckett: his youthful spoof (1930?), 'Le Concentrisme', had pondered 'des morts et des moribonds' (*Disjecta*, 36). John Fletcher deplored this turn in Beckett's translation of *Molloy*: 'the occasional pithy

'A ponderous chronicle of moribunds *in their courses*': this honours the poor old draggers of themselves across the surface of the earth by aligning them with the divine wheelings of the stars; this music of the spheres should come as strangely no surprise, given that Beckett's sentence has just spoken of hearing 'such a music'. And yet 'in their courses' does not burke their being moribunds all right, since in their courses are to be found *corses*, itself a word which, being a perfectly understandable archaism and a Shakespearean *memento mori*, is both dead and alive.

Guillaume Apollinaire ended *Zone* (1913) with the line

Soleil cou coupé

There the French words suffer a gruesomely surrealistic elongation even as the neck is severed, *cou* being the opposite of cut when extended to *coupé*. Beckett's translation in 1950 incarnates a different paradox of life in death and death in life:

Sun corseless head[77]

This gives its own body to the thought. The early stage of translation must have been to turn Apollinaire's sun, a head cut off at the nape, into a head without a body. But 'without a body' is wordy, has none of the cutting economy of 'cou coupé'. And 'bodiless' would not do, since it suggests the disembodied, the incorporeal. Thanks to archaism's moribundity, Beckett—tracking Apollinaire back—has a dour triumph:

Sun corseless head

The sun is wrenched from its corse. The corse revives. The dead word for a dead body can convey still the fire in its ashes.

Beckett's grim felicity in giving us a turn is held by some commentators to be no more than Irishism, the ordinary Irish way of putting things. Even if this were so, it would not extinguish the

---

slang of the original is rarely fully rendered: *quelle galerie de crevés* pales to "gallery of moribunds"' (*The Novels of Samuel Beckett*, 134). But *pales to* is an unwitting tribute to Beckett's deathly pallor of phrasing. (*Molloy* in French, 212: 'Quelle tourbe dans ma tête, quelle galerie de crevés'. Preceding *Molloy*, 188: 'What a rabble in my head, what a gallery of moribunds'.) It was left to B. S. Johnson, in his novel *Travelling People* (1963), to father a character called Maurice Bunde, ripe for abbreviation to Maurie and so due to die.

[77] *Collected Poems*, 153.

linguistic life-in-death in such a deathwards progress as 'this old so dying woman'.

If only she could be pure figment. Unalloyed. This old so dying woman. So dead.[78]

Why can we say *old* and *dying* and *so old* but not *so dying*? How wretchedly alive the thought is, so dying.

For though Beckett is an Irishman, he writes in English, and he never writes without a sense of setting his figures against the ground of the English language. *Ill Seen Ill Said*: but things would be even more ill seen and more ill said were it not that English and French are more alive to Beckett than Irish is.

It is *Ill Seen Ill Said* which presents, as a sentence without a verb: 'This old so dying woman'. And Beckett's syntax of weakness is confirmed, further infirmed, on the next page by the sudden flurry of an unanticipated verb, a verb 'doomed no sooner lit to be extinguished'.

She is done with raising her eyes. Nearly done. But when she lies with them open she can just make out the rafters. In the dim light the skylights shed. An ever dimmer light. As the panes slowly dimmen.[79]

Why is it that in English there is no difficulty about bright/brighter/brighten, but more than a difficulty about dim/dimmer/dimmen? What does this tell us about a language's giving body to a people's hopes and fears? Beckett's original French has no such encroachment as his English makes out, dim light ... dimmer light ... dimmen. In French, 'le demi-jour' darkens, with its own inspissation, into 'toujours': 'Demi-jour toujours plus faible.' But

---

[78] *Ill Seen Ill Said*, 20. Following *Mal vu mal dit*, 24:

Si seulement elle pouvait n'être qu'ombre. Ombre sans mélange. Cette vieille si mourante. Si morte.

Marjorie Perloff, in Alan Warren Friedman *et al.* (eds.), *Beckett Translating/Translating Beckett* (1987), 41:

The syntactic oddity of the English phrase ('old so dying'), which is not present in its French counterpart, is standard Irish ballad diction and turns up in both Yeats and Joyce.

(Where, exactly?)

[79] *Ill Seen Ill Said*, 21. Following *Mal vu mal dit*, 25:

Elle ne lève plus guère les yeux. Mais allongée les yeux ouverts elle entrevoit les combles. Dans le demi-jour qui tombe des jours. Demi-jour toujours plus faible. Les vitres s'opacifiant toujours plus.

this has no sombre climax of flat oddity, of 'dimmen', at once perfectly clear and utterly improbable. Where in English 'the panes slowly dimmen', in French, 'Les vitres s'opacifiant toujours plus.'

The great dictionary Littré in the nineteenth century knew the verb *s'opacifier*, and the English language has long permitted us (though not encouraged us) to opacate and, less anciently, to opacify. But how opaque such a word is in comparison with 'dimmen', how abstracted.

The *OED* recognizes the word, albeit with one citation only:

dimmen
v. rare. To grow dim. 1828–30 W. TAYLOR *Surv. Germ. Poetry* I. 301 Scenery . . on which his dimmening eyes are preparing to close for ever.

So 'dimmen' is no more an idiosyncrasy of Beckett's mere own than is that intimation of Beckettian mortality itself: 'Scenery . . on which his dimmening eyes are preparing to close for ever.' The verb *dimmen* catches many contradictions: it did once exist and yet is '*v. rare*': it feels like a coinage of Beckett's, and yet at the same time, because of medieval verb-forms like *maken* where the later language has *make*, it feels ancient, in more than one way archaic and with archaism's mingling of acknowledged death and enduring life.

'As the panes slowly dimmen'. The noun's pun is not painful, it is a calmative (one of Beckett's best stories, 'The Calmative'). 'The eye glued to one or the other window has nothing but black drapes for its pains.'[80]

Such a verb as 'dimmen' is at once grave and comical in its unostentatious challenge, its straddling so succinctly the easily comprehensible and the continuingly ill-at-ease. Beckett offers many such unfussy fusions, many of them likewise resisting the privileges of lively colours or states:

Watt saw, in the grate, of the range, the ashes grey. But they turned pale red, when he covered the lamp, with his hat. The range was almost out, but not quite. A handful of dry chips and the flames would spring,

---

[80] *Ill Seen Ill Said* again, 12. Following *Mal vu mal dit*, 15:

L'œil collé à l'une et à l'autre fenêtre ne voit que rideaux noirs.

The French, 'ne voit que', is transparent, unlike the-through-a-glass-darkly of 'for its pains'.

merry in appearance, up the chimney, with an organ note. So Watt busied himself a little while, covering the lamp, less and less, more and more, with his hat, watching the ashes greyen, redden, greyen, redden, in the grate, of the range.[81]

There is no problem about *understanding* 'greyen', only the difficulty, first, of admitting it, and then of understanding why the language has taken against it. No such lucid perturbation of mind attends upon Beckett's French here, which veers equably, handy-dandy, 'au gris, au rouge, au gris, au rouge'.

It is not that grey does not permit of a verb; there is, simply enough, the verb to grey. But the asymmetry of 'greyen, redden, greyen, redden', prompts some conjunction of death and life, as in those ashes.[82]

The verb greyen is another of those words which have never been really born. (The *OED* doesn't admit it even as still-born.) This makes it amenable to Beckett's apprehension of death in life and life in death. Those ashes watched by Watt. Or the ashes

---

[81] *Watt*, 37–8. Preceding *Watt* in French, 37:

Watt voyait, dans le foyer du fourneau, les cindres grises. Mais elles viraient au rouge pâle quand il masquait la lampe, avec son chapeau. Le fourneau était presque éteint, mais pas tout à fait. Une poignée de copeaux secs et les flammes jailliraient, joyeuses en apparence, dans la cheminée, avec un ronflement d'orgue. Ainsi Watt s'affaira quelque temps, masquant la lampe de moins en moins, de plus en plus, avec son chapeau, regardant les cindres virer au gris, au rouge, au gris, au rouge, dans le foyer du fourneau.

[82] The conjunction of the murky verb 'greyening' with something quirky as to death ('when dying in London', where 'living in London' would have a more familiar ring) recurs in *Watt*, 212:

So Watt suspected that it was in the depths of the night, when the risk of disturbance was small, that Mr Knott organised his exterior for the day to come. And what went far to strengthen this suspicion in the heart of Watt was this, that when sometimes, in the small hours of the morning, unable or unwilling to sleep he rose and went to the window, to look at the stars, which he had once known familiarly by name, when dying in London, and breathe the night air, and listen to the night sounds, of which he was still extremely curious, he sometimes saw, between him and the ground, lightening the darkness, greyening the leaves and, in wet weather, tinseling the rain, a fascia of white light.

Preceding *Watt* in French, 219–20:

Ainsi Watt soupçonnait que c'était au plus profond de la nuit, où le risque d'être dérangé était minime, que Monsieur Knott organisait son extérieur pour la journée à venir. Et ce qui contribuait à renforcer ce soupçon dans le cœur de Watt était ceci, que lorsque, passé minuit, ne pouvant ou ne voulant pas dormir, il se levait et allait à la fenêtre, pour regarder les étoiles qu'il avait si bien connues, et jusqu'à leurs noms, a l'époque où il se mourait à Londres, et pour respirer l'air de la nuit, et pour écouter les rumeurs de la nuit dont il était toujours très amateur, il voyait quelquefois qui pâlissait l'obscurité, grisaillait les feuilles et, quand il pleuvait, argentait la pluie, entre lui et le sol un faisceau de lumière blanche.

which had formerly been Murphy, his cremated ashes bandied about the pub:

By closing time the body, mind and soul of Murphy were freely distributed over the floor of the saloon; and before another dayspring greyened the earth had been swept away with the sand, the beer, the butts, the glass, the matches, the spits, the vomit.[83]

But then Murphy had always borne witness to his creator's freedom from prejudice in matters of colour.

When after some little time he still had not spoken nor made any movement she turned her head to see was anything amiss. All the colour (yellow) had ebbed from his face, leaving it ashen.[84]

Ashen to ashes, dust to dust.

THE ANTITHETICAL SENSE

Beckett sees these things by peering out of his deadlight.

> what would I do what I did yesterday and the day before
> peering out of my deadlight looking for another
> wandering like me eddying far from all the living
> in a convulsive space
> among the voices voiceless
> that throng my hiddenness

The English is darker than the original French: 'regardant par mon hublot'.[85]

---

[83] *Murphy*, 275. Preceding *Murphy* in French, 196:

Tant et si bien que, longtemps avant l'heure de la fermeture, le corps, l'esprit et l'âme de Murphy étaient librement distribués sur le sol; et avant que l'aube ne vînt encore répandre sa grisaille sur la terre, furent balayés avec la sciure, la bière, les mégots, la casse, les allumettes, les crachats, les vomissures.

[84] *Murphy*, 31. Preceding *Murphy* in French, 28:

Après qu'il fut resté un moment sans parler ni faire le moindre mouvement, elle tourna la tête pour voir s'il y avait du nouveau. Toute la couleur (jaune) s'était retirée de son visage, le laissant couleur de galet.

[85] 'what would I do without this world faceless incurious' (1948), *Collected Poems*, 61. Following 'que ferais-je sans ce monde sans visage sans questions' (1948), 'Six Poèmes 1947-1949', *Collected Poems*, 60:

> que ferais-je je ferais comme hier comme aujourd'hui
> regardant par mon hublot si je ne suis pas seul
> à errer et à virer loin de toute vie

Lawrence Harvey, though he is easily the most informative commentator on Beckett's poems, does the usual thing of reducing a general thought to a circumstantial particularity:

Beckett's English translation for 'hublot' is 'deadlight,' which has both the meaning of 'porthole' and 'skylight,' the latter term suggesting the microcosm of his studio apartment.[86]

This reduces man's estate, and a dead man's estate, to real estate. Not that Harvey is insensitive to the mortality exactly: ' "Deadlight" also has the advantage of reinforcing the phrase "far from all the living".' But more is at stake than just reinforcement. For the energies of germination grow incorporate with corruption.

The *OED* has under *deadlight* not only

1. *Naut.* A strong wooden or iron shutter fixed outside a cabin-window or port-hole in a storm, to prevent water from entering

—not exactly, as Harvey has it, a porthole—and then

2. A skylight not made to open

—not exactly, as Harvey has it, a skylight—but also

3. A luminous appearance seen over putrescent bodies, in grave-yards, etc.; a 'corpse-light' or 'corpse-candle'.

Ill met by corpse-light.

Malone Dies begins at once with the sense of an ending, 'a luminous appearance'.

I shall soon be quite dead at last in spite of all.[87]

> dans un espace pantin
> sans voix parmi les voix
> enfermées avec moi

Where the French has yesterday and today ('comme hier comme aujourd'hui'), the English extends the backward glance, regressive and recessive and without the here-and-now of today: 'what I did yesterday and the day before'. Such vistas often arrive in Beckett's English; compare the move from 'plus mort que vif' to 'even more dead than alive than usual' (p. 86 above).

[86] *Samuel Beckett Poet and Critic*, 244 n.
[87] Beckett's earlier translation, as the second of 'Two Fragments' (*transition fifty* (Oct. 1950), 105), did not press on in this syntax of weakness; it was crisp, rather, with nothing after 'at last':

I shall soon be quite dead at last.

And at once, doomed no sooner lit to be extinguished, the indubitability of 'quite dead' is disturbed. For, reading it by the light of a corpse-candle, does it not suggest not only altogether dead but somewhat dead? There is no such doubt about the original French:

Je serai quand même bientôt tout à fait mort enfin.

We may assure ourselves that it, 'quite dead', must mean altogether dead, since the wish to be altogether dead is both more comprehensible and more common than the wish to be somewhat dead. But whatever Beckett may be as a writer, he is never remiss. He is not likely to have failed to notice, or to have decided to ignore, the wrinkling of the flat statement which is introduced in the English by 'quite dead'. If, as the opening of this novel at once goes on to say, the teller of stories can be 'almost lifeless' ('they will be almost lifeless, like the teller'[88]), why can't he be quite, only quite, dead?

Is there a comparative form of *dead*? Scarcely. Or not altogether purely.

Or if I'm guilty let me be forgiven and graciously authorized to expiate, coming and going in passing time, every day a little purer, a little deader.[89]

All the living are partially dead: the cells, the feelings. Beckett is said to have said, not of himself but with himself among those in mind, that there are some human beings who cannot be happy until quite a lot of them has died. (This is a stage towards what it will be to know happiness.) Nor is this extraneous to the books; in the uncompleted play *Human Wishes*, a steely eighteenth-century lady insists: 'I am dead enough myself, I hope, not to feel any great respect for those that are so entirely.'[90] Death inflicts a

---

[88] *Malone Dies*, 2. Following *Malone meurt*, 8: 'elles seront presque sans vie, comme l'artiste'. Beckett's earlier translation, *transition fifty*, was more literal in one way ('they will be almost without life') and less so in another (it ended there, and rendered nothing of 'comme l'artiste').

[89] 'Text for Nothing 8', *Stories and Texts for Nothing*, 113. Following *Nouvelles et textes pour rien*, 184:

Ou qu'on me gracie, si je suis coupable, et me laisse expier, dans le temps, en allant et venant, chaque jour un peu plus pur, un peu plus mort.

[90] *Disjecta*, 162.

retort upon the still living in *More Pricks than Kicks*: 'As for her, it was almost as though she had suffered the inverse change. She had died in part.'[91]

Malone fears that he may end up not *quite dead* ('quite' as a maximizer) but quite dead ('quite' as a compromiser or a diminisher). Malone is not alone in this fear, whether in life, in thought of the afterlife, or in Beckett's literature. Georges Bataille, in his review of *Molloy* in 1951, insisted that Molloy 'is not precisely a dead man. The profound apathy of death, its indifference to every possible thing, is apparent in him, but this apathy would encounter in death itself its own limit.'[92]

But if the antithesis of life and death is not quite what it claims, this contingency is criss-crossed with the antithetical energies of the word 'quite', a word of which Freud could have made much in his brief profound essay on the antithetical sense of primal words.[93]

Many a word or device can be an axis and not a direction; but the words of antithetical sense are unremitting reminders that we may be faced not by a direction but by an axis.

Freud savoured the antithetical senses of such words because they establish language as intimate with dreams, where there are no contraries. Beckett's way with antithetical senses is such as to suggest that their propensity to short-circuit is further intimate with mortality. As organisms, such words might be myrmidons enlisted within that other argument of Freud's:

What we are left with is the fact that the organism wishes to die only in its own fashion. Thus these guardians of life, too, were originally the myrmidons of death. Hence arises the paradoxical situation that the living organism struggles most energetically against events (dangers, in fact) which might help it to attain its life's goal rapidly—by a kind of short-circuit.[94]

'Quite dead'—'I shall soon be quite dead at last in spite of all'—offers within *quite* an antithesis both true and false, a quirk within 'languages, both dead and living'. Witness the *OED*.

---

[91] 'Draff', *More Pricks than Kicks*, 273.

[92] *Critique* (15 May 1951); *Samuel Beckett: The Critical Heritage*, 58, trans. Jean M. Sommermeyer.

[93] 'The Antithetical Sense of Primal Words' (1910); *Collected Papers*, iv (1925), 184–91.

[94] See p. 107 above.

quite

I. Completely, wholly, altogether, entirely; to the fullest extent or degree.

II. Actually, really, truly, positively (implying that the case or circumstances are such as fully justify the use of the word or phrase thus qualified). [e.g. 1805 'she was quite ill and restless'.]

III. In a weakened sense: rather, to a moderate degree, fairly. This sense has developed out of sense II, and is often difficult to distinguish from it. [e.g. 1854 Thoreau, 'when quite young'.]

It is extraordinary that sense III was not admitted until the recent Supplement (1976); this sense is not recorded in the original *OED* or in the Supplement of 1933.

The uses of 'quite' are distinguished by the grammarians as maximizer, compromiser, and diminisher, and the inflections and functions have been amiably teased out:

As well as being a maximizer, especially with units that are either nongradable or are seen as being at the end of the scale (*quite perfect*), we see that *quite*, apparently contradictorily, has two further roles, whether used as a modifier or as an adverbial. As compromiser, it is usually stressed only lightly; as diminisher, it is heavily stressed or actually made nuclear; with verbs, the usage is especially British English. For example:

> The book is quite GÒOD. [compromiser or amplifier]
> It seems that they quite LÌKE her. [compromiser]
> The book is QUÌTE GÓOD.
> It seems that they QUÌTE LÍKE her. [diminisher]

There is however considerable variation idiolectically. Note that with negatives, only the maximizer use is found: 'She didn't *quite* approve'.[95]

It is on such occasions that one takes pleasure in the fact that the etymological root of glamour is grammar. The grammarians' information gleams with critical applicability. The contradiction within 'quite' (or rather, 'apparently contradictorily'); the oddity that with negatives there is only the maximizer use; the crucial part played by stress and intonation: to these illuminations, there can be germanely added, in the case of Beckett's 'quite dead', the grammarians' reminder that, as a maximizer, *quite* belongs 'especially with units that are either nongradable or are seen as being at the end of the scale (*quite perfect*)'. For where does this leave death? To be or not to be nongradable, that is the question.

[95] Randolph Quirk *et al.*, *A Comprehensive Grammar of the English Language*, 599.

(Biodegradable, yes.) And is death 'at the end of the scale (*quite perfect*)'? A consummation devoutly to be wished. Perfected in death.

Such are some of the intimations of mortality, and intimidations, which lurk within the innocence and equivocation of the opening words of Beckett's great novel:

I shall soon be quite dead at last in spite of all.

There are many contrarieties which have their power within our language: the fact that *to best* someone and *to worst* someone may come to the same thing, or that to say something *roundly* may amount to saying it *squarely*. But these engaging anomalies are not as central, do not strike their roots as deep, as does the antithetical sense of primal words.

For by something which itself partakes of the oxymoron, the antithetical sense is at once fully an oxymoron and yet not one at all (rather as *rime riche* may be poverty-stricken). The two senses which in an oxymoron are two words ('precious bane' or 'open secret' or 'literary theorist') are here compacted to the point at which there disappears that two-ness postulated of an oxymoron.

At the level of mere journalistic indignation, you can hear it in the accusing question (accusing the Senate of negligence) which ended an article by William Safire in the *New York Times* (9 April 1990): 'Where is the Senate's oversight?'

At a deeper level of certainty and uncertainty, there is Beckett's attention to that old favourite, *certain*. Again the *OED*:

certain

I.1. Determined, fixed, settled; not variable or fluctuating; unfailing.

II.7. Used to define things which the mind definitely individualizes or particularizes from the general mass, but which may be left without further identification in description; thus often used to indicate that the speaker does not choose further to identify or specify them.

Different as this seems to be from sense I, it is hardly separable from it in a large number of examples: thus in the first which follows [1300 Ilk dai a certain hore], the *hour* was quite 'certain' or 'fixed', but it is not communicated to the reader; to him it remains, so far as his knowledge is concerned, quite indefinite; it may have been, *as far as he knows*, at any hour; though, *as a fact*, it was at a particular hour.[96]

---

[96] There has entered a misprint in *OED* 2nd edn., 'indentification' for 'identification'. In fronting the equivocations of *certain*, this entry twice has recourse to the equivocal word *quite* ('quite "certain"' and 'quite indefinite').

Belacqua awaits what should be no more than a minor operation, nursing his grievances.

Now two further women, there was no end to them, the one of a certain age, the other not, entered, ripping off their regulation cuffs as they advanced.[97]

The great Dictionary is circumspect, shows a certain delicacy, as to this use of 'certain':

Sometimes euphemistically: Which it is not polite or necessary further to define. *a certain age*: an age when one is no longer young, but which politeness forbids to be specified too minutely: usually, referring to some age between forty and sixty (mostly said of women).

It is part of *How It Is* that we should have grown accustomed to the fact that 'certain' may mean withheld from us so as to be in some way *un*certain, *un*specified; at one point in *How It Is* 'certain age' finds itself riven asunder, and we are left by no means certain as to whether the 'cries' are all too indubitable or airily left unparticularized for our ears:

good a fellow-creature more or less but man woman girl or boy cries have neither certain cries sex nor age [. . .][98]

How to punctuate that with its cries? Roughly:

Good: a fellow-creature, more or less—but man, woman, girl or boy . . . ? Cries have neither—(certain cries)—sex nor age.

What this has gained in stride it has lost in eerie lameness.

I need to cite several of these words of antithetical sense, such as 'quite' and 'certain', as they pitch their contrary claims in Beckett, for it is only by getting some feeling for how ubiquitous they are that one can judge their field of force—a field of force, more than incidentally, much more marked in Beckett's English than in his French, and this because more marked in English than in French.

The words 'quite still', often called for by Beckett, compound

[97] 'Yellow' (the one-but-last story in the book), *More Pricks than Kicks*, 250; 'a lady of a certain age who had found being young and beautiful and pure more of a bore than anything else' figures in the first story in the book ('Dante and the Lobster', 15).
[98] *How It Is*, 60. Following *Comment c'est*, 67:

c'est bon c'est un semblable plus ou moins mais homme femme fille garçon les cris n'ont ni certains cris ni sexe ni âge [. . .]

the process, since not only does 'quite' have eyes in the back of its head, 'still' does too. The French 'tout immobile', to which Beckett is sometimes reduced, has no such antithetical energy in either of its words.

In the poetry of T. S. Eliot, 'still' and its compounds are the occasion for grave delight and wonder at the life of art.

> Only by the form, the pattern,
> Can words or music reach
> The stillness, as a Chinese jar still
> Moves perpetually in its stillness.
>
> ('Burnt Norton', V)

But in Beckett the contrariety within 'still' can offer something different, a glimpsed release from the dreadful prospect of never dying, since antithetical senses can, in a word, stifle, even put to death one another—and yet sometimes *not* a release, since the opposite senses may only paralyse (fascinate) one another.

It is not, then, simply a matter of 'ambiguity' but of a particular energy of it. Brian Fitch, though his study of bilingualism in Beckett is indefatigably thoroughgoing, stops short of saying how these contrarieties stop themselves short—immobilize themselves. ('Immobile' is the French for 'Still' under one of its aspects, as Beckett acknowledged when he translated his elegiac piece *Still* as *Immobile*, obliged to sacrifice the contrarious energy of the English.) Fitch remarks:

There are, however, a number of cases where the ambiguity of the English is much more pronounced, as in the example of the word 'still' in the sentence 'Even still in the timeless dark you find figures a comfort' (*Company*, p. 55), which could refer either to spatial immobility or to temporal continuity. The French opts for the latter: 'Encore maintenant dans le noir hors du temps les chiffres te réconfortent' (*Compagnie*, p. 54).[99]

Yet Fitch's word 'ambiguity' will not, of itself, record the impact when the immobile meets the continuing, there within the unassuming word 'still'.

---

[99] *Beckett and Babel*, 105. Of discrepancies of meaning in *Still* as against *Immobile*, Fitch notes: 'The most striking is the omission no less than five times of the adverb "quite" in the expression "quite still" and the omission twice of the whole expression' (p. 91).

What is it, when contemplating someone who may be alive now in memory only, for that time of hers to be 'still current', where not only does 'still' have its own internal cross-currents but where one of the senses of *still*, the unmoving one, precipitates a further oxymoron as it moves on into 'still current'?

Then a time when within her walls she did not appear. A long time. But little by little she began to appear. Within her walls. Darkly. Time truth to tell still current. Though she within them no more. This long time.[100]

The French has no such currency, nothing which feels the torpedo-touch with which the English word 'still' may sting itself to paralysis or to death: 'A vrai dire ce temps dure encore.'[101]

What is it to *go still*? To continue to move and to leave? To cease to move? The latter, no doubt, but how firmly the former may need to be beaten back, in the ill-willed walled world of *Malone Dies*:

A kind of air circulates, I must have said so, and when all goes still I hear it beating against the walls and being beaten back by them.[102]

—when all goes still | I hear it beating?
Or
—when all goes | still I hear it beating?
The French keeps its own counsel, silent as to any such goings-on: 'et quand tout se tait je l'entends'.

'To think there is still life in this age.'[103] The English sentence catches—in the flicker of its shutter—a still life. The engraved French does not bat an eyelid: 'Dire qu'il y a des vivants dans ce siècle.'

---

[100] *Ill Seen Ill Said*, 13–14. Following *Mal vu mal dit*, 16:

Ensuite un temps où dans ses murs elle ne paraissait pas. Un temps très long. Mais peu à peu elle se mit à y paraître. Obscurément. A vrai dire ce temps dure encore. Malgré qu'elle n'y soit plus. Depuis longtemps.

[101] Again: 'Encore. Tu sens sur ton visage la frange de ses longs cheveux noirs se remuer dans l'air immobile.' (*Compagnie*, 65). This cannot effect what is within the reach of the English 'Still . . . still': 'Still. You feel on your face the fringe of her long black hair stirring in the still air'. (*Company*, 66). Stirrings still.

[102] *Malone Dies*, 47. Following *Malone meurt*, 78:

Une sorte d'air y circule, j'ai dû le dire, et quand tout se tait je l'entends qui se jette contre les cloisons qui le rejettent naturellement.

[103] *Ill Seen Ill Said*, 11. Following *Mal vu mal dit*, 13.

Beckett came to consummate the paradoxical capacities of *still* in his very late, exquisitely beautiful, prose work: *Stirrings Still* (1988). He had earlier entertained, first, *Fragments*, then *Still Stirrings*.[104] His subsequent French title has its own insinuating power but is quite other than *Stirrings Still*: *Soubresauts*. This makes a sudden leap, is less stirring.

I must resist the temptation to summon all such antithetical words, and must limit myself to those which peer from their deadlight, and which shed a luminous appearance of death in life, much favoured by Beckett.

One such is 'inexistence'/'inexistent'. Not only is this profoundly its own antithesis (inherently existing vs. not existing at all), but it ministers to cries which are never 'certain cries' but always undecidable as to their tone, their being laments or asseverations, or the proportion of the one to the other. In *How It Is*, the absence of punctuation gives rise to profound uncertainties, doubts as to what goes with what, pauses which give you pause.

orgy of false being life in common brief shames I am not dead to inexistence not irretrievably time will tell it's telling [. . .]

What are we to make of 'I am not dead to inexistence'? Not dead to the point of inexistence, non-existence, not (alas) *that* dead? Or not dead to—that is, not oblivious of—inexistence? (Perhaps 'time will tell'—but what immediately follows, 'it's telling', may be a grimly telling observation.)

'Dead to inexistence': George Herbert had faith, less that time will tell, than that eternity will:

> Who would have thought my shrivel'd heart
> Could have recover'd greennesse? It was gone
> Quite under ground; as flowers depart
> To see their mother-root, when they have blown;
> Where they together
> All the hard weather,
> Dead to the world, keep house unknown.
>
> ('The Flower')

'Dead to the world' has come to be, since 1899, a 'colloquial phrase: unconscious or fast asleep; unaware of the external world'.

---

[104] Brater, *why beckett*, 136.

In the world of George Herbert's flowers, it had meant something very different: seeming in the eyes of the world to be dead—but alive at root, below ground, biding its time in the confidence of eternity.

It might be thought that the seventeenth-century world of Herbert's flowers, 'Dead to the world', is too remote from Beckett's 'dead to inexistence'; but if this be so, it is because it is not Herbert's flowers but rather Herrick's that are in common.

orgy of false being life in common brief shames I am not dead to inexistence not irretrievably time will tell it's telling but what a hog's wallow pah not even not even pah brief movements of the lower face profit while ye may silence gather while ye may deathly silence patience patience[105]

Herrick:

> Gather ye Rose-buds while ye may,
>   Old Time is still a flying:
> And this same flower that smiles to day,
>   To morrow will be dying.

If only one could be sure of that.

The fear in *How It Is* is not of dying but of an eternity ('To morrow, and to morrow, and to morrow') arriving not at death but at an endless dying, deathwards progressing to no death, like Keats's Moneta.

>   Then saw I a wan face,
> Not pin'd by human sorrows, but bright blanch'd
> By an immortal sickness which kills not;
> It works a constant change, which happy death
> Can put no end to; deathwards progressing
> To no death was that visage;

>   ('The Fall of Hyperion', i. 256–61)

Keats, too, knew How It Is; knew what it would be to implore happy death to put an end to us.

'Old Time is still a flying':

---

[105] *How It Is*, 76. Following *Comment c'est*, 85:

orgie de faux être vie commune courtes hontes je ne suis pas perdu à l'inexistence pas sans retour l'avenir le dira il est en train mais une telle souille bah même pas même pas bah brefs mouvements du bas du visage profitons silence cueillons silence de mort patientons

I am not dead to inexistence not irretrievably time will tell it's telling

'To the Virgins, to make much of Time': To the Reader, to make much of Time's being the mercy of Eternity.

And *inexistence* in all this, here and in the afterlife? What exactly is 'an inexistent peace'?

and if it may seem strange that without food to sustain us we can drag ourselves thus by the mere grace of our united net sufferings from west to east towards an inexistent peace we are invited kindly to consider[106]

Or, existent for Beckett for sure, centrally:

The cabin. Its situation. Careful. On. At the inexistent centre of a formless place.

Minimally less. No more. Well on the way to inexistence. As to zero the infinite.[107]

For the cruelly apt thing about *inexistent* or *inexistence* is its duplicity. The pincer-jaws gleam in the *OED*.

inexistent
Existing or having its being in something else; inherent. 1553; 1678 CUDWORTH Empedocles and Democritus . . say that Generation is not the Production of any new Entity, but only the Secretion of what was before Inexistant.

Obs. Not existing; having no existence; non-existent. 1646 BROWNE mixtures inexistent.

inexistence
The fact or condition of existing in something; inherence. 1635; 1654 WARREN There was an inexistence, or being of all men in Adam. 1871 FRASER *Life Berkeley* Separate inexistence in perception is one phase of the dualism of Berkeley.

---

[106] *How It Is*, 156. Following *Comment c'est*, 173:

et s'il peut paraître étrange que sans vivres pour nous soutenir nous puissions ainsi nous traîner à la faveur de nos souffrances net réunies d'ouest en est vers une paix inexistante nous sommes priés de bien vouloir considérer

[107] First, *Ill Seen Ill Said*, 8. Following *Mal vu mal dit*, 8–9:

Le cabanon. Son emplacement. Attention. Aller. Le cabanon. A l'inexistant centre d'un espace sans forme.

Second, *Ill Seen Ill Said*, 54. Following *Mal vu mal dit*, 69:

Moindre minimement. Pas plus. Bien parti pour l'inexistence comme pour zéro l'infini.

The dualism of Berkeley pales beside the dualism of *inexistence*,
for the Dictionary continues:

inexistence
Now *rare*. The fact or condition of not existing; non-existence.
1623 The not Being of a thing, *Inexistence, Inessence*; 1725 BROOME *On
Odyssey* He calls up the heroes of former ages from a state of inexistence
to adorn and diversify his poem. 1830 W. PHILLIPS *Mt. Sinai* Till..
Death drop stricken on his latest prey, To inexistence starved.

Beckett's sense of life makes two-faced 'inexistence' a crux for
him. Will we, at death, enter upon inexistence or inexistence? The
OED, even while it juxtaposes one sense of 'inexistency' with
the opposite sense, cites within the former sense a theological
ambidexterity.

1768–74 TUCKER *Lt. Nat.* (1834) The ancients held forms, ideas, and
truths, to be eternal..in the Divine Mind..They were not God, nor
attributes, nor yet distinct substances, but inexistencies in Him: which
inexistency was a very convenient term, implying something that was both
a substance and not a substance, and so carrying the advantages of
either.

For Beckett, *inexistence* is a very convenient term, implying
something that both is and is not, and so carrying the misadvantages of either.

'Men . . . seem to have a design to hasten their misadvantages'
(1649).[108] Beckett has a design to hasten men's sense of their
misapprehended advantages: their prospects of the wiser inexistence, the having no existence.

In Beckett, the words 'inexistent' and 'inexistence' announce
themselves, patently expect that we will 'scrute' them (another
macabre resurrection by Beckett).[109] Other, more everyday, words
do no more than cast sidelong glances—both sides at once. There
is, for instance, the innocent little word 'over', with its antithetical
energies.

---

[108] Cited by the *OED* under *misadvantage*.
[109] *Ill Seen Ill Said*, 55: 'With in second sight the shack in ruins. To scrute together
with the inscrutable face'. Following *Mal vu mal dit*, 70–1: 'Avec en seconde vue les
ruines du cabanon. A scruter en même temps que l'inscrutable visage'. *OED*: 1536
Primer Eng. & Lat. 121 My synne and inequite why doste thou scrute so.

Oh I know I too shall cease and be as when I was not yet, only all over instead of in store, that makes me happy,[110]

—'all over': discharged, defunctus, finished with, once and for all. But also the opposite, on occasion: *all over* as yet to be done again, all over again, all over.

you are there somewhere alive somewhere vast stretch of time then it's over you are there no more alive no more then again you are there again alive again it wasn't over an error you begin again all over more or less in the same place or in another as when another image above in the light you come to in hospital in the dark[111]

How excruciatingly the longing to be done—'then it's over'—is succeeded by the cruel continuity: 'you begin again all over'. The cruel contrariety of *all over* (no such thing) is at one with those unpunctuated refusals to provide the surety which is craved.

The French language, which was first in the infernal field of *Comment c'est*, chooses something other than the dubious light of these shilly-shallyings: instead of *over*, *all over*, with their fiery flickering murk, there is the clarity, differently valuable, of this, a true reminder of something *nouveau* because in another tongue:

[...] puis c'est fini on n'y est plus puis de nouveau on est là de nouveau de n'était pas finie une erreur c'est à recommencer plus ou moins [...]

Whether Beckett's French is as apt an instrument as his English, or rather his Irish English, and whether this would be because of something about Beckett or about French: these are less important than our enjoying his bilingual myriad-mindedness as evincing a true wit, wit as T. S. Eliot understood it: 'It involves, probably, a recognition, implicit in the expression of every experience, of other kinds of experience which are possible.'[112] The

---

[110] *From an Abandoned Work*, 17. Preceding 'D'un ouvrage abandonné', trans. Ludovic and Agnès Janvier in collaboration with Beckett; *Têtes-mortes*, 21:

Oh je sais que moi aussi je vais finir et être comme avant d'être, sauf que tout bu au lieu d'à boire, ça fait mon bonheur

[111] *How It Is*, 24. Following *Comment c'est*, 26–7:

on est là quelque part en vie quelque part un temps énorme puis c'est fini on n'y est plus puis de nouveau on est là de nouveau ce n'était pas fini une erreur c'est à recommencer plus ou moins au même endroit à un autre comme lorsque nouvelle image là-haut dans la lumière on reprend à l'hôpital connaissance dans le noir

[112] 'Andrew Marvell', *Selected Essays*, 203.

experience of another language is a supreme instance of such a recognition.

The two senses of a workaday phrase—*all over* [again] or *all over* [finished]—may beckon the afterlife. On this earth we may hope for summary mercy, but it too will need to avail itself of this turn. Plus 'all over' as 'very characteristic of'.

Scrupulous to the last, finical to a fault, that's Malone, all over.[113]

Ah Moran, he said, what a man! I was staggering with weakness. If I had dropped dead at his feet he would have said, Ah poor old Moran, that's him all over.[114]

The French, appositely the same as ever, is: 'Ah ce vieux Moran, toujours le même.'

Alive to all these paralysing possibilities of antithetical senses, Beckett works unusual wonders with the usual condition that *cleave* can mean either stick together or cut apart (there's another mortal liveliness for you); and with the fact, no less pertinent to his lifelong preoccupation with whether or not one is going to be allowed to say 'thanks for the nice time and go', that *leave* and *left* may be likewise equivocal. (Get to go, or get to stay?)

Beckett does not scorn as nugatory the smaller pleasures of these words.[115] He finds not only pleasure but profit in the awareness that even prepositions may palter with us in a double sense. It is agreeably confounding that to slow down is hard to distinguish from slowing up, and that saving against your old age turns out to resemble saving for it.

---

[113] *Malone Dies*, 60. Following *Malone meurt*, 98:

Scrupuleux jusqu'à la fin, voilà Malone, à cheval sur les cheveux.

[114] *Molloy*, 224. Following *Molloy* in French, 254:

Sacré Moran! dit-il. Je chancelais de faiblesse. Je serais décédé à ses pieds qu'il aurait dit, Ah ce vieux Moran, toujours le même.

'Staggering' has its comic possibilities; the BBC once praised Nureyev as 'a staggering dancer'.

[115] In a letter to the *New York Times*, John Train said that he takes 'a modest pride [ah] in having invented the application of the obsolete word, antilogies', and he listed, among others: apparent, buckle, to dust, enjoin, handicap, moot, and overlook. There might be added the phrases of Janus, such as the American 'could care less', which strikes oddly on the English ear, and 'there's no love lost between them', of which the *OED* says: 'an ambiguous phrase, which has been employed with two contrary implications. (*a*) Their affection is mutual. *Obs.* (*b*) Now always: They have no love for each other.'

The small single window condensed its changes, as half-closed eyes see the finer values of tones, so that it was never quiet in the room, but brightening and darkening in a slow ample flicker that went on all day, brightening against the darkening that was its end.[116]

And how gratifying that 'in charge of' can equivocate as to who exactly is the warder and who the wardee—or the loonie:

Now the loonies poured out into the sun, the better behaved left to their own devices, the others in herds in charge of warders.[117]

OED: '*in charge (of)* is used both actively and passively; *e.g.* to leave children *in charge of* a nurse, or a nurse *in charge of* the children'. Beckett, along with the better behaved, leaves the phrase to its own devices. Meanwhile the *loonies* are illuminated by the *sun*.

One especial triumph by Beckett in the art of miniature negation turns upon—turns round—the happy coincidence that a lack can be positively felt, mysterious and tangible, valuable as alien.

I also discovered a little packet tied up in age-yellowed newspaper. It reminds me of something, but of what? I drew it over beside the bed and felt it with the knob of my stick. And my hand understood, it understood softness and lightness, better I think than if it had touched the thing directly, fingering it and weighing it in its palm. I resolved, I don't know why, not to undo it. I sent it back into the corner, with the rest. I shall speak of it again perhaps, when the time comes. I shall say, I can hear myself already, Item, a little packet, soft, and light as a feather, tied up in newspaper. It will be my little mystery, all my own. Perhaps it is a lack of rupees. Or a lock of hair.[118]

---

[116] *Murphy*, 66. Preceding *Murphy* in French, 53:

L'unique petite fenêtre en condensait les changements, comme des yeux à moitié fermés voient mieux les nuances des tons, de sorte que, dans la chambre, la lumière n'était jamais tranquille, mais allait s'éclaircissant et s'obscurcissant dans un tremblement lent et ample qui durait toute la journée.

[117] 'Fingal', *More Pricks than Kicks*, 31.

[118] *Malone Dies*, 21. Following *Malone meurt*, 37–8:

J'ai découvert aussi un petit paquet enveloppé dans du papier journal jauni et ficelé. Il me dit quelque chose, mais quoi? Je l'ai amené tout près de moi, à côté du lit, et je l'ai tâté avec le gros bout du baton, en m'en servant comme d'un pilon, mais doucement. Et ma main a compris, elle a compris mollesse et légèreté, mieux je crois que si elle y avait touché directement, palpant et soupesant. Je n'ai pas voulu le défaire, je ne sais pourquoi. Je l'ai renvoyé dans le coin, avec le reste. J'en reparlerai peut-être, le moment venu. Je dirai, je m'entends d'ici, Item, un petit paquet, mou, et léger comme une plume, ficelé dans du

Once again the French reads as if, far from being the original, it had not really been born, unable to counterchange the antithetical 'lack', leave alone to plait the lovely *packet/lack/lock* strands.

C'est peut-être un lack de roupies. Ou une mèche de cheveux.

But last of these antithetical words, with their truths and their ability to lie like truth, is the word 'last'. It may mean the final one, or only the latest one (and open to be succeeded).[119] Let us not be as sure as some critics are that *Krapp's Last Tape* has to be his final one. And *last* may mean finality and extinction or, rather the reverse, endurance and continuance.

'After all' [after all]—

After all it is not important not to finish, there are worse things than velleities. But is that the point? Quite likely. All I ask is that the last of mine, as long as it lasts, should have living for its theme, that is all, I know what I mean.[120]

Where the English makes 'the last of mine' and 'as long as it lasts' cleave together as disconcertingly one, dismayingly declining to assure us of any final relief and release, the original French cleaves the constituents apart:

Je veux seulement que ma dernière parle jusqu'au bout de vivre

This too is *How It Is*:

a little more to last a little more untwine the rope make two ropes tie the bottom of the sack fill it with mud tie the top it will make a good pillow it will be soft in my arms brief movements of the lower face would they were the last

papier journal. Ce sera mon petit mystère, bien à moi. C'est peut-être un lack de roupies. Ou une mèche de cheveux.

The first American edition of *Malone Dies* (1956) has 'a lack of rupees' (p. 21), as does the English edition (1958, p. 21) and the English edition of the trilogy (1959, p. 197). The Penguin *Malone Dies* (1962, p. 28) has 'lac'; the American edition of the trilogy (1959, p. 269) has 'lakh'. *OED* records all these spellings and others, under 'lakh': 'One hundred thousand: a. of things in general; *occas.* used for an indefinite number; b. *spec.* of coins, esp. in *a lac of rupees*'.

[119] Where *Mal vu mal dit*, 56, has 'par encore les derniers rayons', *Ill Seen Ill Said*, 44, renders this as 'by the latest last rays'.

[120] *Malone Dies*, 22. Following *Malone meurt*, 39:

Après tout il importe peu de finir, j'ai dû le dire. La velléité n'a en soi rien de spécialement déshonorant. Mais s'agit-il de cela? Il y a des chances. Je veux seulement que ma dernière parle jusqu'au bout de vivre, j'ai dû changer d'avis. C'est tout. Je me comprends.

when the last meal the last journey what have I done where been that
kind mute screams abandon hope gleam of hope [. . .][121]

The Dantesque 'abandon hope' is given a last twist of the knife.
Abandon hope of entering upon the last, because

a little more to last

keeps horribly open the matter.

Freud cited the antithetical sense of primal words[122] to lend
warrant to the notoriously absurd derivation *lucus a non lucendo*: 'a
grove, (so called) from the absence of *lux*, light' (*OED*). This is
illuminating. No less valuably negative, and available to any
psychoanalyser of dreams, is the reflection in *A Midsummer Night's
Dream*: 'I will get *Peter Quince* to write a ballet of this dreame, it
shall be called *Bottome's Dreame*, because it hath no bottome'
(IV. i). Dreams have their own sequiturs. 'Following darkenesse
like a dreame.'

THE COUNTER-POISON

Much more than finest verbalism is involved in such an axis of the
language as the antithetical sense of primal words. So here is
the last of the antitheses which are at once true and false, and
which are active in languages, both dead and living: Beckett's
counterpoison.

It is said by some, these days, that whether or not words alone
are certain good, words alone are certain—and that Beckett Our
Contemporary has no truck with any positing of the *real*, anything
beyond the text. But Beckett, sceptical even of scepticism, is not
party to the pyrrhonistic complacency of our age's sages.

Such equal liars both. Real and—how ill say its contrary? The counter-
poison.

---

[121] *How It Is*, 52. Following *Comment c'est*, 56–7:

petite suite pour durer encore détortiller la corde en tirer deux ficeler le fond du sac le
remplir de boue en ficeler le haut ça fera un bon oreiller ça fera doux dans mes bras brefs
mouvements du bas du visage s'ils pouvaient être les derniers

quand le dernier repas le dernier voyage qu'ai-je fait où suis-je passé ce genre hurlements
muets abandon lueur d'espoir [. . .]

[122] *Collected Papers*, iv. 189: 'In this way perhaps the much derided derivation *lucus a
non lucendo* would have some real meaning'.

'Counter-poison' is far better stocked, better written as a prescription, than was the more conventional and expansive pairing in Beckett's book on Proust:

Memory—a clinical laboratory stocked with poison and remedy, stimulant and sedative.[123]

'Counter-poison' is alive to the now-much-mentioned *pharmakon* of Derrida, or rather of Plato's *Phaedrus*. The *OED* allows that the two senses of *counterpoison* counteract one another:

1. A medicine that counteracts the influence of a poison; an antidote. [e.g. *fig.* 1603 CARTWRIGHT Unlesse by the counterpoyson of the word of God. 1656 COWLEY *Pind. Odes, To Dr. Scarborough*, A Med'cine and a Counter-poyson to the Age.]

2. An opposite poison [e.g. 1852 SOUTHEY The men whose heart.. revolted against intolerance.. were themselves infected with the counterpoison of French philosophy.]

'Real and—how ill say its contrary?' No, better to find the word which well says its own contrary.

The whole paragraph in *Ill Seen Ill Said* is central to a comprehension of where Beckett's art stands, especially as his late fiction is often all-too-accommodatingly spoken of as if it were abstracted, not to death, but to that impercipient living death which constitutes one of the present fashions in academic literary studies: the flaccid assurance that everything is fictive and verbal, and that the real has finally been shown the door. Things shown the door have a way of coming back in through the window, and the insistent rhetoric of *in fact* is much deployed by those who deny the existence of facts or who don the rubber-gloves of inverted commas—the 'facts'—except when it is their own fact-finding which is promulgated.

Opposition to this glee at the irreal can fasten upon its self-contradiction (if all is fictive, against what does the fictive define itself?) and can diagnose galloping logomania. But it is art, not argumentation, which constitutes the best, the most enduring opposition to such airiness.

Beckett—'A Med'cine and a Counterpoyson to the Age'—is not satisfied to rebound. His paragraph deplores the confusion which it acknowledges.

[123] *Proust*, 22.

On resumption the head is covered. No matter. No matter now. Such the confusion now between real and—how say its contrary? No matter. That old tandem. Such now the confusion between them once so twain. And such the farrago from eye to mind. For it to make what sad sense of it may. No matter now. Such equal liars both. Real and—how ill say its contrary? The counter-poison.[124]

This finds it impossible, impossible in honesty, to discard not only the unnamable contrary to the real, but the real.

Beckett wrote of the gouaches of Henri Hayden:

Leur beauté est le fait d'un artiste qui a su, toute sa vie et comme peu d'autres, résister aux deux grandes tentations, celle du réel et celle du mensonge.[125]

One currently tempting lie is that there is no such thing as the real. Beckett takes care to resist this temptation too, this easing of the mind and of life.

Here are four moments in Beckett's fiction when something horribly real is set before us, and when it would seem to me a perverse derogation from the art to insist that words, oh fascinatingly used of course, are all there is. These moments speak of the body's failing, as well as of the brain's failing to get its instructions heeded by the body. Delays. Thwartings. Chalk.

And how in her faint comings and goings she suddenly stops dead. And how hard set to rise up from off her knees.[126]

A man would wonder where his kingdom ended, his eye strive to penetrate the gloom, and he crave for a stick, an arm, fingers apt to grasp and then release, at the right moment, a stone, stones, or for the power to utter a cry and wait, counting the seconds, for it to come back to him, and suffer, certainly, at having neither voice nor other missile, nor limbs submissive to him, bending and unbending at the word of command, and

---

[124] *Ill Seen Ill Said*, 40. Following *Mal vu mal dit*, 49–50:

A la reprise la tête est sous la couverture. Cela ne fait rien. Plus rien. Tant il est vrai que réel et—comment dire le contraire? Enfin ces deux-là. Tant vrai que les deux si deux jadis à présent se confondent. Et qu'au compère chargé du triste savoir l'œil ne signale plus guère que désarroi. Cela ne fait rien. Plus rien. Tant il est vrai que les deux sont mensonges. Réel et—comment mal dire le contraire? Le contrepoison.

[125] 'Henri Hayden' (1960); *Disjecta*, 150.
[126] *Ill Seen Ill Said*, 14. Following *Mal vu mal dit*, 17:

Et dans ses menues allées et venues cette façon soudain de se planter là. Et ses interminables agenouillements.

perhaps even regret being a man, under such conditions, that is to say a head abandoned to its ancient solitary resources.[127]

The man has not yet come home. Home. I have demanded certain movements of my legs and even feet. I know them well and could feel the effort they made to obey. I have lived with them that little space of time, filled with drama, between the message received and the piteous response.[128]

She sits on erect and rigid in the deepening gloom. Such helplessness to move she cannot help.[129]

In all of these, supremely in the last (from *Ill Seen Ill Said*), it is not simply the 'syntax of weakness' but the incarnation of the human reality of it all, of piteous bodily weakness, and of the strength to contemplate it, and to realize it, which is so moving.

Many recent critics of Beckett will have none of this. They *make nothing* of his art.

There are for Beckett, as there are, contrarieties which gnaw.

Gautama, avant qu'ils vinssent à lui manquer, disait qu'on se trompe en affirmant que le moi existe, mais qu'en affirmant qu'il n'existe pas on ne se trompe pas moins.[130]

---

[127] *The Unnamable*, 103. Following *L'innommable*, 152:

Un homme se demanderait où finit son royaume, son œil s'efforcerait de sonder les ténèbres, il donnerait cher pour avoir une pierre, un bras, des doigts sachant prendre et lâcher, au bon moment, une pierre, beaucoup de pierres, ou pour pouvoir crier et attendre, en comptant les secondes, que son cri revienne, et il souffrirait certainement, de n'avoir ni voix ni autre missile, ni membres à son obéissance, se pliant et se détendant au commandement, et il regretterait peut-être d'être un homme, dans ces conditions, c'est-à-dire une tête abandonnée, à ses seules vieilles ressources.

In the English, 'bending and unbending' has is antithetical movements, as in the old line that 'He was a stiff and unbending man, but he could unbend on occasion'; odd that to unbend can mean to bend.

[128] *Malone Dies*, 15. Following *Malone meurt*, 28:

L'homme n'est pas encore rentré. J'ai demandé certains mouvements à mes jambes, à mes pieds. Je les connais si bien que j'ai pu sentir l'effort qu'ils faisaient pour m'obéir. J'ai vécu avec eux ce petit espace de temps où tout un drame tient, entre le message reçu et la réponse desolée.

Again an antithetical impulse in the English, 'certain movements', now sadly uncertain, soon to be all too sadly certain, unforthcoming.

[129] *Ill Seen Ill Said*, 7. Following *Mal vu mal dit*, 7:

Droite et raide elle reste là dans l'ombre croissante. Tout de noir vêtue. Garder la pose est plus fort qu'elle.

The last sentence in the French has a piercing simplicity, something different from the loving exasperation, and rebuke to loving exasperation, in the English.

[130] Beckett, 'Henri Hayden, homme-peintre' (written 1952, published 1955); *Disjecta*, 146.

But such contraries, of social reality or of individual being, contraries from which no human enterprise can escape unbesieged, are now held to have been 'refused', 'put in question', dissolved.

Here is the professionalized orthodoxy.

If there were such things as pardons to be had, they could only be 'seen' and might only be imaginary (since the text has conclusively demonstrated, like most of the late Beckett texts, that seeing is imagining).[131]

The inverted commas around 'seen' are not imaginary and should not be pardoned (they are the *au-courant* thinker's regressive way out). And 'seeing is imagining'? No Beckett text has 'conclusively demonstrated' any such thing. The fact that seeing entails the imagination does nothing to abolish the distinction between the imaginative and the imaginary, or between the imaginary and the seen. And, were the distinction to vanish, there would be lost—among much else—the sombre comedy of such a thought as this, depending as it does on an acknowledged counterthrust: 'before he could finally make up his imagination on this score'.[132]

Another:

Just as there is no longer a difference between, say, poetry and prose, there is no longer a difference between the real and its opposite. Could it be fiction, as Borges understands it? All is fiction. Language is all that remains.[133]

This is intellectual abdication masquerading as majesty. The protestations are of strenuousness; the air is of abject relief.

Another:

Memory, as every reader of *Molloy* knows, is only another name for invention.[134]

This flick of the critical wrist would blithely annul all the life of the design, all the buttressing by which language braces itself against all else in life, even as literature braces itself against all

---

[131] John Pilling, on *As the Story Was Told*, in *Frescoes of the Skull*, by James Knowlson and Pilling (1979), 184.

[132] *Company*, 73. Preceding and following *Compagnie*, 72–3: 'avant de pouvoir finalement se faire une imagination à ce sujet'.

[133] Monique Nagem, on *Ill Seen Ill Said*, in Robin J. Davis and Lance St J. Butler (eds.), *'Make Sense Who May'* (1989), 88–9.

[134] Victor Sage, in *Beckett the Shape Changer*, ed. Katharine Worth, 97.

else in life. To these *idées reçues* should be preferred the age-old unrelentings of Beckett. 'Memory, as every reader of *Molloy* knows, is only another name for invention'? But this is an invention, a *simplesse*, as readers of *Molloy* can read for themselves:

And truly it little matters what I say, this or that or any other thing. Saying is inventing. Wrong, very rightly wrong. You invent nothing, you think you are inventing, you think you are escaping, and all you do is stammer out your lesson, the remnants of a pensum one day got by heart and long forgotten, life without tears, as it is wept.[135]

This is a great deal more elusively complicated ('Wrong, very rightly wrong') than any laxative announcement that 'Memory is only another name for invention'. That would be intellectual 'life without tears'.

As to invention and the imaginary, this is *How It Is*:

the proportion of invention vast assuredly vast proportion a thing you don't know the threat the bleeding arse the cracking nerves you invent but real or imaginary no knowing it's impossible it's not said it doesn't matter it does it did that's superb a thing that matters[136]

The antithesis of 'real or imaginary' there refuses to be told that any such antithesis has long been exploded: 'you invent but real or imaginary no knowing it's impossible'.

Another commentator:

By everywhere undermining the connection between language and reality, Beckett has deliberately run words aground, leaving them no longer usable as signs for meanings beyond themselves, but oddly free to express meaning by reference to other words... Once the referential function of language has been exposed as a sham, the lyrical is put on an equal footing with the less than lyrical... The language of Beckett's minimalist fiction can, by definition, cut away everything but language. And once language is accepted as relying not on external 'reality' for its

---

[135] *Molloy*, 41. Following *Molloy* in French, 46:

Et que je dise ceci ou cela ou autre chose, peu importe vraiment. Dire c'est inventer. Faux comme de juste. On n'invente rien, on croit inventer, s'échapper, on ne fait que balbutier sa leçon, des bribes d'un pensum appris et oublié, la vie sans larmes, telle qu'on la pleure.

[136] p. 80. Following *Comment c'est*, 89:

la part d'invention énorme assurément une part énorme une chose qu'on ignore la menace le cul à sang les nerfs à vif on invente mais comment savoir imaginaire réel on ne peut pas on ne dit pas quelle importance c'est important ça l'était ça c'est magnifique une chose importante

significance but is understood rather as the source of its own meaning, the more poetic, more conventional use of it lends at least a linguistic significance to what is said.[137]

The tawdry casualness of phrasing ('undermining' is overdue for burial) fits happily with the philosophical presumption ('the referential function of language has been exposed as a sham')— and with the gaping holes in the argument ('*oddly* free'? 'by definition'?). It is wisely unfathomable what it could be to find language 'the source of its own meaning', but it can be understood all too clearly that the easy invoking of 'at least a linguistic significance' is merely the usual gesture. Meanwhile, reality— which is haled in as just another of those shams—is given the usual treatment, the infected hygiene, iatrogenic, of inverted commas: external '*reality*'.

And all this is bent upon a writer who has shown us, through his words, how much more there is to his art than words, how unforgettable his apprehension of suffering though not only of that:

She sits on erect and rigid in the deepening gloom. Such helplessness to move she cannot help.

With which one might further contrast another commentator, on just such a second version as *Ill Seen Ill Said*:

They, even more than their predecessors—difficult though it may be to conceive of such a possibility—are completely cut adrift from any reality other than that which they manifest by their mere presence as language.[138]

In such 'discourse', as it calls itself, we are in another world than that of Beckett's greatness, his being an art which never is so complacent as to deny the existence of 'the without', 'impregnable' as it yet fertilely is. As witness his tribute to the artist Arikha:

Siege laid again to the impregnable without. Eye and hand fevering after the unself. By the hand it unceasingly changes the eye unceasingly changed. Back and forth the gaze beating against unseeable and

[137] Frederik N. Smith, in *Beckett Translating/Translating Beckett*, 138.
[138] Brian Fitch, *Beckett and Babel*, 191.

unmakable. Truce for a space and the marks of what it is to be and be in face of. Those deep marks to show.[139]

Such is what Beckett himself, alive to things and imaginings, has to show for his pains:

Already all confusion. Things and imaginings. As of always. Confusion amounting to nothing. Despite precautions. If only she could be pure figment. Unalloyed. This old so dying woman. So dead. In the madhouse of the skull and nowhere else. Where no more precautions to be taken. No precautions possible. Cooped up there with the rest. Hovel and stones. The lot. And the eye. How simple all then. If only all could be pure figment. Neither be nor been nor by any shift to be. Gently gently. On. Careful.[140]

[139] 'For Avigdor Arikha' (1967); *Disjecta*, 152. Following 'Pour Avigdor Arikha' (1966); *Disjecta*, 152:

Siège remis devant le dehors imprenable. Fièvre œil-main dans la soif du non–soi. Oeil par la main sans cesse changé à l'instant même où sans cesse il la change. Regard ne s'arrachant à l'invisible que pour s'asséner sur l'infaisable et retour éclair. Trêve à la navette et traces de ce que c'est que d'être et d'être devant. Traces profondes.

[140] *Ill Seen Ill Said*, 20. Following *Mal vu mal dit*, 24:

Dèja tout s'emmêle. Choses et chimères. Comme de tout temps. S'emmêle et s'annule. Malgré les précautions. Si seulement elle pouvait n'être qu'ombre. Ombre sans mélange. Cette vieille si mourante. Si morte. Dans le manicome du crâne et nulle part ailleurs. Où plus de précautions à prendre. Plus de précautions possibles. Internée là avec le reste. Cabanon caillasse et tout le bazar. Et le guetteur. Comme tout serait simple alors. Si tout pouvait n'être qu'ombre. Ni être ni avoir été ni pouvoir être. Du calme. La suite. Attention.

4. *The Irish Bull*

The soup before me had stopped steaming. Had it ever steamed?[1]

The English dictionary definitions of the Irish bull take for granted the very thing which is sharply at stake.

bull
A self-contradictory proposition; in modern use, an expression containing a manifest contradiction in terms or involving a ludicrous inconsistency unperceived by the speaker. Now often with epithet *Irish*; but the word had been long in use before it came to be associated with Irishmen. (*OED*)

A blunder, or inadvertent contradiction of terms, for which the Irish are proverbial. (Brewer's *Dictionary of Phrase and Fable*)

But whether the comic or satiric energy of the Irish bull is 'inadvertent', 'unperceived by the speaker', is the nub, and here the definers are manifesting complacency as to their own inadvertencies, as to what may go unperceived by lordly them.

It was said of Byron that he aimed at the suicidal success of extinguishing in laughter the emotions he had raised. The bull is a form of linguistic suicide, and for an Irish writer as occupied with suicide as Beckett, it had its attractions. And its affinities with other linguistic goings-on in the vicinity of life and death:

And though in purposelessness I may seem now to go, yet I do not, any more than in purposelessness then I came, for I go now with my purpose as with it then I came, the only difference being this, that then it was living and now it is dead, which is what you might call what I think the English call six of one and half a dozen of the other, do they not, might you not? Or do I confuse them with the Irish?[2]

---

[1] *Molloy*, 158. Following *Molloy* in French, 179: 'Devant moi la soupe ne fumait plus. Avait-elle jamais fumé?'

[2] *Watt*, 58. Preceding *Watt* in French, 59:

Et si maintenant je peux sembler partir sans but il n'en est pourtant rien, pas plus que je ne suis pas venu sans but alors, car je pars maintenant avec mon but comme avec lui alors je suis venu à ceci près qu'alors il était vivant et que maintenant il est mort, ce qu'on pourrait

Like any other form of oxymoron, the bull raises sharp questions about stupidity, about the moronic. An oxymoron (Greek 'pointedly foolish', sharp + dull) ought at least to prick us into wondering which way the sharpness may be pointing. Is it always itself that the bull absurdly nicks, by accident, or does the bull sometimes turn and gore the goader?

The English tradition, here anti-Irish, of being in no doubt about the matter ('a ludicrous inconsistency unperceived by the speaker', *not* an edged and politic glint at the spoken-to) is sometimes accommodated even by those who write in sympathy with Irishry. Brian Earls, in his hospitable monograph on 'Bulls, Blunders and Bloothers', sets himself reasonably enough to show that many a phrase mocked as an Irish bull is reasonable enough, provided only that the hearer is cognizant of Irish English. But the price paid for this intervention, justified though it be on occasion, is its blunting the penetrative power of a true bull, such as would be justified *not* as not being a bull at all if sympathetically apprehended, but as being, yes, a bull and the better for it. More power to its horns.

Earls, himself unaware of just where this will lead him, goes along with the assumption that the mark of the bull is its utterer's unawareness:

It involves a comic contradiction between two of its component parts of which the speaker is unaware but which is perceived by the person who has recorded the anecdote and by his readers.[3]

But it is sometimes hard to tell how aware a speaker is (this then being perhaps cannily traded upon).

Take the sometime Vice-President of the United States of America.

Mr Quayle, economical with his thinking, has often delivered himself up.

One word sums up probably the responsibility of any vice president, and that one word is 'to be prepared'.

appeler n'est-ce pas ce que sauf erreur les Français appellent bonnet blanc et blanc bonnet. Ou est-ce que je les confonds avec les Belges?

The Belgians can be surrogates for the Irish, but are not confused with them. There is not a Belgian bull.

[3] *Béaloideas: The Journal of the Folklore of Ireland Society* (1988), 1.

From a man of thought, this might well be a provocation to thought—thought, for instance, about how foolish it is to have supposed that one word could sum up the responsibility of a vice-president, one word which we ought 'to be prepared' to acknowledge as three-in-one and one-in-three like the USA.

Given Mr Quayle's penchant, we may ask ourselves whether he is in the habit of asking himself about the evolution of his thought. 'The evolution towards democracy in China is irreversible— but that could change' (May 1989). Jon Elster entertained the possibility of doing the decent thing by this:

We may, out of charity to Mr Quayle, find some kind of poetic wisdom in this statement. The perception of a chain of events as irreversible may itself be reversible.[4]

Mr Quayle might, after all, have been straightfacedly bantering the ludicrous hubris of Sinologists, all too confident that they know irreversibility when they see it. Whether the public perception of Mr Quayle is irreversible—that is another story.

The Irish bull is a big subject, so it may be as well to start by taking a concessive but perhaps apocryphal leaf out of Carlyle's book, *Oliver Cromwell's Letters and Speeches*: 'Some omissions will also appear in this edition'.

As for Jane Welsh Carlyle, she had not only her bear of a husband but her pet bull. She wrote to Charles Gavan Duffy in Dublin:

When one has 'sworn an everlasting friendship' at first sight, one desires, very naturally, that it should not have been on your Irish principle, 'with the reciprocity all on one side.'[5]

For the great thing about the bull is that it does not have the reciprocity all on one side—or the folly all on one side.

The doubt as to which way the bull faces, whether it is two-faced as well as two-horned, whether it is simply foolish or whether with comic duplicity it fools: this might be judged endemic in the word's etymology.

---

[4] *London Review of Books*, 25 Jan. 1990.
[5] 14 Sept. 1845; *Letters and Memorials* (1883), i. 332. J. A. Froude makes his contribution to the Carlyle circle, saying of *Past and Present*: 'The arrangement is awkward—as awkward as that of "Sartor"—for indeed there is no arrangement at all' (*Thomas Carlyle: A History of His Life in London* (1884), i. 284).

The *OED* deems it 'of unknown origin', but compares it with the Old French *boul*, 'fraud, deceit, trickery', and Middle English *bull*, 'falsehood', as well as with that quite other thing the Icelandic *bull*, 'nonsense'. The verb *to bull* is 'to befool, mock, cheat'— where to befool is the opposite of to be a fool or to make a fool of *oneself*. The twisted roots of the word might issue in its flowering as a form of nonsense which is itself tricky and befooling.[6]

The one thing about which the Dictionary is confident is that the Church is not the one foundation: 'No foundation appears for the guess that the word originated in "a contemptuous allusion to papal edicts".' Yet this is the irresistible coincidence of which the polemicist has always taken advantage. The uttered stupidity of the Irish is at one with their utter stupidity in being the willing victims of papal edicts.[7]

Milton pounced upon the contradiction ineradicable in the word *Catholic* once the Reformation had deprived Catholicism of its claimed universality, claimed and etymological. 'Whereas the Papist boasts himself to be a Roman Catholick, it is a meer contradiction, one of the Popes Bulls.'[8]

Milton's animus is unlovely, and yet he has a point. To call Roman Catholics 'Catholics', *tout court*, would be to concede their case, servilely perhaps; to call them 'Roman Catholics' would be to dismiss their case, rudely perhaps, and is moreover to pinion them with an oxymoron. C. S. Lewis the Ulsterman, never one to forgo an advantage, thought it his duty to use what he averred was the neutral term: Papist.

One happy habit, pertinent to an oyxmoron's being itself etymologically constituted as an oxymoron, has long been that of explaining a bull with a bull. To take up the bull in this way, to rally with it, is to make clear that at least on some occasions— notably when dramatized—such foolery may be a wise move. So the *OED* records, as its very first citation, such a rally in 1640 within Richard Brome's *The Antipodes* (and a bull is its own antipodes):

---

[6] Recent, scatological, and reprehensibly gender-specific, *bull*, from *bullshit*, is no relation.

[7] Beckett (a Protestant from the Republic of Ireland) has Murphy refer to his horoscope as 'My little bull of incommunication'. *Murphy*, 31. Preceding *Murphy* in French, 28: 'Ma petite bulle d'incommunication'.

[8] *OED*, Milton (1673), *True Relig.*

Dumbe Speaker! that's a Bull. Thou wert the Bull Then, in the Play.
Would I had seene thee rore.

That's a Bull too, as wise as you are.

It is fitting that there should be the understanding of folly as
paradoxically enjoying its own wisdom, even in earshot of the
retort 'That's a Bull too, as wise as you are'. Fitting, too, that the
incongruity of the bull should be compounded, a bull bred by a
bull, in this, the *OED*'s earliest instance. Likewise in John Collins's
poem:[9]

A Bull and No Bull

A Wag having wager'd, with Teague, half a crown,
About how many Signs of the Bull were in town;
Teague swore there were *Three*, which was flatly denied,
And to point out a Bull more than *Two* was defied;
When he thus 'gan to count:—"There's the Black Bull in Foregate,
"That's One;—then the Second's the White Bull in Norgate;
"And as for the next, which make *Three*, you'll allow,
"In the very next lane, there's the little Brown Cow!"
'A right Irish blunder,' says each Stander-by,
'And your Bet you have lost'.—"Tut," says Teague, "that's a lie";
"I'll be bound, 'stead of losing my wager, I win it,
"For that Blunder's a BULL, or the Devil is in it."

The tradition of bulls-within-bulls is alive within Richard
Steele's reply when he was asked how it happened that his
countrymen made so many bulls: 'It is the effect of climate, sir; if
an Englishman were born in Ireland, he would make as many.' It
sounds as if it makes sense; it looks then as if it doesn't.

Ah, but in a way it does, since it is conceivable that an
Englishman might be born in Ireland. To be born in a stable is
not necessarily to be a horse, leave alone a Houyhnhnm. Jonathan
Swift notoriously wrote from Dublin to the Earl of Oxford:

I loved My Lord Your father better than any other Man in the World,
although I had no obligation to him on the Score of Preferment, having
been driven to this wretched Kingdom (to which I was almost a Stranger)
by his want of power to keep me in what I ought to call my own Country;

---

[9] *Scripscrapologia* (1804), 95.

though I happened to be dropped here, and was a Year old before I left it, and to my Sorrow did not dye before I came back to it again.[10]

That last unsentimental sentiment is a reminder that Swift is in so many ways akin to Beckett; and the turn of phrase is by way of being a bull: 'and to my Sorrow did not dye before I came back to it again'. There *before I came back* has an itch to mean something like 'and so would not have had to come back'. For, had he died, he would not have come back to it again. Only, at most, his remains.

As to the animal-pun opportunity milked by Brome, and thereby the bull's breeding another bull, there is Sir John Pentland Mahaffy's famous reply when asked to distinguish the Irish bull from similar freaks of language: 'The Irish bull is always pregnant'. One cannot imagine anything more pregnant. Not only is there the cross-eyed cross-gendering (a pregnant *bull?*), and the male/female filaments criss-crossed with the English/Irish ones (this, ripe with political application and grievance); there is the dreadful prospect of being *always* pregnant (never coming to term with life); and there is the bizarre relation to life (and to death), since an Irish bull—though happy yet again to service and to breed—is at once pregnant and abortive. The bull, in its self-cancellation, may not be poison and antidote, but it is fecundating and abortifacient. It is another embodiment in language of life in death and death in life.[11]

'Of which the speaker is unaware'? But you could hardly get more aware than was witty Mahaffy. *His* bull is clearly not the common or garden one. For the possibility of inadvertence needs to hang about the casual or casual-seeming bull. And inadvertence is itself worth pondering. J. L. Austin issued a warning:

It does not pay to assume that a word must have an opposite, or one opposite, whether it is a 'positive' word like 'wilfully' or a 'negative' word

---

[10] 14 June 1737; *The Correspondence of Jonathan Smith*, ed. Harold Williams, v (1965), 46–7.

[11] On 'the image of the male pregnant with his own twin' in Beckett's *Rough for Radio II*, *Collected Shorter Plays*, 119 ('my brother inside me'), see Paul Lawley, 'The Difficult Birth' in Davis and Butler (eds.), '*Make Sense Who May*', 2. Lawley remarks, too, 'a comparable suggestion of male pregnancy' in 'Afar a Bird' (1973), *For to End Yet Again and Other Fizzles* (1975). The maleness of the Irish bull is important to it; in the whole of the Edgeworths' *Essay on Irish Bulls* there are hardly any (one or two?) instances of women's uttering bulls, and they are doubtful cases.

like 'inadvertently'. Rather, we should be asking ourselves such questions as why there is no use for the adverb 'advertently'.[12]

The bull makes us advert to inadvertence. It is in the bull's having at least a colour of the naïve, in its lending itself to the charge of unwittingness (and then repaying the loan with interest), that its wit lies. As with Stevie Smith's poems, which depend upon its always being in question to what degree their innocence is mock-innocence, the bull is cousin to the combination of the ingenuous and the ingenious which turns upon us an adroitly unsettling charm.

Replying to a questionnaire, Wallace Stevens answered—in his way—the question, 'As a poet what distinguishes you, do you think, from an ordinary man?':

Inability to see much point to the life of an ordinary man. The chances are an ordinary man himself sees very little point to it.[13]

This rueful bull may look like, but would not have to be, something of a blasphemy against democracy.

THE BULL AND BLASPHEMY

In his Dictionary, Dr Johnson offered a twofold definition of the bull: 'A blunder; a contradiction'. He did not venture on the question of whether in a bull the contradiction has to be a blunder, and his supporting instance, from Pope's letters, has an air of good-naturedly protecting the Irish against English condescension while tacitly insisting, as one does when resisting unjustified scorn, that you know what I *mean*: 'I confess it is what the Irish call a *bull*, in the expression, though the sense be manifest enough.'

Pope's lines on wit in *An Essay on Criticism* had caught Dennis's eye.

> The more his *Trouble* as the more *admir'd*;
> Where *wanted*, scorn'd, and envy'd where *acquir'd*.[14]

---

[12] 'A Plea for Excuses', *Philosophical Papers* (1961), 192.

[13] 'Responses to *New Verse* Questionnaire' (1934); *Opus Posthumous* (rev. edn., ed. Milton J. Bates, 1989), 307.

[14] *An Essay on Criticism* (1711), 502–3; Twickenham Edition, *Pastoral Poetry and An Essay on Criticism*, ed. E. Audra and Aubrey Williams (1961), 295: 'These lines gave

Dennis exulted: 'how can Wit be scorn'd where it is not? Is not this a Figure frequently employ'd in *Hibernian* Land?' Pope conceded bluffly:

'Tis right Hibernian, and I confess it what the English call a bull, in the expression, tho' the sense be manifest enough: Mr Dennis's bulls are seldom in the expression, they are almost always in the sense.[15]

Johnson's Dictionary has itself been charged with harbouring bulls. His definition of a garret as 'a room on the highest floor of the house' might be thought to couple oddly with his definition of a cock-loft as 'the room over the garret'. Well, it depends what you mean by the highest *floor*.[16]

But Johnson's sense of himself would not have taken lightly to

---

Pope much trouble'. The Twickenham edition, which combines final readings with first-edition spelling etc., gives as the final version:

> Then most our *Trouble* still when most *admir'd*,
> And still the more we *give*, the more *requir'd*.

[15] 25 June 1711, to John Caryll; *The Correspondence of Alexander Pope*, ed. George Sherburn (1956), i. 121.

[16] Beckett shows the precisian's pleasure, flecked with a touch of the bull (seeking 'high and low' for a *garret*?):

Murphy had occupied a garret in Hanover, not for long, but for long enough to experience all its advantages. Since then he had sought high and low for another, even half as good. In vain. What passed for a garret in Great Britain and Ireland was really nothing more than an attic. An attic! How was it possible for such a confusion to arise? A basement was better than an attic. An attic!
But the garret that he now saw was not an attic, nor yet a mansarde, but a genuine garret, not half, but twice as good as the one in Hanover, because half as large.

Murphy, 162. Preceding *Murphy* in French, 119:

Murphy avait occupé à Hanovre, assez longtemps pour faire l'expérience de tous ses avantages, une mansarde dans la belle maison renaissance de la Schmiedestrasse où avait vécu, mais surtout où était mort, Gottfried Wilhelm Leibniz. A vrai dire il ne s'en était jamais tout à fait remis, et n'avait cessé d'en chercher une autre, fût-elle seulement à moitié aussi belle. En vain. Ce qui passait pur une mansarde au Royaume Uni n'était en verité qu'un grenier. Un grenier! Comment de telles confusions étaient-elles possibles? Un grenier!
Mais la mansarde où maintenant il se trouvait n'était ni un grenier, ni un galetas, ni une chambre de génie, ni une chambre de bonne, mais une veritable mansarde, et en beauté pas la moitié de celle de Hanovre, mais le double.

An unexpected arrival, there in the French: Leibniz of all people, along with the house where he effected something which trumps living: 'où avait vécu, mais surtout où était mort, Gottfried Wilhelm Leibniz'. Such a translation, born anew, is itself 'une maison renaissance'. Yet the French cannot manage the Irish bull—'a garret in Great Britain and Ireland'—of 'sought high and low'.
In 'The Antithetical Sense of Primal Words', Freud noted that 'In German *Boden* (garret, ground) still means the attic as well as the ground-floor of the house' (*Collected Papers*, iv. 189).

either exculpation or inculpation hereabouts, for robust good sense is bound to be impatient with the bull. Boswell judged unique a lapse by his friend:

He once in his life was known to have uttered what is called a *bull*: Sir Joshua Reynolds, when they were riding together in Devonshire, complained that he had a very bad horse, for that even when going down hill he moved slowly step by step. 'Ay (said Johnson,) and when he *goes* up hill, he *stands still*.'[17]

Johnson's only Boswelled bull is on horseback.

This may have been a nonsensical thing for Johnson to say, but it does gruffly anticipate the Red Queen: 'Now, *here*, you see, it takes all the running *you* can do, to keep in the same place. If you want to get somewhere else, you must run at least twice as fast as that!'[18]

Yet Johnson himself, whose poems pun as often as his criticism deprecates puns, may be thought often to commit—or to achieve— bulls. Of his visit to Wales: 'I am glad that I have seen it, though I have seen nothing, because I now know that there is nothing to be seen'.[19] Of his quarrel with an acquaintance: 'And so I shall have no more good of Colson, of whom I never had any good, but flattery, which my dear Mistress knows I can have at home'[20] Very good, the comma after *good*, so that the bull can pass by; and good, too, the way in which flattery is intimated not to be, on reflection, a good.

In their magnificent *Essay on Irish Bulls* (1802), Maria Edgeworth and Richard Lovell Edgeworth, with characteristic magnanimity, put into the mouth of an Englishman the admission that even an English poet might nod:

It is curious to observe how nearly wit and absurdity are allied. We may forgive the genius of Ireland if he sometimes

'Leap his light courser o'er the bounds of taste.'

Even English genius is not always to be restrained within the strict limits of common sense. For instance, Young is witty when he says,

---

[17] Boswell's *Life of Johnson*, ed. Birkbeck Hill and Powell, iv. 322; June 1784.

[18] *Through the Looking-Glass*, ch. 2.

[19] To John Taylor, 20 Oct. 1774; *The Letters of Samuel Johnson*, ed. Bruce Redford, ii (1992), 151.

[20] To Hester Thrale, 6 June 1775; *Letters*, ed. Redford, ii. 217.

'How would a miser startle to be told
Of such a wonder as insolvent gold.'

But Johnson is, I am afraid, absurd when he says,

'Turn from the glittering bribe your scornful eye,
Nor sell for gold what gold can never buy.'[21]

But from the Edgeworths' 'But' there might extend, as is often the case with the quizzed bull, a further *But*. For not only does Johnson's paradoxical way of putting it make you ask yourself whether you *could* ever buy back certain things which you have sold (your honour, say, once you have taken a bribe), but it further makes you think about the way in which gold may find itself changed by who owns it. Whose gold, exactly? There is a grim alchemy as the line transmutes itself: 'Nor sell for Gold, what Gold could never buy'. *Could*—a larger insistence than, as the Edgeworths have it, 'what gold *can* never buy'.

Like other oxymorons and paradoxes, the bull in its self-contradiction is intimate with the great contradictions of life and death. One such is blasphemy. It was Dr Johnson who mounted the first comprehensive, because comprehending, attack on a bull under this aspect. In its relation to eternal life and oblivion, John Gay's epitaph in Westminster Abbey was judged by Johnson to be flippantly blasphemous:

My own EPITAPH
Life is a jest, and all things show it,
I thought so once; but now I know it.

Johnson was not amused.

Mr Gay has returned from the regions of death not much improved in his poetry, and very much corrupted in his morals; for he is come back with a lie in his mouth, *Life is a jest.*

[21] *Essay on Irish Bulls* (1802), ch. XIII. The Edgeworths' Englishman begins here with a passing tribute to English genius, in 'how nearly wit and absurdity are allied'.

Great Wits are sure to Madness near ally'd;
And thin Partitions do their Bounds divide:

(Dryden, *Absalom and Achitophel*, 163–4)

Johnson, *London*, 87–90:

Turn from the glitt'ring Bribe thy scornful Eye,
Nor sell for Gold, what Gold could never buy,
The peaceful Slumber, self-approving Day,
Unsullied Fame, and Conscience ever gay.

Mankind, with regard to their notions of futurity, are divided into two parties: a very small one that believes, or pretends to believe, that the present is the only state of existence; and another, which acknowledges that in some life to come, men will meet rewards or punishments according to their behaviour in this world.

In one of the classes our poet must be ranked: if he properly belonged to the first, he might indeed think life a jest, and might live as if he thought so; but I must leave it to acute reasoners to explain how he could in that case *know* it after death, being for my part inclined to believe that knowledge ceases with existence.

If he was of the latter opinion, he must think life more than a jest, unless he thought eternity a jest too; and if these were his sentiments, he is by this time most certainly undeceived. These lines, therefore, are impious in the mouth of a Christian, and nonsense in that of an atheist.

But whether we consider them as ludicrous or wicked, they ought not to stand where they are at present; buffoonery appears with a very ill grace, and impiety with much worse, in temples and on tombs.[22]

Bull: 'A blunder; a contradiction'. But Gay's contradiction, though it may have been a mistake, was not a blunder. He had written to Pope:

I begin to look upon myself as one already dead; and desire, my dear Mr. *Pope*, (whom I love as my own Soul) if you survive me, (as you certainly will) that you will, if a Stone should mark the Place of my Grave, see these Words put on it:

> Life is a Jest, and all Things show it;
> I thought so once, but now I know it.

With what more you may think proper.

If any Body should ask, how I could communicate this after Death? Let it be known, it is not meant so, but my present Sentiment in Life.

Gay's editors have noted: 'When Gay's monument in Westminster Abbey was unveiled, there were objections, and the epitaph was omitted from the engraving of the monument in the frontispiece to the *Fables* of 1738. The monument was moved from the Poet's Corner to the triforium in 1938, to expose a medieval fresco, so that Gay's grave is now unmarked'.[23] Unmarked, now, the grave;

---

[22] *Gentleman's Magazine*, Oct. 1738; included in the Oxford Authors *Samuel Johnson* (1984), ed. Donald Greene.

[23] John Gay, *Poetry and Prose*, ed. Vinton A. Dearing with the assistance of Charles E. Beckwith (1974), i. 253, ii. 597, where Gay's letter to Pope is described as 'variously

and not going unmarked then, the epitaph: God is not mocked.

Gay had been moved to attempt, or to pretend to attempt, a down-to-earth explanation of his *outré* flash from the *outre-tombe*: 'If any Body should ask, how I could communicate this after Death? Let it be known, it is not meant so, but my present Sentiment in Life.' This should be taken with many a grain of salt. It is then the salt that preserves such a jest.

'My own Epitaph' did not die with Gay, but, preserved, its tradition lives on in Beckett. The narrator of *First Love* contemplates his truly lasting love:

My other writings are no sooner dry than they revolt me, but my epitaph still meets with my approval. There is little chance unfortunately of its ever being reared above the skull that conceived it, unless the State takes up the matter. But to be unearthed I must first be found, and I greatly fear those gentlemen will have as much trouble finding me dead as alive. So I hasten to record it here and now, while there is yet time:

> Hereunder lies the above who up below
> So hourly died that he lived on till now.

The second and last or rather latter line limps a little perhaps, but that is no great matter, I'll be forgiven more than that when I'm forgotten.[24]

---

dated 1727 and 1729'. There is a dry touch of another bull in 'if you survive me, (as you certainly will)'.

[24] *First Love*, 10–11. Following *Premier amour*, 9–10:

Mes autres écrits, ils n'ont pas le temps de sécher qu'ils me dégoûtent déjà, mais mon épitaphe me plaît toujours. Elle illustre un point de grammaire. Il y a malheureusement peu de chances qu'elle s'élève jamais au-dessus du crâne qui la conçut, à moins que l'État ne s'en charge. Mais pour pouvoir m'exhumer il faudra d'abord me trouver, et j'ai bien peur que l'État n'ait autant de mal à me trouver mort que vivant. C'est pour cela que je me dépêche de la consigner à cette place, avant qu'il ne soit trop tard:

> Ci-gît qui y échappa tant
> Qu'il n'en échappe que maintenant

Il y a une syllabe de trop dans le second et dernier vers, mais cela n'a pas d'importance, à mon avis. On me pardonnera plus que cela, quand je ne serai plus.

The French comes to an end with something more final than 'when I'm forgotten': 'quand je ne serai plus'. There is no counterpart in the English to the grammarian's funeral arrangement ('Elle illustre un point de grammaire'); but, in compensation, the English has a skewer denied to the French: instead of 'le second et dernier vers', there is a flash of Beckett's unending play with last things: 'The second and last or rather latter line'.

For another epitaph with a glinting preposition, see *Malone Dies*, 101: 'Here lies Malone at last', 'Here lies a ne'er-do-well, six feet under hell'. Following *Malone meurt*, 162–3: 'Ci-gît Malone enfin', 'Ci-gît un pauvre con, tout lui fut aquilon'.

Johnson judged Gay's self-addressed epitaph blasphemous. But then there is no penetrative religious literature that does not—as crucial to its enterprise—raise the question of whether it is open to the charge of blasphemy, as there is no true erotic art which does not raise the possibility of being rebuked as pornography. If the charge of blasphemy were simply to stick, then the religious art would have failed in some respect, in respect; but were the charge not even to be imaginable, then the religious art would not be alive with imagination's disconcerting force.

> Hail holy light, ofspring of Heav'n first-born,
> Or of th' Eternal Coeternal beam
> May I express thee unblam'd?

> *(Paradise Lost*, iii. 1–3)

Unblamed: without being blamed for blasphemy, *blaspheme* being the etymological root of *blame*, and blasphemy being a blaming which is to be blamed. The *OED* has *blaspheme*:

1. To utter profane or impious words, talk profanely.
2. To speak irreverently of, utter impiety against (God or anything sacred).
3. To speak evil of, revile, calumniate, abuse.

Likewise *blasphemy*:

1. Profane speaking of God or sacred things; impious irreverence.
b. *fig.* (against anything held 'sacred').

The Dictionary moves from the unhedgedly sacred—God or sacred things—to that for which the Dictionary gives a *fig.*, with its double hedging in 'anything *held* "sacred"' (my italics, but tacitly theirs, and their *noli-me-tangere* tweezer-commas).

Blasphemy's crux is shaped here. Where, other than in God, naturally (supernaturally), does a particular society locate the sacred, or, with a caveat, the 'sacred'?

The three figurative citations in the *OED* speak volumes about the mutation of that which comes to be held sacred. The first is from Bacon in 1605: 'He was well punished for his blasphemy against learning'. The second, in 1873, is from John Morley, who has a sense that these days are not those days: 'You are drawing an indictment against nature,—no trifling blasphemy in those days'. And the third is from Philip Hamerton in 1875: 'This doctrine sounds like blasphemy against friendship'. *God or sacred things*—and thereafter a further trinity takes shape, open now to blasphemy: learning, nature, and friendship.

As T. S. Eliot saw, blasphemy is possible only to a believer—or rather either to a believer or to someone who half-fears that he or she may be a believer, and who kicks against the pricks. *More Pricks than Kicks*: with his first work of fiction, Beckett at once joined the great Irish writers who have earned the tribute of being banned in the Republic of Ireland.[25]

Beckett's witty blasphemy of title was only partly a matter of his having touched with obscenity the godly moment ('It is hard for thee to kick against the pricks'). For what will also have goaded the authorities, and many a gentle reader, was the shape Beckett gave to his thought. *More Pricks than Kicks* intersects the road to Damascus with an English byway: 'More kicks than halfpence', glossed by the *OED* as 'more harshness than kindness' (and quoted from Scott, Darwin, and Trollope).

Blasphemy is, among other things, an exacerbated acknowledgement of an unignorable external power (omnipotence, even) and of one's ability completely to deny it. This underlies the violent indignation usual to *both* sides, just because there lurks some such acknowledgement, this constituting at once a mitigation in the eyes of the blasphemer—aggrievedly, I'm acknowledging it, aren't

---

[25] See Beckett's acerb essay, 'Censorship in the Saorstat', written in 1935, on Irish censorship (*Disjecta*, 84–8). *More Pricks than Kicks* is alive with particular blasphemies. One heartening instance is Beckett's play with *sursum corda* (*OED*: 'In Latin Eucharistic liturgies, the words addressed by the celebrant to the congregation at the beginning of the Eucharistic Prayer; in English rites, the corresponding versicle, "Lift up your hearts"'). For Belacqua the Peeping Tom, it is not the heart which rises to these occasions. 'Walking Out', *More Pricks than Kicks*, 150:

'Then I thought' he said at last 'that the best thing to do was to go to the wood for a little sursum corda.'
This was another falsehood, because the wood had been in his thoughts all day. He told it with a kind of miserable conviction.
'Corda is good' said Lucy.
As she uttered these words with one of her smart smiles the truth, or something that seemed very like it, struck her with such violence that she nearly fell out of the saddle.

And pp. 153–4:

Poor little Lucy! The more she struggled to eject the idea that possessed her ever since those careless words: 'Corda is good', the more it seemed to prevail to the exclusion of all others. The derogation of her gentle Belacqua from one whom she had loved in all the shadows and tangles of his conduct to a trite spy of the vilest description was not to be set aside by a girl of her mettle merely on account of its being a great shock to her sentimental system.

I?—and an aggravation in the eyes of the devout—You even acknowledge it, don't you?

Eliot wrote, à propos of Baudelaire:

Genuine blasphemy, genuine in spirit and not purely verbal, is the product of partial belief, and is as impossible to the complete atheist as to the perfect Christian. It is a way of affirming belief.[26]

Hence, it might be added, the fact that the *possibility* of being accused of blasphemy is essential to Christian literature, since without such a possibility the literature would announce itself as that of 'the perfect Christian', a self-negating belief since to be a Christian is to acknowledge one's imperfection. *De Imitatione Christi*, yes; but such an imitation must never arrive at the sincerest form of self-flattery.

'I think', wrote Eliot, 'that there is an interesting subject of investigation, for the student of traditions, in the history of Blasphemy, and the anomalous position of that term in the modern world.'

It is certainly my opinion that first-rate blasphemy is one of the rarest things in literature, for it requires both literary genius and profound faith, joined in a mind in a peculiar and unusual state of spiritual sickness. I repeat that I am not defending blasphemy; I am reproaching a world in which blasphemy is impossible.[27]

Eliot had earlier rehearsed this brief, adducing

the twelfth century anomaly—and yet the essential congruity—of the finest religious verse and the most brilliant blasphemous verse. To the present generation of versifiers, so deficient in devotion and so feeble in blasphemy, the twelfth century might offer an edifying subject of study.[28]

---

[26] 'Baudelaire', *Selected Essays*, 421.

[27] *After Strange Gods* (1934), 51–2. Eliot would have found surprising, in Sara Suleri's account of blasphemy, only her being surprised by what she comes to think: that *The Satanic Verses* 'perversely demands to be read as a gesture of wrenching loyalty, suggesting that blasphemy can be expressed only within the compass of belief'. But it would not follow from this, as she supposes, that 'the term *blasphemy* itself must be reread as a gesture of reconciliation toward the idea of belief rather than as the insult that it is commonly deemed to be'. There are other possibilities than those two, and to kick against the pricks is exactly not *reconciliation*. Suleri, 'Contraband Histories: Salman Rushdie and the Embodiment of Blasphemy', *Yale Review*, 78 (1989), 606–7.

[28] *Times Literary Supplement*, 11 Aug. 1927, reviewing C. H. Haskins, *The Renaissance of the Twelfth Century*.

The anomaly and yet the essential congruity: such a contradictory compacting is what animates both blasphemy and the bull.

Christianity has thriven on such contradiction and paradox. The Fall of Man was a Felix Culpa. The Christian God is One and Three, thereby gaining in the Trinity all the advantages of both monotheism and polytheism. The Mother of the Son of God is both mother and virgin (or used to be accounted so, in the robust days of the religion), thereby gaining all the advantages of both mother-worship and virgin-worship.

Beckett did not suppose that a Christian upbringing could ever be lightly shucked. Charles Juliet[29] reports a conversation in 1977:

We discuss religion, and I ask whether he has been able to free himself from its influence.

SB: Perhaps in my external behavior, but as for the rest...

A telling ellipsis.

It is here that a bull may express the necessary outrage, authentic and absurd.

NAGG.   (*clasping his hands, closing his eyes, in a gabble*). Our Father which art—

HAMM.   Silence! In silence! Where are your manners? (*Pause*). Off we go. (*Attitudes of prayer. Silence. Abandoning his attitude, discouraged*). Well?

CLOV.   (*abandoning his attitude*). What a hope! And you?

HAMM.   Sweet damn all! (*To Nagg*). And you?

NAGG.   Wait! (*Pause. Abandoning his attitude*). Nothing doing!

HAMM.   The bastard! He doesn't exist![30]

---

[29] *TriQuarterly* 77 (1989–90), 27, trans. Suzanne Chamier. On these matters William Empson wrote with his usual staunchness when *Waiting for Godot* was first performed in London:

Mr Bagby was quite right, I think, to point out the radical ambiguity of *Waiting for Godot*, but not all ambiguity is good. Here it expresses the sentiment: We cannot believe in Christianity and yet without that everything we do is hopelessly bad. Such an attitude seems to be more frequent in Irish than either English or French writers, perhaps because in Ireland the religious training of children is particularly fierce. A child is brought up to believe that he would be wicked and miserable without God; then he stops believing in God; then he behaves like a dog with its back broken by a car, screaming and thrashing on the public road, so that a passer-by can only wish for it to be put out of its misery. Surely we need not admire this result; the obvious reflection is that it was a very unfairly risky treatment to give to a child.

Times Literary Supplement, 30 Mar. 1956; *Argufying* (1987), 593. Empson, turning the old God/dog axis, hit upon an image recurrent in Beckett; see p. 119 above.

[30] *Endgame*, 38. Following *Fin de partie*, 75–6:

You can just imagine the studiedly patient remonstration: Come now, if He doesn't exist, He can scarcely be a bastard, now, can He? But, oh, you know what Hamm means. There is the simple relief of the self-cancellation, there in the bull, at one with the complicated blasphemy (the Son of God was, in His unique way, a bastard; His uppercase Father did not *marry* His lowercase mother). Not, of course, that Beckett leaves it at that.

HAMM.   The bastard! He doesn't exist!
CLOV.   Not yet.[31]

Hamm's spirited senselessness is a temptation deliciously yielded to. Murphy was made of sterner stuff.

He closed his eyes and fell back. It was not his habit to make out cases for himself. An atheist chipping the deity was not more senseless than Murphy defending his courses of inaction, as he did not require to be told.[32]

As always in comedy, the timing is all. If I had had the imagination to come up with the lovely thought of Murphy's defending his courses of *in*action, I fear that I'd have stopped there for a small drum-roll of self-congratulation: 'An atheist chipping the deity was not more senseless than Murphy defending his courses of inaction'. But no, the sentence has its own course of action, proceeding as if it had not said anything out of the way at all: 'than Murphy defending his courses of inaction, as he did not

NAGG. (*joignant les mains, fermant les yeux, débit précipité*).—Notre Père qui êtes aux...
HAMM.—Silence! En silence! Un peu de tenue! Allons-y. (*Attitudes de prière. Silence. Se décourageant le premier.*) Alors?
CLOV. (*rouvrant les yeux*).—Je t'en fous! Et toi?
HAMM.—Bernique! (*A Nagg.*) Et toi?
NAGG.—Attends. (*Un temps. Rouvrant les yeux.*) Macache!
HAMM.—Le salaud! Il n'existe pas!

[31] *Endgame*, 38. Following *Fin de partie*, 76:

HAMM.—Le salaud! Il n'existe pas!
CLOV.—Pas encore.

The French 'salaud' was less tailored to Christ's conception than is 'bastard'. The Lord Chamberlain ruled that 'bastard', in the performance of *Endgame*, be changed to 'swine'. A different deity, Lord Chamberlain of the Flies.

[32] *Murphy*, 38. Preceding *Murphy* in French, 33–4:

Il ferma lex yeux et se laissa retomber sur le lit. Se justifier n'était pas son genre. Un athée blaguant Dieu n'était pas plus ridicule que Murphy défendant sa manière de ne pas agir, et il le savait mieux que personne.

require to be told'. Rounding aggressively on a putative censurer, this is a new lease of lifelessness.

An atheist chipping the deity is a walking bull, a blasphemy against good sense as well as against the good Lord. Yet how charmingly chipper 'chipping' is, while itself being so inappropriate in its linguistic register as to constitute something of a blasphemy in itself.

chip at
to aim a blow at, peck at, hit at, pick a quarrel with; also, to poke fun at. Hence *trans.* (by omission of *at*), to make (a person) the object of a joke, to chaff, banter.

To make (a person) the object of a joke is one thing; to make (the deity) the object of a joke is to take on more-than-one more-than-person.

Yet God must by now be hardened to blasphemous bulls. See C. C. Bombaugh in his maggoty-headed compendium *Gleanings for the Curious* (1890):

Here is an American Hibernicism, which is entitled to full recognition:— Among the things that Wells & Fargo's Express is not responsible for as carriers is one couched in the following language in their regulations: 'Not for any loss or damage by fire, *the acts of God*, or of Indians, *or any other public enemies of the government*'.[33]

Not the best way of putting it, unless it be a dark and blasphemous jest. But then the cream of the jest is that Wells & Fargo expressly associate themselves with the dictionary (*OED*) definition of an act of God:

action of uncontrollable natural forces in causing an accident, as the burning of a ship by lightning.

Only the supernatural would be able to control such natural forces. But God may weary of hearing such calamities (rather than providential beneficences) described as acts of God. Not that Wells & Fargo are alone in bringing God perilously, all but blasphemously, close to public enemies:

1882 *Charter-party*: The Act of God, the Queen's Enemies, Fire, and all and every other Dangers and Accidents of the Seas .. always excepted.

---

[33] Excerpted by Martin Gardner and published as *Oddities and Curiosities of Words and Literature* (1961), 258, under 'Hiberniana'.

God must stand in a unique relation to the bull (but then to what does He not?), in that contradictions amounting to impossibility can be meat and drink to Him. To Him, all things are possible, including the impossible.

In this, the creative poet may resemble his creator. The Edgeworths have this as part of a dialogue:[34]

Scotchman.—'The same trope is employed in the following metaphorical expression:—the seeds of the Gospel have been *watered* by the *blood* of the martyrs.'

Englishman.—'That does seem an absurdity, I grant; but you know great orators *trample on impossibilities*.'

Scotchman.—'And great poets *get the better of them*. You recollect Shakspeare says,

> "Now bid me run,
> And I will strive with things *impossible*,
> Yea, *get the better of them*." '

It is the paradox that the impossible is possible to God which is turned to beautiful account by Christina G. Rossetti, when she imagines, superlatively, that the lowest place may be not the lowest.

The Lowest Place

Give me the lowest place; not that I dare
  Ask for that lowest place, but Thou hast died
That I might live and share
  Thy glory by Thy side.

Give me the lowest place: or if for me
  That lowest place too high, make one more low
Where I may sit and see
  My God and love Thee so.

This carries to sublime depths the contradictions of the bull, coming to rest at the end upon the exquisite double meaning of *so* in 'and love Thee *so*'—so humbly stationed, and so ineffably much.

'The Lowest Place' is the heavenly counterpart to the hellish paradox in *Paradise Lost*:

> Which way I flie is Hell; my self am Hell;
> And in the lowest deep a lower deep

---

[34] Ch. XII, with a note attributing to Lord Chatham *'trample on impossibilities'*.

> Still threatning to devour me opens wide,
> To which the Hell I suffer seems a Heav'n.

(iv. 75–8)

If the lowest, how can there be a lower one, whether a lower deep or a lower place? Because such bulls are acts of God, the God who conceives of Christina Rossetti's Heaven, and of Milton's Hell—and Beckett's, with its so-called lowest depths:

part one before Pim the journey it can't last it lasts I'm calm calmer you think you're calm and you're not in the lowest depths and you're on the edge I say it as I hear it and that death death if it ever comes that's all it dies[35]

THE BULL AND DEATH

There is a bull in the Bible, or rather in the King James Bible:

Then the angel of the LORD went forth, and smote in the camp of the Assyrians a hundred and fourscore and five thousand: and when they arose early in the morning, behold, they were all dead corpses.

(Isaiah 37: 36)

With pronouns, careless talk costs lives.

The bull, like the cliché, gravitates naturally towards death, partly because the bull is itself a form of suicidal self-cancellation and partly because death teems with contradictions and oxymorons.[36] So there is many a death-based bull.[37] An Irish MP is said to have been outraged by a minister's avarice:

I verily believe ... that if the honorable gentleman were an undertaker, it would be the delight of his heart to see all mankind seized with a common mortality, that he might have the benefit of the general burial, and provide scarfs and hat-bands for *the survivors*.

---

[35] *How It Is*, 22. Following *Comment c'est*, 25:

première partie avant Pim je voyage ça ne peut plus durer ça dure je suis plus calme on croit qu'on est calme et on ne l'est pas au plus bas et on est au bord je le dis comme je l'entends et que la mort la mort si jamais elle vient c'est tout ça meurt

[36] On death (especially death these days) and oxymorons, see Edwin S. Schneidman (ed.) *Death: Current Perspectives* (1976), pp. xix, xx, 12, 136, 138, 473. The editor: 'Professor of Thanatology, Director, Laboratory for the Study of Life-Threatening Behavior'. (Yet death does not have a monopoly of threats.)

[37] Earls, *Béaloideas* (1988), 22–4, gives two pages of bulls 'which cluster around the theme of death' and speaks of their popularity.

So avaricious, the honourable gentleman, that even in an impossible situation he would manage somehow to kill the geese that lay the golden eggs?

A Hibernian gentleman, when told by his nephew that he had just entered college with a view to the church, said, 'I hope that I may live to hear you preach my funeral sermon.'[38]

It sounds equably sensible enough; whereupon it gutters into absurdity; but then there survives about it a happy relish of hoping against hope.

Beckett has his own two minds about the fact that where there's hope, there's life.[39]

Then it will be all over with the Murphys, Merciers, Molloys, Morans and Malones, unless it goes on beyond the grave. But sufficient unto the day, let us first defunge, then we'll see.[40]

But, in this posited future, *seeing* is believing that we will not then have sufficiently defunged. Seeing is keeping us in existence—*esse est percipi*, too.[41]

It is the contradiction of our needing somehow to imagine ourselves, in death, but without the good offices of imagination, which puts our own death beyond reach. In speaking cannily of this, Freud anticipates the absurdity of 'we really survive as spectators' with his 'we can perceive':

Our own death is indeed unimaginable, and whenever we make the attempt to imagine it we can perceive that we really survive as spectators.[42]

Pondering 'Our Fear of Death and Desire for Immortality', F. H. Bradley, whose thinking here is ample as ever, concluded that we are deeply confused.

---

[38] Bombaugh, *Oddities and Curiosities*, ed. Gardner, 256–7.

[39] Beckett left untranslated the poem in which he suggested as much (*Collected Poems*, 82):

> plus loin un autre commémore
> Caroline Hay Taylor
> fidèle à sa philosophie
> qu'espoir il y a tant qu'il y a vie
> d'Irlande elle s'enfuit aux cieux
> en août mil neuf cent trente-deux

[40] See p. 120 above.

[41] Beckett took Berkeley's gnome and placed it at the head of the scenario for *Film* (1963).

[42] See p. 43 above.

This conclusion is obscured by the weakness of our imagination, and by this I mean our difficulty in realizing what elements are and what are not actually present in our object. There is a constant tendency to import into the object feelings and ideas which are incompatible with that object, and may even have been formally excluded from its being. And to this tendency we, many of us, seem a helpless prey. Thus, to shrink from pain and from partial annihilation is rational, while, if the annihilation really is total, there is nothing either to shrink or to shrink from. Our fear comes from imagining ourselves present where we are explicitly set down as absent. What we actually fear is the process where that which clings to itself is rudely torn away and apart; while, on the other hand, the pain of sheer negation is an inconsistent and illusory idea. At sunset where, sunk before our eyes,

> Le soleil s'est noyé dans son sang qui se fige,

we listen in our hearts to the complaining of

> Un cœur tendre qui hait le néant vaste et noir,
> Du passé lumineux recueille tout vestige.

But once the heart has ceased to beat, it is but folly to dream that it feels. And again to suppose that I seek *merely* 'to go on' after death, while at the same time I refuse to 'go on' as another man, seems (to use plain words) to be something like stupidity. For obviously I am here desiring for myself a great deal more than merely to 'go on'.[43]

It is not just the pertinence to Beckett ('I can't go on, I'll go on') which makes me feel such gratitude to Bradley for his lucid poignancy. How chastened the accents, and how perfect the sunset.[44] Yet even Bradley, for all his wisdom, cannot escape the enmeshing contradictions. For what in the world is *partial annihilation*? So that when the next sentence arrives at 'if the annihilation really is total', a reader who honours Bradley for his wonted stringency will have to ask of him how *annihilation* could ever be anything other than *total*?

The dilemma is the old one. When annihilation is, as it has to be, total, then we cannot imagine it. And when we imagine 'partial annihilation', we may succeed in imagining all right, but it is not annihilation that we are imagining.

If it were not that philosophers have to set their faces pro-

---

[43] 'Supplementary Note B' to ch. XV of *Essays on Truth and Reality* (1914), 456–7. Bradley quotes Baudelaire, 'Harmonie du soir'.

[44] See p. 119 above.

fessionally against bulls, I should say that Bradley effects a bull when he says that 'to shrink from pain and from partial annihilation is rational'. That way of putting it is not rational.

The poets have made play with the paradoxes, whether Rochester in 'Upon Nothing', or Marvell in 'The Garden':

> Mean while the Mind, from pleasure less,
> Withdraws into its happiness:
> The Mind, that Ocean where each kind
> Does streight its own resemblance find;
> Yet it creates, transcending these,
> Far other Worlds, and other Seas;
> Annihilating all that's made
> To a green Thought in a green Shade.

It is with the utmost dexterity that the humble word *To* performs its duty here, the duty of holding together (straight and strait) the acknowledged totality of annihilation and the glimpsed chimera of partial annihilation. For 'To a green Thought' is famously sly. Does the couplet mean 'Annihilating all that's made | [In comparison] To a green Thought in a green Shade'? Or 'Annihilating all's that made | [Down] To a green Thought in a green Shade'? For a thought is not exactly a something, and is not exactly made.

Marvell never blunders. And a blunder, an impercipience, may sometimes move us as no perfect feat could. Coleridge, fascinated by the bull, limns the meeting of time, eternity, death, and human sorrow in a tender blunder.

Grave stones tell truth ~~yet~~ scarce 40 years—that ⟨many⟩ an Oak if it could but tell the birthday of its Grandfather might laugh to scorn the heraldry of our oldest families are cold consolations to the Student of Perpetuity, even in the dead & so even ~~lasting~~ living languages—'A little while to perpetuate my memory' Mrs Cowley's instructive Bull in Tiverton Church Yard, on the Tomb of her Daughter— [45]

Coleridge clearly finds this bull not only instructive but touching, as he should. His revision of *lasting* into *living* ('even in the dead & so even ~~lasting~~ living languages') is likewise instructive. And as to perpetuity, Moran knows not only what perpetuity is but what a plot is:

[45] *The Notebooks of Samuel Taylor Coleridge*, ed. Kathleen Coburn, iii (1973), entry 4371 (1817–18).

Some twenty paces from my wicket-gate the lane skirts the graveyard wall. The lane descends, the wall rises, higher and higher. Soon you are faring below the dead. It is there I have my plot in perpetuity. As long as the earth endures that spot is mine, in theory.

It is a great thing to own a plot in perpetuity, a very great thing indeed. If only that were the only perpetuity.[46]

But then, 'as long as the earth endures': what kind of perpetuity is that?

Napoleon, resisting flattery for once, enquired what his immortality of fame was estimated at, and being told about eight hundred years, snorted 'Bah! telle immortalité'.

'A little while to perpetuate my memory': this is not remote from the thought to which Beckett gave expression, a cousin to 'partial annihilation', *relative immortality*.

The mortal microcosm cannot forgive the relative immortality of the macrocosm. The whisky bears a grudge against the decanter.[47]

The absurdity of such a grudge is at one with the absurdity of positing relative immortality. But with Beckett's commentators, it is harder to be sure that they have noticed how they have just put it: 'a story, then stories within the story and meta-stories around them, and so almost *ad infinitum*'.[48] Hard to tell which is harder to imagine, infinity or things proceeding 'almost *ad infinitum*'.

Ad infinitum is a turn we owe to that oddly living thing, a dead language. According to Bombaugh, Dr Johnson once let slip a bull here:

Every monumental inscription should be in Latin; for that being a dead language, it will always live.[49]

---

[46] *Molloy*, 145, 187. Following *Molloy* in French, 208–9:

A quelque vingtaine de pas de mon guichet la ruelle se met à longer le mur du cimetière. La ruelle descend, le mur s'élève de plus en plus. Passé un certain point on chemine plus bas que les morts. C'est là que j'ai ma concession à perpétuité. Tant que durera la terre, cette place sera à moi, en principe.

And p. 269:

C'est beau d'avoir une concession à perpétuité. C'est une bien belle chose. S'il n'y avait que cette perpétuité-là.

[47] *Proust*, 10.

[48] Andrew Kennedy, *Samuel Beckett* (1989), 138.

[49] Bombaugh, *Oddities and Curiosities*, ed. Gardner, 255. I have not traced this bull in Johnson, though the sentiment is his; 'Dr. Johnson said, the inscription should have

But then the bull is naturally entangled in perplexities of life and death.

To a gentleman who expressed himself in disrespectful terms of Blackmore, one of whose poetick bulls he happened just then to recollect, Dr. Johnson answered,—I hope, Sir, a blunder, after you have heard what I shall relate, will not be reckoned decisive against a poet's reputation: When I was a young man, I translated Addison's Latin poem on the Battle of the Pigmies and the Cranes, and must plead guilty to the following couplet:

> Down from the guardian boughs the nests they flung,
> And kill'd the yet unanimated young.

And yet I trust I am no blockhead. I afterwards changed the word *kill'd* into *crush'd*.[50]

Perhaps *kill'd* was a mere blunder; perhaps it was what is sometimes better, a bull. For birds' eggs which have been fertilized both are and are not animated. So that *crush'd* is more flat than *kill'd*. The abortive has gone.

Boswell was likewise moved to defend Blackmore; not, though by inculpating himself for a similar blunder, but by exculpating Sir Richard.

I defended Blackmore's supposed lines, which have been ridiculed as absolute nonsense:

> 'A painted vest Prince Voltiger had on,
> Which from a naked Pict his grandsire won.'

I maintained it to be a poetical conceit. A Pict being painted, if he is slain in battle, and a vest is made of his skin, it is a painted vest won from him, though he was naked.[51]

---

been in Latin, as every thing intended to be universal and permanent, should be' (Boswell, *The Tour to the Hebrides*; *Life*, ed. Birkbeck and Powell, v. 154). On Beckett and dead languages, see the opening of Chapter 3, above.

[50] *Poems*, ed. E. L. McAdam, Jr., with George Milne (1964), 22; quoting George Steevens, from *St. James's Chronicle*, 15 Jan. 1785. The editors note: 'Since the newly recovered poem reads "crush'd" (l. 49), it is clear that the change was made while Johnson was at Stourbridge, and perhaps because his blunder was pointed out by his schoolmaster.'

[51] Boswell's *Life of Johnson*, ed. Birkbeck Hill and Powell, ii. 108; 27 Oct. 1769. In the introduction to their *Essay on Irish Bulls*, the Edgeworths brand these lines of Blackmore's 'a laughable confusion of ideas', merely.

Such is the rescue of a bull. But notice here too the matters of life
and death, the extra layer of skin, dead but living on. Beckett's
Moran was leather-wise:

My boots became rigid, from lack of proper care. So skin defends itself,
when dead and tanned. The air coursed through them freely, preserving
perhaps my feet from freezing.[52]

The skin of Moran's boots is sympathized with, doing no more
after all than defend itself in the only way known to it; the
cadence is heroic-elegiac, Shakespearean even: 'So skin defends
itself, when dead and tanned'. Whereupon, grateful as ever for
small mercies, a Beckett character acknowledges that even here he
may be not only victim but beneficiary: 'The air coursed through
them freely, preserving perhaps my feet from freezing.' All things
work together for good to them that love God.

The vanity of human wishes may be seized in a momentary
absurdity:

> With listless Eyes the Dotard views the Store,
> He views, and wonders that they please no more;
> Now pall the tastless Meats, and joyless Wines,
> And Luxury with Sighs her Slave resigns.
>
> (*The Vanity of Human Wishes*, 263–6)

If they are *tasteless* and *joyless*, the meats and wines, how then can
they *pall*? Compacting the tenses (which would expand as: Now
pall into tastelessness what had been tasty meats), the bull captures
the moment ('Now pall') of grim metamorphosis, and skewers the
hedonism which once mistakenly supposed that true taste and true
joy could be found in epicureanism. Such palling is a kind of
death, a foretaste of it; the suppliant

> shuns to know,
> That Life protracted is protracted Woe.
>
> (*The Vanity of Human Wishes*, 257–8)

Life can be living death. The Edgeworths, keen to defend the
Irish bull by adducing English freaks and sports of language, were
not afraid to call as witnesses Milton, Pope, and Shakespeare.

---

[52] *Molloy*, 183. Following *Molloy* in French, 264:

Mes chaussures se firent raides, faute d'entretien. C'est la façon de se défendre de la peau
morte et tannée. L'air y circulait librement, empêchant peut-être mes pieds de geler.

One step further in hyperbole is reserved for him, who, being buried, carries about his own sepulchre.

> 'To live a life half dead, a living death,
> And buried; but oh, yet more miserable!
> Myself my sepulchre, a moving grave!'

No person, if he heard this passage for the first time from the lips of an Irishman, could hesitate to call it a series of bulls; yet these lines are part of the beautiful complaint of Samson Agonistes on his blindness. Such are the hyperboles sanctioned by the genius, or, what with some judges may have more influence, the name of Milton. The bounds which separate sublimity from bombast, and absurdity from wit, are as fugitive as the boundaries of taste. Only those who are accustomed to examine and appraise literary goods are sensible of the prodigious change that can be made in their apparent value by a slight change in the manufacture. The absurdity of a man's swearing he was killed, or declaring that he is now dead in a ditch, is revolting to common sense; yet the *living death* of Dapperwit, in the 'Rape of the Lock,' is not absurd, but witty; and representing men as dying many times before their death is in Shakspeare sublime:

> 'Cowards die many times before their death;
> The brave can never taste of death but once.'

The most direct contradictions in words do not (*in English writers*) destroy the effect of irony, wit, pathos, or sublimity.[53]

As a writer exacerbatedly sensitive to living death, Beckett appreciates that it is not only cowards who die many times before their death.

And he realises with horror that his grandmother is dead, long since and many times, that the cherished familiar of his mind, mercifully composed all along the years by the solicitude of habitual memory, exists no longer, that this mad old woman, drowsing over her book, overburdened with years, flushed and coarse and vulgar, is a stranger whom he has never seen.[54]

Too bleak for a bull, this, but in the same field.

For the blatancy of a death-based bull, A. E. Housman is the man. 'Of an argument that had no sense in it he wrote: "I shall

---

[53] *Essay on Irish Bulls*, ch. VI.
[54] *Proust*, 15.

never understand it—not if I live till I die".[55] Housman, 'the lover of the grave', so keen in the detection of nonsense in classical studies, and in the creation of nonsense verse, relished the nonsensical acumen of the Irish bull.[56] To his brother Basil Housman, he wrote at the festive costive costly season:

Don't trouble to acknowledge what my banker sends to yours at the New Year,—unless he doesn't as the Irishman would say.[57]

Housman relished blasphemy no less. His 'Fragment of a Greek Tragedy' is itself something of a blasphemy, since it scores not only off the ruling translators but off the plays themselves; and its opening incarnates a bull, one peculiarly appropriate to the dramatic medium, since, as Ezra Pound insisted, the medium of drama is not words but persons moving about on a stage using words:

> *Chorus*:   O suitably attired in leather boots
> Head of a traveller, wherefore seeking whom
> Whence by what way how purposed art thou come
> To this well-nightingaled vicinity?
> My object in inquiring is to know.
> But if you happen to be deaf and dumb
> And do not understand a word I say,
> Nod with your hand to signify as much.[58]

This is delicious. To prompt Housman to a more acerb bull, it takes the absurd mistake of ever having been born. His is a vision of non-existent happiness.

> Sweat ran and blood sprang out and I was never sorry:
> Then it was well with me, in days ere I was born.
>
> (*A Shropshire Lad* XLVIII)
>
> But I will go where they are hid
> That never were begot,

---

[55] Laurence Housman, *A.E.H.* (1937), 90–1.

[56] ' "I am not a bird" said the Irishman "to be in two places at once"; and it is another injustice to his distressful country that we call this speech a bull. The bird which is in two places at once is the Virgilian swan.' Housman, 'A Note on Virgil', *The Classical Papers of A. E. Housman*, ed. J. Diggle and F. R. D. Goodyear (1972), i. 348.

[57] 29 Dec. 1927; *The Letters of A. E. Housman*, ed. Henry Maas (1971), 257.

[58] Written and published 1883; *Collected Poems and Selected Prose*, ed. Christopher Ricks (1988), 236.

To my inheritance amid
    The nation that is not.

    (*More Poems* II)

Finest of these profound absurdities, meeting what is for Housman the absurdity of life with the courage of a bull, is what he was moved to make of the great apophthegm in *Oedipus Coloneus*. It is better to be dead than alive, best of all never to have been born.[59] In Housman's translation, this becomes immitigably other.

> Thy portion esteem I highest,
>   Who wast not ever begot;
> Thine next, being born who diest
>   And straightway again art not.

It is remarkable how the simple addition of direct address ('Thy portion ... Thine next'), which is *not* in the Greek, promptly converts Sophocles into an Irishman. Thy bull esteem I highest, Housman.

THE BULL, IDENTITY, AND POSTERITY

Horace Walpole identified a favourite of his.

I will give you what I call the king of bulls. An Irish baronet, walking out with a gentleman who told me the story, was met by his nurse, who requested charity. The baronet exclaimed vehemently, 'I will give you nothing. You played me a scandalous trick in my infancy.' The old woman, in amazement, asked him what injury she had done him? He answered, 'I was a fine boy, and you changed me.'
    In this bull even personal identity is confounded![60]

The Edgeworths report Walpole's happiness, and then venture slyly upon the philosophical niceties which vex the relationships.

---

[59] See pp. 10–11. There is a very different weight to the Gnomic Verses of Theognis. In Dudley Fitts's translation (*From the Greek Anthology* (1957), 72):

> The best of all things it were, never to be born,
> Never to know the light of the strong sharp sun;
> But being born,
> The best of all is to pass as soon as may be
> To Hadês' gate,
>   there to lie dead,
> Lost, locked close beneath the world's huge weight.

[60] *Walpoliana* (1819), 74–5.

Lord Orford particularly admires this bull, because in the confusion of
the blunderer's ideas he is not clear even of his personal identity.
Philosophers will not perhaps be so ready as his lordship has been to call
this a blunder of the first magnitude. Those who have never been
initiated into the mysteries of metaphysics may have the presumptuous
ignorance to fancy that they understand what is meant by the common
words *I*, or *me*; but the able metaphysician knows better than Lord
Orford's changeling how to prove, to our satisfaction, that we know
nothing of the matter.

'Personal identity,' says Locke, 'consists not in the identity of substance,
but in the identity of consciousness'.

—and so into the Edgeworths' gallant and only half-ironical claim
that 'there was no continuity of identity between the infant and
the man who expressed his hatred of the nurse for perpetrating
the fraud'.[61]

But the strong case for such an inspired fatuity or quasi-fatuity
is not that it is not really, upon reflection, absurd at all, but that its
absurdity is telling. 'When first I saw you I thought it was you, but
now I see it is your brother.' It will be a dour world which feels
compelled to find such an observation either simply sensible or
simply senseless. Beckett is more capacious.

He acknowledges having effaced himself more and more from his work.
SB: Finally one no longer knows who is speaking. The subject disappears completely. That's where the crisis of identity ends.[62]

Or, less schematic, there is the world of Beckett's art (as against
his rare wan comments on it), where the crisis of identity is often
happy to end not in solemnity but in comedy, sometimes in a bull.
As when a dead dog, its uncrisised identity now over, is buried:

It was she put him in the hole, though I was the gentleman. For I cannot
stoop, neither can I kneel, because of my infirmity, and if ever I stoop,
forgetting who I am, or kneel, make no mistake, it will not be me, but
another.[63]

---

[61] *Essay on Irish Bulls*, ch. I.
[62] Conversation with Charles Juliet, 1975; *TriQuarterly*, 77 (1989–90), 22; trans.
Suzanne Chamier.
[63] *Molloy*, 48. Following *Molloy* in French, 53:

Ce fut elle qui le mit dans le trou, moi je ne peux pas me pencher, ni m'agenouiller, à cause
de mon infirmité, et si jamais cela m'arrive, oublieux de mon personnage, de me pencher ou
de m'agenouiller, n'en croyez rien, ce ne sera pas moi, mais un autre.

Nothing in the French about Molloy's being 'the gentleman', perhaps because the

The bull is constituted partly of extinction, since it is self-extinguishing; partly of procreation, since the bull always begets a further round or two of thought, while often breeding a new bull; and jointly of posterity and the preposterous. 'What has posterity done for me, that I should do so much for posterity?'[64] In proffering this, the Edgeworths may have taken quiet pleasure in the fact that their book, by daughter and father, was itself an incarnation of posterity.

But always the bull strikes awe, even if only at its own fatuity. The Augustan compendium of such moments is, famously, *The Art of Sinking in Poetry* (1727):

So astonishing as these are, they yield to the following, which is *Profundity* itself,

> None but *Himself* can be his Parallel.
>
> Theobald, *Double Distress*.

unless it may seem borrow'd from the Thought of that *Master of a Show* in *Smithfield*, who writ in large Letters, over the Picture of his Elephant,

This is the greatest Elephant in the World, except Himself.[65]

Yet the thought of profundity, however ironically introduced ('*Profundity* itself'), refuses to go quietly. Sydney Smith, who wrote with characteristic brilliance about the Edgeworths' Essay, sought to assure himself that 'it certainly is not very necessary that a writer should be profound on the subject of bulls'.[66] But the

thought is not French, and is not the same as his being the man about the place.

[64] Quoted by the Edgeworths, ch. X: 'the same sort of humour and sophistry that appears in the Irishman's celebrated question'.

[65] *The Art of Sinking in Poetry*, ch. VII; *Selected Prose of Alexander Pope*, ed. Hammond, 182. In *The Dunciad* (1728, iii. 271–2), Pope savaged Theobald's line:

> For works like these let deathless Journals tell,
> 'None but Thy self can be thy parallel'.

Dr. Johnson genially took the absurdity up within his great affection for Mrs. Thrale's Streatham:

This is the course of my life. You do not think it much makes me forget Streatham. However it is good to wander a little, lest one should dream that all the world was Streatham, of which one may venture to say *None but itself can be its parallel*. (29 May 1779; *Letters*, ed. Redford, iii. 166)

[66] *Edinburgh Review* (1803); *Works* (1839), i. 71.

Edgeworths had seized the bull. They were not intimidated by
Paradise Lost:

Englishman.—'And in Paradise Lost we have, to speak in *fashionable*
language, two *famous* bulls. Talking of Satan, Milton says,

> "God and his Son except,
> Created thing nought valued he nor shunn'd."

And speaking of Adam and Eve, and their sons and daughters, he
confounds them all together in a manner for which any Irishman would
have been laughed to scorn:—

> "Adam, the goodliest man of men since born,
> His sons; the fairest of her daughters Eve."

Yet Addison, who notices these blunders, calls them only little blemishes.'

(ch. XII)

But Milton knew that it was his duty, though not to court, yet to
accept, the accusation of blasphemy. The Edgeworths in their
turn risk blaspheming against Milton when they suppose him to
be blaspheming against the Trinity.

Can the Creator be further understood under the auspice of the
created, and his Son likewise? Samuel Butler flippantly flipped
Pope's line so that it became 'An honest God's the noblest work
of man'. Samuel Beckett more darkly compressed his mind.

Devised deviser devising it all for company. In the same figment dark
as his figments.[67]

As for the second of the Edgeworths' '*famous* bulls' from Milton,
it too is about creation and birth, and it might be judged to catch
as no other poet has done the mystery by which we stand uniquely
to these forebears, and they to themselves.

> So hand in hand they passd, the lovliest pair
> That ever since in loves imbraces met,
> *Adam* the goodliest man of men since born
> His Sons, the fairest of her Daughters *Eve.*

(*Paradise Lost*, iv. 321–4)

---

[67] *Company*, 64. Preceding and following (see ch. 2 n. 34) *Compagnie*, 63:

Imaginant imaginé imaginant le tout pour se tenir compagnie. Dans le même noir
chimérique que ses autres chimères.

This may be a bull, or it may be the apprehension of a mystery, this sense that Eve was not simply fairer than her daughters but was the fairest of her daughters. 'That ever since ... since born': Milton knows what he is doing when he takes our unimaginable relationship with Adam and Eve, and acknowledges it, with entire equanimity, as beyond the reach of our knowledge and of our imagination.

The great Irishman James Henry (classical scholar, doctor, crusader against the cruel god, and poet) declined to let Milton's bull pass. The unrelenting permutation-games of Beckett are anticipated in Henry's happily obdurate poem of 1858.

> 'Adam, the goodliest man of men since born
> His sons, the fairest of her daughters Eve.'
>
> PARADISE LOST, IV, 323.

So father Adam was his own born son,
And her own fairest daughter, mother Eve:
And father Adam was his own sons' brother,
And sister of her daughters, mother Eve.
And father Adam of himself was father,
And mother of herself was mother Eve:
And father Adam was his own grandfather,
And great grandfather, and great great grandfather,
And great great great grandfather—without end:
And mother Eve was her own grandmother,
And great grandmother, and great great grandmother,
And great great great grandmother—without end.
But mother Eve was father Adam's wife,
And father Adam's sons were mother Eve's,
So mother Eve was father Adam's mother,
And grandmother of father Adam's sons,
And grandmother of father Adam's self,
And great grandmother, and great great grandmother,
And great great great grandmother—without end.
And father Adam—being the lawful husband
Of mother Eve, and father of her daughters—
Was mother Eve's own father and grandfather,
And great grandfather, and great great grandfather,
And great great great grandfather—without end.
And mother Eve was father Adam's sister,
Aunt and grand-aunt and niece and cousin-german;
And father Adam, mother Eve's own brother,

> Uncle, grand-uncle, nephew, and full cousin.
> And father Adam was his own sons' cousin;
> And cousin of her daughters, mother Eve:
> And father Adam's sons and mother Eve's
> Daughters were cousins, all, among each other,
> And, intermarrying had sons and daughters,
> Goodliest of whom was still old father Adam,
> Fairest of whom was still old mother Eve.[68]

This levels its own absurd dignity at Milton's dignified absurdity. But the cursed mutterings of *Watt* grate on their scrannel windpipes.

And the poor old lousy old earth, my earth and my father's and my mother's and my father's father's and my mother's mother's and my father's mother's and my mother's father's and my father's mother's father's and my mother's father's mother's and my father's mother's mother's and my mother's father's father's and my father's father's mother's and my mother's mother's father's and my father's father's father's and my mother's mother's mother's and other people's fathers' and mothers' and fathers' fathers' and mothers' mothers' and fathers' mothers' and mothers' fathers' and fathers' mothers' fathers' and mothers' fathers' mothers' and fathers' mothers' mothers' and mothers' fathers' fathers' and fathers' fathers' mothers' and mothers' mothers' fathers' and fathers' fathers' fathers' and mothers' mothers' mothers'. An excrement.[69]

The line stretches back to the crack of doom. There are life and death in the chain, and repetition intimate with mortality.

Repetition as it stands to death is pondered by Neil Hertz in a

---

[68] *Poematia* (1866). For a gentler, elegiac, way with these vistas, see another poem of James Henry's, 'Another and another and another' (1854), in *The New Oxford Book of Victorian Verse*, ed. Christopher Ricks (1987), 331–2.

[69] *Watt*, 46–7. Preceding *Watt* in French, trans. Ludovic and Agnès Janvier in collaboration with Beckett, 47:

Et cette pauvre vieille pouilleuse de vieille terre, la mienne et celle de mon père et de ma mère et du père de mon père et de la mère de ma mère et de la mère de mon père et du père de ma mère et du père de la mère de mon père et de la mère du père de ma mère et de la mère de la mère de mon père et du père de la mère de ma mère et de la mère du père de mon père et du père de la mère de ma mère et du père du père de mon père et de la mère de la mère de ma mère et des pères et mères d'autres infortunés et des pères de leurs pères et des mères de leurs mères et des mères de leurs pères et des pères de leurs mères et des pères des mères de leurs pères et des mères des pères de leurs mères et des mères des pères de leurs pères et des pères des mères de leurs mères et des mères des pères de leurs pères et des pères des pères de leurs mères et des mères des pères de leurs pères et des pères des mères de leurs mères et des pères des pères de leurs pères et des mères des mères de leurs mères. Une immondice.

book with the grimly hopeful title *The End of the Line*. Hertz considers the relation in Freud of the 'compulsion to repeat' to his understanding of death:

> When, in *Beyond the Pleasure Principle*, Freud developed his more abstract conception of a compulsion to repeat and argued for the existence of 'death instincts' . . . he was obliged to acknowledge that evidence for such an instinctive force was hard to find: the drive was, in his words, never 'visible,' it 'eluded perception' except (he added in *Civilization and its Discontents*) when it was 'tinged or colored' by sexuality.[70]

The colour of sexuality in that permutant passage from *Watt* is black; the death instinct, virulently repetitive, sees life itself (lurking and working in all those predecessors) as an excrement, a black humour. At conception, life is sifted out from one body into the other, and in due course a baby is sifted out from a body into the world. An excrement. A posteriority.

Yet it is only a short step from the Freudian sublime to the genially ridiculous. As the haggard parent of a new-born baby, I was once given this Irish-American advice: Sleep every waking moment.

COLERIDGE AND THE BULL

The greatest thinker to be preoccupied by the bull was Coleridge, who was drawn to confront its oddity in many realms of literary thought: in his domestic records, in his critical speculation, and in his political engagement. He appreciated that poetic hyperbole of any kind is close kin to the bull. Yet is this the kinship of legitimacy or of bastardy? Is the bull akin as itself one form of poetry, or as a travesty of the poetic imagination, perhaps a blasphemy upon poetry?

A mere record of comings and goings could prompt Coleridge here. In 1802 he anticipated Wordsworth's arrival with his wife and sister. But how to convey their impossible position, hurried and harried?

> If they stay longer than tomorrow they will call—if not, you will be good enough to consider this as a mere accident—as their *apparitions* only— for in truth they hoped to have concealed their rapid *in and out* even from

[70] *The End of the Line* (1985), 100.

themselves, by way of a poetic Hyperbole which often borders very near on an Irish Bull, you know.[71]

But it was not friends, it was children, who showed themselves most at home with the self-contradictions of the bull, and this because of the endemic contradictoriness of children. It is not only Mary who is quite contrary.

Derwent (Nov. 6. Tea time) came in, & all the *Cake* was eat up, & he way by no means willing to accept dry Toast & butter as a Substitute. 'Don't eat all the Cake!'—Well, we will not tomorrow!—'O but don't eat the Cake! You have eat the cake! O but don't eat up all the cakes!'— His Passion had compleatly confounded his Sense of Time, & its Consequences—He saw that it was done; & yet he passionately entreated you not to do it—& not for the time to come/but for the Present & the Past. 'O but you have! O but don't now!'—This Mem. for ~~my~~ the effect of the Passions on the reasoning power imprimis in producing *Bulls*

Derwent's *Bull* from eager Desire & Disappointment [. . .]—at the same time I noticed the remarkable disposition of all Children of his Age, who are any way kindly treated, to *contradict*—the pleasure they find in it/when there is any plausibility in their own counterassertion it often rises into passion & self-willedness; when none, it is *fun*—& *wit*—. It hangs in a String with their love of calling white black, &c. as Derwent when he had scarce a score of words in his whole Tonguedom comes holding up a pair of filthy Pawlets, & lisps—Here's *clean white* Hands!— & then laughed immoderately.[72]

Bulls, like childish contrarinesses, are 'their own counterassertion', where passion and self-willedness hang in a string with fun and wit. But Coleridge knew that the man was father of the child, and that he himself was prey to bulls. He dreamed of a child of his being contrary again (Hartley this time), and of God, and of time ticking away, and he understood that bulls share the nature of dreams:

Frid. Morn. 5 o'clock—Dosing, dreamt of Hartley as at his Christening— how as he was asked who redeemed him, & was to say, God the Son/he went on, humming and hawing, in one hum & haw, like a boy who knows a thing & will not make the effort to recollect it—so as to irritate me greatly. Awakening ⟨gradually I ~~found~~ I was able compleatly to detect,

---

[71] To William Calvert, 13 Oct. 1802; *Collected Letters*, ed. E. L. Griggs, vi (1971), 1015.

[72] *Notebooks*, ed. K. Coburn, i (1957), entries 1643 and 1645; Nov. 1803.

that⟩ it was the Ticking of my Watch which lay in the Pen Place in my Desk on the round Table close by my Ear, & which in the ~~nervous~~ diseased State of my Nerves had *fretted* on my Ears—I caught the fact while ~~it~~ Hartley's Face & moving Lips were yet before my Eyes, & his Hum & Ha, & the Ticking of the Watch were each the other, as often happens in the passing off of Sleep—that curious modification of Ideas by each other, which is the Element of *Bulls*.—I arose instantly, & wrote it down—it is now 10 minutes past 5.[73]

The bull is an inspired act of contradiction (inspired by and to contradiction), and is alive with naïve acumen; it is therefore for Coleridge—and for all who follow him in this—naturally childlike and preternaturally poetic.

Childlike, and thereby in a close affinity with poetry, at least for so great a Romantic as Coleridge.

The bull namely consists in the bringing together two incompatible thoughts, with the *sensation*, but without the *sense*, of their connection. The psychological condition, or that which constitutes the possibility of this state, being such disproportionate vividness of two distant thoughts, as extinguishes or obscures the consciousness of the intermediate images or conceptions, or wholly abstracts the attention from them. Thus in the well known bull, '*I was a fine child, but they changed me;*' the first conception expressed in the word '*I*,' is that of personal identity—*Ego contemplans*: the second expressed in the word '*me*,' is the visual image or object by which the mind represents to itself its past condition, or rather, its personal identity under the form in which it imagined itself previously to have existed.—Ego contemplatus. Now the change of one visual image for another involves in itself no absurdity, and becomes absurd only by its immediate juxta-position with the first thought, which is rendered possible by the whole attention being successively absorbed in each singly, so as not to notice the interjacent notion, 'changed' which by its incongruity with the first thought, '*I*,' constitutes the bull. Add only, that this process is facilitated by the circumstance of the words '*I*,' and '*me*,' being sometimes equivalent, and sometimes having a distinct meaning; sometimes, namely, signifying the act of self-consciousness, sometimes the external image in and by which the mind represents that act to itself, the result and symbol of its individuality. Now suppose the direct contrary state, and you will have a distinct sense of the connection between two conceptions, without that *sensation* of such connection which is

---

[73] *Notebooks*, i, entry 1620.

supplied by habit. The man *feels*, as if he were standing on his head, though he cannot but *see*, that he is truly standing on his feet.[74]

This is profound, not only in the justified seriousness with which it takes the bull (rather as the modern thinker about perception has come to take optical illusions very seriously), but also in the details of its wording: for instance, 'conceptions' twice as the nub, and 'extinguished' too. The one point at which Coleridge must be challenged is his determination that, in the bull, the attention is wholly abstracted from the incongruity—'so as not to notice'. The bull, certainly the bull of penetrative power, leaves it profoundly uncertain what kind or degree of noticing is active. That is its point.

Yet in the same year that saw the publication of *Biographia Literaria*, with its puzzled admiration of the bull, Coleridge's *Lay Sermon* associated the capricious thing with blasphemy against order and government.

For mobs have no memories. They are in nearly the same state as that of an individual when he makes (what is termed) *a Bull*. The passions, like a fused metal, fill up the wide interstices of thought, and supply the defective links: and thus incompatible assertions are harmonized by the *sensation*, without the *sense*, of connection.[75]

But, for a different political sympathy, the bull might be associated with a different philosophy, since the bull has its dialectic: first, on the face of it, sense; then nonsense or non-sense; but then, it may be, a further sense. This is genuinely a dialectic, and would make for a politics of the dialectic such as is sometimes genuine.

The Irish bull has even been invoked by the editor of Coleridge's

---

[74] *Biographia Literaria*, ed. James Engell and W. Jackson Bate (1983), i. 72–3; ch. 4. For the 'well known bull', see p. 181 above.
[75] *A Lay Sermon* (1817); *Lay Sermons*, ed. R. J. White (1972), 153. Compare the earlier political nightmare of Coleridge:

here French faces, some with red caps and with crosses, and behind them an Hibernian variety of the Centaur genus, composed of a deranged man and a mad *bull*;

The Courier, 31 Aug. 1811; *Essays on His Times*, ed. David V. Erdman (1978), ii. 269. The Centaur phantasmagorically becomes a Minotaur. Erdman notes: 'a double pun on an Irish bull and the papal bull of 1648 after the massacre granting absolution to all Irish who had taken up arms in the cause of the Catholic faith'.

notebooks to suggest why Coleridge may have jotted something down in the first place.

All the Linen at the Bridgewater Arms mark'd 'Stoln from the Bridgwater Arms.'

[Ed.] Noted as an example of an Irish bull?[76]

Property is theft.

SYDNEY SMITH AND THE IRISH

The Edgeworths' *Essay on Irish Bulls* (1802) is a wise and witty work of humane protest, an anthology and an argument. It moved Sydney Smith to good-natured dissent. He makes you think, not least because of his clarity and his freedom from misgivings.

Though the question is not a very easy one, we shall venture to say, that a bull is an apparent congruity, and real incongruity, of ideas, suddenly discovered. And if this account of bulls be just, they are (as might have been supposed) the very reverse of wit; for as wit discovers real relations, that are not apparent, bulls admit apparent relations that are not real. The pleasure arising from wit proceeds from our surprise at suddenly discovering two things to be similar, in which we suspected no similarity. The pleasure arising from bulls proceeds from our discovering two things to be dissimilar, in which a resemblance might have been suspected.

In both these cases of bulls, the one verbal, the other practical, there is an apparent congruity, and real incongruity of ideas. In both the cases of wit, there is an apparent incongruity and a real relation.[77]

But Smith's lucidity conceals from him and from his readers that the bull may know what it is up to when it muddies the waters. Or that it prompts a further round of thought, by which the apparent congruity, succeeded by a real incongruity, then issues in an unexpected congruity.

Smith suffuses, both in class terms and in national terms, a simple superiority: so the bull may bring together 'two actions, which more correct understandings immediately perceive to have no relation at all':

---

[76] *Notebooks*, ed. K. Coburn, ii (1961), entry 3024; Feb.–May 1807. Compare John Sparrow's insistence that a sign which says 'Put Your Litter Here' ought to say 'Put Here What, If You Threw It on the Ground, Would Be Litter'.

[77] *Works*, i. 66–7, 69.

A great deal of the pleasure experienced from bulls, proceeds from the sense of superiority in ourselves. Bulls which we invented, or knew to be invented, might please, but in a less degree, for want of this additional zest.

As there must be apparent connexion, and real incongruity, it is seldom that a man of sense and education finds any form of words by which he is conscious that he might have been deceived into a bull.[78]

But this is complaisant, even complacent. He values the Edgeworths' *Essay*, as he should, for its humanity, but his own humanity is coloured with condescension, towards both the Edgeworths and the Irish at large, so that his closing words are exasperatingly unruffled:

Whatever be the deficiencies of the book, they are, in our estimation, amply atoned for by its merits; by none more, than that lively feeling of compassion which pervades it for the distresses of the wild, kind-hearted, blundering poor of Ireland.

It is true, as Brian Earls has noticed, that the Edgeworths are themselves caught within something of a contradiction:

Edgeworth attempted to clear the Irish from the charge of making bulls by arguing that these are to be found in all countries and that those of other nations have been attributed to the Irish. Simultaneously, if somewhat contradictorily, he suggested that Irish bulls are to be explained by reference to specifically Irish circumstances and verbal habits.[79]

This is too cagey ('if somewhat contradictorily') and is not open enough to catch the bull's—and therefore bull-study's—pleasure in contradiction. The same goes for Earls's over-cautious remarking such a thing in William Carleton in 1843:

The passage might initially appear to contain an element of self-contradiction in that Carleton simultaneously denies the existence and explains the origins of the bull.[80]

As with many an ethnic stereotyping, one question is Who is outwitting Whom? The Irish bull is constituted of pressure, such

[78] *Works*, i. 67, 69.
[79] *Béaloideas* (1988), 13. It is to be regretted that Sydney Smith speaks as if Richard Lovell Edgeworth alone had written the *Essay*. It is also to be regretted that recent literary historians have taken to speaking as if Maria Edgeworth alone had written it. She herself said: 'no book was ever written more completely in partnership'. *Memoirs of Richard Lovell Edgeworth* (1820), ii. 336.
[80] *Béaloideas* (1988), 45.

as may amount to oppression, and of resistance. The resistance is genuine, as is the resistance manifested by blasphemy, but it is also *not* revolutionarily resistant any more than blasphemy is, because it too acknowledges realities and is obliged both to manifest and to contain reluctance.

The bull is the resource of a pressed, suppressed, or oppressed people, a people on occasion pretending to be self-subordinated by foolishness so as the better to keep alive a secret self-respect and to be insubordinate and even safely provocative. Safely, because the powerful find themselves presented with a choice between finding you a stupid blunderer and finding you a clever needler— and the powerful will usually choose the former, because it is your stupidity which is held to validate their persisting paternalism. The tactic is a risky one, since in some ways it plays into the hands of the powerful invigilators, and even may confirm their bigotries; and yet it keeps open its communications with the future. It wins its way by yielding to the tide—in the words of a Catholic satirist well aware of the punitive censorship threatened by Sir Robert Walpole.

'The Bliss of Ignorance', the Edgeworths dubbed their chapter V. Where politic ignorance is feigned, or *may* be feigned, it would be folly to seem wise.[81]

Recent Irish turmoil has fathered the great bull, 'Whatever you say say nothing', a graffito which is not only a fine saying in itself but also furnishes the title for a fine poem by Seamus Heaney.

On occasion the English have been suspicious of English self-congratulation:

Mr. Ruskin had no patience, in face of disasters like those of the *London* and the *Captain*, with all the talk about our splendid British seamanship. It was bombastic English blarney—not Irish, for there was always wit in an Irish bull, but only a double blunder in an English one—all that talk about sweeping the fleets of all other nations off the seas.[82]

---

[81] *Mercier and Camier*, 61:

An example of bliss in ignorance, bliss at having recovered an essential good, ignorance of its nature.

Following *Mercier et Camier*, 98:

Ce sera la joie dans l'ignorance (combinaison fréquente, entre parenthèses), la joie d'avoir récupéré un bien essentiel, dans l'ignorance de sa nature.

[82] *The Pleasures of England: The Pleasures of Truth*; the report of a lecture: *Works*, ed. E. T. Cook and Alexander Wedderburn, xxxiii (1908), 508–9.

The generous conviction that 'there was always wit in an Irish bull' is too round; for one thing, the Irish—like anybody else— may sometimes merely blunder, for another the bull, when not a mere blunder, depends on its not being beyond dispute that wit is at work.

The political pains of Ireland have called forth not only violence but friendship, the politics of brotherhood. There can be 'a blasphemy against friendship'.[83] And hence the opportunity for a staunch bull.

'Two Irishmen having travelled on foot from Chester to Barnet, were confoundedly tired and fatigued by their journey; and the more so when they were told that they had still about ten miles to go. "By my shoul and St. Patrick," cries one of them, "it is but five miles a-piece." '

On which the Edgeworths commented handsomely:

Here, notwithstanding the promise of a jest held forth by the words, 'By my shoul and St. Patrick,' we are ultimately cheated of our hopes. To the ignorant, indeed, the word of promise is kept to the mind as well as to the ear; but others perceive that, instead of a bull, they have only a piece of sentimental arithmetic, founded upon the elegant theorem, that friendship doubles all our pleasures, and divides all our pains.[84]

Our hopes of sneering are dashed, or so the Edgeworths hope. And they reinforce this by invoking from *Macbeth* a passage which provides not only what is always a 'double sense', allusion, but also the double sense which attends upon the true bull (could it be a double sense in 'cow'd' which brought these lines to the Edgeworths' mind?):

> Accursed be that tongue that tels mee so;
> For it hath Cow'd my better part of man:
> And be these Jugling Fiends no more beleev'd,
> That palter with us in a double sence,
> That keepe the word of promise to our eare,
> And breake it to our hope.

> (v. viii)

De Quincey found sentimental in the bad sense the Edgeworths' categorizing the Irish exchange as 'a piece of sentimental arithmetic'.

---

[83] See pp. 165–6 above.   [84] *Essay on Irish Bulls*, ch. V.

The idea of a *bull* is even yet undefined; which is most extraordinary, considering that Miss Edgeworth has applied all her tact and illustrative power to furnish the *matter* for such a definition; and Coleridge all his philosophic subtlety (but in this instance, I think, with a most infelicitous result) to furnish its *form*. But both have been too fastidious in their admission of bulls. Thus, for example, Miss Edgeworth rejects, as no true bull, the common Joe Miller story, that, upon two Irishmen reaching Barnet, and being told that it was still twelve miles to London, one of them remarked, "Ah! just six miles *apace*." This, says Miss E., is no bull, but a sentimental remark on the maxim that friendship divides our pains. Nothing of the kind: Miss Edgeworth cannot have understood it. The bull is a true representative and exemplary specimen of the *genus*.[85]

Nothing of the kind: such, when De Quincey is in this mood, is what passes for argument.

Beckett does not argue the toss, but he has his own un-sentimental understanding of such 'sentimental arithmetic' as the Edgeworths smile upon.

That we thought of ourselves as members of a vast organization was doubtless also due to the all too human feeling that trouble shared, or is it sorrow, is trouble something, I forget the word.[86]

Again:

'Do not tell me any more,' he said, 'if it gives you so much pain.'
'Two in distress,' said Neary, 'make sorrow less.'[87]

SOME BULLS FROM BECKETT

Here is a bouquet of Beckett's bulls:

Ticklepenny had unscrewed the ladder, so that now he could draw it up after him. Do not come down the ladder, they have taken it away.[88]

---

[85] A note in *Autobiographic Sketches*, ch. VIII.
[86] *Molloy*, 147. Following *Molloy* in French, 166:

Si nous nous voyions membres d'un immense réseau, c'était sans doute aussi en vertu du sentiment très humain qui veut que le partage diminue l'infortune.

When Beckett shared this in translation, he rendered it unclear-cut: '. . . that trouble shared, or is it sorrow, is trouble something, I forget the word'. He had had the word, untroubled, but that was French, not Irish.

[87] *Murphy*, 51–2. Preceding *Murphy* in French, 42–3:

—Ne m'en raconte pas davantage, dit-il, si cela te fait tant de peine.
—Peine partagée, dit Neary, peine perdue.

[88] *Murphy*, 188. Preceding *Murphy* in French, 137:

It was as though the brakes were jammed, and heaven knows they were not, for my bicycle had no brakes.[89]

For just as I had difficulty in sitting on a chair, or in an arm-chair, because of my stiff leg you understand, so I had none in sitting on the ground, because of my stiff leg and my stiffening leg, for it was about this time that my good leg, good in the sense that it was not stiff, began to stiffen.[90]

I put down the tray and looked for a few stamps at random [. . .] They were all there. That proved nothing. It only proved that those particular stamps were there.[91]

If I sometimes cut a branch, a flower, it was solely for their good, that they might increase in strength and happiness. And I never did it without a pang. Indeed if the truth were known, I did not do it at all, I got Christy to do it.[92]

For coat and hat have this much in common, that whereas the coat is too big, the hat is too small.[93]

You'll get down, Mrs. Rooney, you'll get down. We may not get you up, but I warrant you we'll get you down.[94]

Ticklepenny avait dévissé la base de l'échelle, de sorte que maintenant il pouvait la ramener derrière lui. Ne descendez pas par l'échelle, Louis, ils l'ont enlevée.

Amazing how much can turn upon the humble article ('*the* ladder'), breaking all the rungs of the thought. A different version of the warning (Welsh, Beckett told John Fletcher in 1961) is in *Watt*, 44, preceding *Watt* in French, 44.

[89] *Molloy*, 62. Following *Molloy* in French, 70:

> On aurait cru les freins serrés à bloc, ce qui n'était pourtant pas le cas, car ma bicyclette n'avait pas de freins.

[90] *Molloy*, 95. Following *Molloy* in French, 108:

Car autant je m'asseyais difficilement sur une chaise, ou dans un fauteuil, à cause de ma jambe raide vous comprenez, autant je m'asseyais facilement par terre, à cause de ma jambe raide et de ma jambe raidissante, car c'est vers cette époque que ma bonne jambe, bonne dans le sens qu'elle n'était pas raide, se mit a raidir.

[91] *Molloy*, 165–6. Following *Molloy* in French, 187:

Je posai le plateau et cherchai quelques timbres au hasard [. . .] Ils étaient à leur place. Cela ne prouvait rien. Cela prouvait seulement que ces timbres-là étaient à leur place.

[92] *Molloy*, 174–5. Following *Molloy* in French, 197:

Si j'en rentrenchais quelquefois une branche, une fleur, c'était uniquement pour leur bien, pour qu'ils poussent plus drus et plus heureux. Mais je ne le faisais que le cœur serré. D'ailleurs c'est simple, je ne le faisais pas, je le faisais faire par Christie.

[93] *Malone Dies*, 55. Following *Malone meurt*, 89:

Car manteau et chapeau ont ceci de commun, que si celui-là est trop grand, celui-ci est trop petit.

[94] *All That Fall*, 14. Preceding *Tous ceux qui tombe*, 23:

Carry if necessary this process of compression to the point of abandoning all other postulates than that of a deaf half-wit, hearing nothing of what he says and understanding even less.[95]

Less than nothing would be quite something. But then these postulates thrive upon impossibilities.

They were hundreds of pieces, large and small, in the end they blocked the door, making egress impossible, and *a fortiori* ingress, to and from the corridor.[96]

The impossible would not seem, on the face of it, to lend itself to an ensuing *a fortiori*. But the Latin, living on to this day, puts a good face on it, backed as it is by ingress and egress (very different from the plain French).

The bulls in Beckett are on good terms with all his other ways of writing askew, each of which contradicts less itself than all that we have learned to expect. Or to foresee, as in this rebuke to wishfulness:

I'm making progress, it was time, I'll learn to keep my foul mouth shut before I'm done, if nothing foreseen crops up.[97]

One of these bags was the grousebag, already perhaps mentioned. In spite of the straps, and buckles, with which it was generously provided, Watt held it by the neck, as though it were a sandbag.

The other of these bags was another and similar grousebag. It also Watt held by the neck, as though it were a club.[98]

Vous descendrez, madame, vous descendrez. Nous n'arriverons peut-être pas à vous faire monter, mais je vous garantis que nous arriverons à vous faire descendre.

[95] *The Unnamable*, 144. Following *L'innommable*, 211:

Pousser au besoin cette compression jusqu'à ne plus envisager qu'un sourd exceptionnellement débile d'esprit, n'entendant rien de ce qu'il dit, ni avant ni trop tard, et n'y comprenant, de travers, que le strict minimum.

[96] *First Love*, 47. Following *Premier amour*, 42:

Il y en avait des centaines, grands et petits. Ils arrivaient à la fin jusque devant la porte, de sorte qu'on ne pouvait plus sortir de la chambre, ni à plus forte raison y entrer, par là.

[97] 'Text for Nothing 4', *Stories and Texts for Nothing*, 93. Following *Nouvelles et textes pour rien*, 157:

Je suis en progrès, il était temps, je finirai par pouvoir fermer ma sale gueule, sauf prévu.

[98] *Watt*, 217. Preceding *Watt* in French, 225:

L'un de ces sacs était la gibecière déjà évoquée peut-être. Au mépris des courroies et des

It must not be forgotten that all this time I was lying down. He did not know I was ill. Besides I was not ill.[99]

Do you feel like singing? said Camier.
Not to my knowledge, said Mercier.[100]

He advanced towards Mercier who promptly recoiled. I was only going to embrace you, said Camier. I'll do it some other time, when you're less yourself, if I think of it.[101]

Speak up, said Mercier, I'm not deaf.[102]

This last exasperation refuses to offer either of the usuals: You don't have to shout, I'm not deaf; or Speak up, I'm a bit deaf. But Mercier's way of putting it posits a world in which if they think you are deaf, they deliberately lower their voices so as to frustrate you, drive you mad. And here too the turn, Irish in its acute perversity, thrives in the English version but is absent from the original French, which has simply:

Parle plus fort, dit Mercier, je n'entends rien.

It makes very good sense, the French, but do we really hear a thing? Whereas the English, lowering its voice, makes very good nonsense, and it speaks volumes:

Speak up, said Mercier, I'm not deaf.

---

boucles dont elle était généreusement pourvue, Watt la tenait par l'oreille, à la manière d'un sac de sable.

L'autre de ces sacs était une autre gibecière, semblable en tous points à la première. Elle aussi Watt la tenait par l'oreille, à la manière d'un gourdin.

[99] *Molloy*, 194. Following *Molloy* in French, 219:

J'étais toujours allongé, ne l'oublions pas. Il ne savait pas que j'étais malade. D'ailleurs je n'étais pas malade.

[100] *Mercier and Camier*, 25. Following *Mercier et Camier*, 36:

As-tu envie de chanter? dit Camier.
Pas à ma connaissance, dit Mercier.

[101] *Mercier and Camier*, 30. Following *Mercier et Camier*, 47:

Il s'approcha de Mercier qui recula vivement. J'allais seulement t'embrasser, dit Camier. Je le ferai une autre fois, quand tu seras mieux, si j'y pense.

The French advances straightforwardly ('quand tu seras mieux'); it is in Englishing this that Beckett does his U-turn ('when you're less yourself').

[102] *Mercier and Camier*, 85. Following *Mercier et Camier*, 143.

THE BULL AND POWER

The bull at its best is an act of principled self-defence, of guise and guile. He that plays the King: he that plays the Fool. So there is something odious about the bull when it is wielded by the powerful. ('He unsheathed his truncheon'.) The self-contradictions of those in power are often a way of proclaiming their tyrannical confidence that they may, if they so choose, ride roughshod over protest and protestation. *They* don't have to deign to make sense—indeed nothing could more establish their power than their flaunting their not being accountable to the ordinary rules. Do I contradict myself? Very well then I contradict myself (I am large, I constrain multitudes). Then the bull, instead of being an ironic catachresis, becomes a sarcastic catabolism.

Take the opening of Kipling's 'How the Rhinoceros Got His Skin':

Once upon a time, on an uninhabited island on the shores of the Red Sea, there lived a Parsee from whose hat the rays of the sun were reflected in more-than-oriental splendour.

This, with its more-than-occidental superiority, is too thick with the prejudice that an island inhabited by a Parsee is, to our intents and purposes, uninhabited. How the Bull Got His Thick Skin. Just so.

What protects the bull against being calculatingly perverse is its being a self-protection, called-for and aware of its dubiety. But in Kipling the boot is on the longstanding foot. There ought to be some danger from the bull, since it is a way of dealing with danger. The bull is busy sawing off the branch we and it are sitting on. A risky comic turn, and one which is creepily factitious when down below there are flunkeys with cushions to break your fall.

Within literary studies, the institutionalizing of deconstruction is not only itself something of a paradox, but has the unhappy effect of abolishing the felicities of the bull, since in the eyes of the deconstructionist all language is a bull anyway, unremittingly engaged in self-contradiction. Similarly with 'the antithetical sense of primal words': Freud's insight is swallowed up and lost in the insistence that there are no words which are not constituted of antithetical senses. This victory is both pyrrhic and pyrrhonist.

Since deconstruction is in its own pastures a sacred cow, to disparage it may constitute blasphemy. But then, turns within turns, deconstruction, like some allied movements of mind, itself constitutes a blasphemy, kicking against the pricks. Complacent in its unquestioned scepticism, deconstruction—like other forms of pyrrhonism—is a blasphemy against not only sense (which is always involved in some way in the non-sense cum supra-sense which is a bull) but against language, and against literature.

What such systematized scepticism manifests, or rather betrays, is an exacerbated acknowledgement of the power which such theories are up against, and even an acknowledgement of the irremovable though limited validation of the power they are up against, the power for instance of the old understandings in all their suspect commonsensicality. But what is not acknowledged, unfortunately, by the destabilizers is their own current power or privilege.

Nor, human nature being what it is (essentialist), are such uneasy contradictions limited to deconstruction. Harold Bloom has contradictory relations with deconstruction, but he is happy to play his paradoxes along the same lines: 'There are no interpretations but only misinterpretations.'[103]

Stanley Fish, having decided to his own satisfaction that the poems of George Herbert are self-consuming artifacts, soon found that his logic—his then logic, since he is an elusive Pimpernel—looked like requiring all texts to be so.

In Beckett's hands, the bull works wonders. But it does so because it distinguishes the bull not only from other solecisms but from all which is not solecism. As with this authorial pronouncement:

All the puppets in this book whinge sooner or later, except Murphy, who is not a puppet.[104]

The authority of so masterly an author permits him these straight-faced outfrownings, whether about his characters or about writing.

---

[103] *The Anxiety of Influence* (1973), 95.
[104] *Murphy*, 122. Preceding *Murphy* in French, 92:

Ils pleurnichent tous tôt ou tard, les pantins de cette histoire, à l'exception de Murphy, qui n'est pas un pantin.

I did not look closely. I drew a line, no, I did not even draw a line, and I wrote, Soon I shall be quite dead at last, and so on, without even going on to the next page, which was blank.[105]

It was astonishing how much the article *the* could effect by way of the bull ('Do not come down the ladder, they have taken it away'); here it is no less astonishing what *and* can be up to when it gets down to it.

I drew a line, no, I did not even draw a line, and I wrote

—*and* I wrote?
The illuminating absurdities of writing, like those of characterization, meet those of reading:

At such times I never read, any more than at other times, never gave way to revery or meditation[106]

In the seventy years since the appearance of the first issues of the *Criterion* (Beckett was to publish a review there in 1934), the convictions of T. S. Eliot have often found themselves challenged, and lately slighted or ignored. Yet his words should at least be judged to be the expression of a coherent and dignified evocation of a lifetime's effort:

It is the function of a literary review to maintain the autonomy and disinterestedness of literature, and at the same time to exhibit the relations of literature—not to 'life,' as something contrasted to literature, but to all the other activities, which, together with literature, are the components of life.[107]

Among the components of life is death. Together with language, and the relations of language both to life and to death. Words might then be valued, not as a hermetic system, something contrasted to life or to reality, but in their relations to all that is *not* words.

---

[105] *Malone Dies*, 34. Following *Malone meurt*, 58:

Je n'ai pas bien regardé. J'ai tiré un trait, non je n'ai même pas tiré un trait, j'ai écrit, Bientôt je serai tout à fait mort enfin, sans même aller à la page suivante qui était vierge.

[106] *First Love*, 16. Following *Premier amour*, 14:

Je ne lisais jamais, pas plus là qu'ailleurs, je ne rêvais ni ne réfléchissais

[107] 'Notes', *The Criterion*, 1 (1923), 421.

Arsène assures Watt that those who attend upon Mr Knott are good-natured men,

> whatever may escape us now and then in the way of bitter and I blush to say even blasphemous words and expressions, and perhaps also because what we know partakes in no small measure of the nature of what has so happily been called the unutterable or ineffable, so that any attempt to utter or eff it is doomed to fail, doomed, doomed to fail.[108]

Blasphemous words and expressions. T. S. Eliot had his tentative insistence: 'It may be said that no blasphemy can be purely verbal'.[109] Except the allied blasphemies of the post-Eliot consensus, first, that everything is purely verbal, and second, that the verbal is purely a bull?

Yet there are those of us who have confidence that the witty resilient aplomb of the Irish bull will outlive its theoretical immolation or immobilization; will decline to be reduced to being nothing more than yet another instance of the usual thing, language's indeterminacy-mongering. The bull will resist even the blandishments which would assure it that all language aspires to the condition of the bull.

Like the other ways in which Beckett's very words embody a doing right by death as well as by life, the bull is itself an imaginative embodiment of a principled living death, not one-sidedly 'the living principle' but the making friends with the necessity of dying.

Beckett's art puts in their place the merely professional manifestations of living death. It minds them. The best of the small *professional* Irish bulls was voiced by a friend of mine, contemplating his English Department: 'There are plenty of vacancies but they're all filled.'

The best of the large Irish bulls is the thought of vacancy to which Beckett often and diversely returned: 'Nothing is more real than nothing.'

---

[108] *Watt*, 62. Preceding *Watt* in French, 64:

quelles que soient les brèves paroles qui de temps en temps nous échappent voire expressions entières frappées au coin de l'amertume et même—j'en rougis—blasphématoires, et peut-être aussi parce que ce que nous savons relève en grande partie de l'inexprimable ou ineffable, si bien que toute tentative pour l'exprimer ou pour l'effer est vouée à l'échec, vouée vouée à l'échec.

[109] *After Strange Gods*, 12.

I know those little phrases that seem so innocuous and, once you let them in, pollute the whole of speech. *Nothing is more real than nothing.* They rise up out of the pit and know no rest until they drag you down into its dark.[110]

Come now, nothing can be only as real as nothing, nothing can be neither more nor less real than *nothing*. But not only do you know what he means, you sense the chilly comfort of the thought.

[110] *Malone Dies*, 16. Following *Malone meurt*, 29–30:

Je connais ces petites phrases qui n'ont l'air de rien et qui, une fois admises, peuvent vous empester toute une langue. *Rien n'est plus réel que rien.* Elles sortent de l'abîme et n'ont de cesse qu'elles n'y entraînent.

Allied, there had been *Murphy*, 246, which by distinguishing 'Nothing' from 'naught' precludes a straight bull: 'the Nothing, than which in the guffaw of the Abderite naught is more real'. Preceding *Murphy* in French, 176, which differentiated the two nothings only as cases of the upper and the lower: 'au Rien, ce Rien dont disait le farceur d'Abdère que rien n'est plus réel'. Beckett wrote to Sighle Kennedy, 14 June 1967: 'If I were in the unenviable position of having to study my work my points of departure would be the "Naught is more real..." and the "Ubi nihil vales..." both already in *Murphy* and neither very rational' (*Disjecta*, 113). Beckett began this letter with a bull of a plea: 'Please forgive unforgivable delay in answering your letter'. On Democritus the Abderite and his word-play, see Sighle Kennedy, *Murphy's Bed*, 23–4.

5. *Postscript*

Thoughts of Beckett at news of his death. The unforgettable Hardy title has been knocking. 'Thoughts of Phena at News of Her Death'. It had previously come to mind at news of another death, Philip Larkin's, because of his once pin-pointing essentially the birth of his own art: the moment when he stopped condescending to Hardy's. 'As regards his verse I shared Lytton Strachey's verdict that "the gloom is not even relieved by a little elegance of diction". This opinion did not last long; if I were asked to date its disappearance, I should guess it was the morning I first read "Thoughts of Phena at News of Her Death".'

'And age, and then the only end of age': how recent seems Larkin's end, though four years have gone. In my mid-fifties, everything proves to have happened three times longer ago than I first think (a death, a book, a trial), whereas only yesterday it was but twice as long ago.

Thoughts of Beckett. What scenes spread around his last days?

The word had been abroad, a day or two before he died, that he was soon to. A phone-call from a London newspaper broke to me the likelihood, and asked if I would write something. Against his dying. I said no, because I was bespoken in that I had already set down my say. A couple of years ago the *Sunday Times* had asked me to write, not an obituary, but a tribute, to wait the day. I remember that it was a discomposing experience, writing it, and new to me, this speaking of someone as if he or she were already dead. I haven't ever written a pickled obituary for *The Times* proper; haven't been asked to. It must require a flexile touch, the plaiting of prospect and retrospect, the unnamable's familiarity.

'Emotion anticipated in tranquillity'. So it was that Geoffrey Madan distilled his obituary-on-phial. 'In the words of an obituary notice, intended for the *Times* but never sent: "A genius for friendship with all and sundry, infectious enthusiasm, selfless devotion to progressive causes, a deep and touching love of animals and of natural beauty"—he would not have claimed for himself any of these so frequent attributes of the lately dead.'

These anonymous lapidations always have a Beckett-like *vigor mortis*. I have long collected them, as apt for Beckett's key-cold charity. When not insinuatingly derogatory ('He never married'), the obituaries are informed by a co-operative subconscious, and therefore are rich in the happy infelicities which the Irish employ so adroitly. Verging on the Bull. Philip Larkin had an eye for these; it was he who sent in to the *New Statesman*, for monumental mockery ('This England'), the obituary which said plummily: 'Any sketch of David Glass's work would be incomplete without reference to his *amour propre*, the history of his subject'. Over in America, I miss the *Times* obituaries more than anything else from the public prints. The USA has no counterpart. The *New York Times* reduces its necrology to a final spasm of public relations, if not by the very deceased, then by what Beckett called the 'nearest if not dearest'.

'I am always glad when one of those fellows dies, for then I know I have the whole of him on my shelf' (Lord Melbourne, speaking of Crabbe).

Beckett and I go back a long way. Not, though, in one another's company. Did I meet him? (Until just now, it was 'have you ever met him?' Students have a way of asking.) Twice. Briefly. Not to be forgotten, not to be memorialized either. 'I live in another world where life and death are memorised.' The reminiscences of Beckett already flourish apace. Best not to join this cortège industry.

In the Rue de Seine in Paris there was an English bookshop. 'The English Bookshop' rather. Long gone. Given over now to anthropological artwork. A student, on holiday in Paris in 1954, I flushed out *Watt*, carmine, published the year before in the Collection Merlin of the Olympia Press, the friendly-neighbourhood softish-porn people. A numbered edition of 1,125 copies. I stood there reading the first two pages, I fretted and winced and smiled (I still think them among Beckett's best), and I bought Number 885 for 25 shillings. Also *En attendant Godot*, published in October 1952 but not performed till January 1953. I had heard of Beckett, though not much. He had been sighted and cited by Anthony Hartley—in the *Spectator*, I suppose; Hartley had a great nose and a fine ear for things French, and he let the British in on his finds—I can't think that there is anyone around today who does this work so well.

Waiting for Godot, as the world knows, opened at the Arts Theatre on 3 August 1955. I attended it with impatient young up-and-coming Anthony Howard; he soon came to cease attending to the play, though I can't now remember whether his exasperation moved him to quit, physically. Theatregoers went, during the performance. But then theatregoers are not the only people who go to theatres, and they too much know what they like and want what they know.

Isis, the undergraduate magazine at Oxford, ran a short small series, 'Dust-Jacket'. Beckett, dust to dust, felt appropriate. The series was mostly bent upon, oh, such as Nigel Balchin. Beckett seemed to me more acutely Mine Own Executioner. So I wrote about him in *Isis*, 16 November 1955. Thirty-four years ago. It is disconcerting to think that he was then appreciably younger than I now am.

Re-reading my youthful cocky piece, I am neither proud nor ashamed of it, or perhaps am equally both. I am glad (slightly different) to have written back then about the novels, *Watt* and *Molloy*, neither yet published in England (1963 and 1960 respectively). 1955 was early days, except for Beckett himself, though he was inured to neglect. My testimony was embarrassingly brash, even then, and yet I am not sorry to have said simply that Beckett is very difficult to understand but that his isn't a small voice. I think, too, that I quoted some very good bits. On love-making:

What I do know for certain is that I never sought to repeat the experience, having, I suppose, the intuition that it had been unique and perfect, of its kind, achieved and inimitable, and that it behoved me to preserve its memory, pure of all pastiche, in my heart, even if it meant my resorting from time to time to the alleged joys of so-called self-abuse.

And on Godsmiths:

And I would never do my bees the wrong I had done my God, to whom I had been taught to ascribe my angers, fears, desires, and even my body.

True, in reverting to 1955 I am remembering me, but that doesn't mean that I am not remembering Beckett too. Less a diary than a snatch of partial annals.

In 1968 I was mildly thrilled to receive a letter of enquiry from the Nobel Committee of the Swedish Academy. I did not then know that so many such letters get sent out as to make them little more than the thinking man's junk-mail. Though I had no need of weighing whom to nominate, I took pains with how best to do so. My letter of twenty years ago ended in the same terms in which I still wished to praise him in the week of his death: for 'the dignity and integrity of his career, both in artistic terms (his work has never swerved from the aims, at once high and profound, which it set itself in "Dante . . . Bruno. Vico . . Joyce", 1929), and in personal terms: with single-minded dedication and dignity, and without either bitterness or elation, he has lived through forty years of neglect and through twenty years of recognition, manifestly his own man and manifestly, too, a man of supreme loyalty to his art.' About the only change which I had to make to this, in December 1989 as against December 1968, was to match the forty years of neglect with, now, forty years of recognition. In 1969, Beckett won the Nobel Prize. Thanks to me and whose army. He owed it to me? No, I owed it to him.

Over the years I wrote to him from time to time, and he wrote back. This is a less misleading way of putting it than speaking as if we enjoyed a correspondence. I was the one who enjoyed it, and who enjoined it by making an enquiry, never interpretative and almost always textual. Is 'then' a misprint for 'than'? Which wording would he wish to stand by, that of the English or of the US edition? And he would answer the enquiry, on one of those crisp cards with his name, severely elegant, alone at the head. These unmassive missives moved me. From 1972 to 1989.

Often they were deliciously lugubrious. Of the English wording versus the American one in *Company*: 1. 'Yet a certain activity of mind however slight is a necessary complement of company'. 2. 'Yet a certain activity of mind however slight is a necessary adjunct of company'. Beckett: 'I don't know which I dislike more.'

Best was his admission that the cardiac arithmetic in *Company* goes wrong. Ever since people registered that Beckett doesn't tell us what the seventh scarf at the beginning of *Murphy* is up to, the critics have been devoted to his numeracy, and in particular to its anomalies. Such anomalies are found more fun if they are believed to be intentional, especially by critics who don't believe in intentionality: an arithmetical anomaly in Beckett is held to intimate to us, surprise, surprise, that Deconstruction rules. I prefer to take Beckett's word for his words, and to see therefore

A SELECTIVE CHRONOLOGY OF BECKETT'S PUBLISHED VOLUMES[1]

[1] Within the one year, ordered alphabetically by title.

1963 *Film*
      Oh les beaux jours
1964 *Comédie*
      How It Is
      Play
1965 *Imagination Dead Imagine*
      Imagination morte imaginez
      No's Knife: Collected Shorter Prose 1945–1966
1966 *Dis Joe*
      Eh Joe
      Va et vient
1967 *Come and Go*
      D'un ouvrage abandonné
      Stories and Texts for Nothing
      Têtes-Mortes
1968 *Watt* (translated into French)
1969 *Sans*
1970 *Lessness*
      Mercier et Camier
      Premier amour
1971 *Le dépeupleur*
1972 *The Lost Ones*
1973 *First Love*
      Not I
1974 *Mercier and Camier*
1975 *For to End Yet Again and Other Fizzles*
1976 *All Strange Away*
      Pour finir encore et autres foirades
1980 *Compagnie*
      Company
1981 *Ill Seen Ill Said*
      Mal vu mal dit
1983 *Disjecta: Miscellaneous Writings and a Dramatic Fragment*
      Worstward Ho
1984 *Collected Poems 1930–1978*
      Collected Shorter Plays
      Collected Shorter Prose 1945–1980
1988 *Stirrings Still*
1989 *Nohow On (Company, Ill Seen Ill Said, Worstward Ho)*
      Soubresauts
1990 *As the Story Was Told: Uncollected and Late Prose*
1992 *Dream of Fair to Middling Women*

ACKNOWLEDGEMENTS

Beckett's writings in French are quoted by permission of Les Éditions de Minuit.

Acknowledgement is given to the Beckett Estate and to The Calder Educational Trust, London, for permission to quote from the following titles:

Collected Poems 1930–1978, translated by Samuel Beckett, © 1930–84 Samuel Beckett, published by John Calder (Publishers) Ltd., London. Also by permission of Grove Press, Inc.

Company, from *Nohow On*, © 1979, 1980, 1992 The Samuel Beckett Estate, published by Calder Publications Ltd., London. Also by permission of Grove Press, Inc.

Disjecta, © 1983 John Calder (Publishers) Ltd., published by John Calder (Publishers) Ltd., London. Also by permission of Grove Press, Inc.

First Love, translated by Samuel Beckett, from *Collected Shorter Prose 1945–1980*, © 1970, 1973, 1984 Samuel Beckett, published by John Calder (Publishers) Ltd., London. Also by permission of Grove Press, Inc.

How It Is, translated by Samuel Beckett, © 1964 Samuel Beckett, published by Calder & Boyars Ltd., London. Also by permission of Grove Press, Inc.

Ill Seen Ill Said, translated by Samuel Beckett, © 1981, 1982 Samuel Beckett, published by John Calder (Publishers) Ltd., London. Also by permission of Grove Press, Inc.

Malone Dies, translated by Samuel Beckett, © 1958, 1975, 1987 Samuel Beckett, published by John Calder (Publishers) Ltd., London. Also by permission of Grove Press, Inc.

Mercier and Camier, translated by Samuel Beckett, © 1974 Samuel Beckett, published by Calder & Boyars Ltd., London. Also by permission of Grove Press, Inc.

Molloy, translated by Samuel Beckett and Patrick Bowles, © 1955, 1959, 1966, 1971, 1976 Samuel Beckett, published by John Calder (Publishers) Ltd., London. Also by permission of Grove Press, Inc.

More Pricks than Kicks, © 1934 Samuel Beckett, published by

Calder & Boyars Ltd., London. Also by permission of Grove Press, Inc.

Murphy, © 1938, 1963, 1977 Samuel Beckett, published by John Calder (Publishers) Ltd., London. Also by permission of Grove Press, Inc.

Proust and Three Dialogues with Georges Duthuit, © 1931, 1987 Samuel Beckett, published by John Calder (Publishers) Ltd., London. Also by permission of Grove Press, Inc.

Texts for Nothing, translated by Samuel Beckett, from *Collected Shorter Prose 1945–1980*, © 1967, 1984, 1984 Samuel Beckett, published by John Calder (Publishers) Ltd., London. *Stories and Texts for Nothing*, by permission of Grove Press, Inc.

The Unnamable, translated by Samuel Beckett, © 1958, 1975 Samuel Beckett, published by John Calder (Publishers) Ltd., London. Also by permission of Grove Press, Inc.

Watt, © 1953, 1963, 1970, 1976 Samuel Beckett, published by John Calder (Publishers) Ltd., London. Also by permission of Grove Press, Inc.

Permission to quote from *All That Fall* and *Endgame* by Samuel Beckett has been given by Faber & Faber Ltd., and by Grove Press, Inc.; and from *Anthology of Mexican Poetry*, translated by Samuel Beckett, by permission of Thames & Hudson Ltd., and of Indiana University Press.

Permission to quote Philip Larkin's 'Wants', from *The Less Deceived*, has been given by George Hartley, The Marvell Press, England and Australia; and by Farrar Straus Giroux, for Larkin's *Collected Poems*, 1988. Permission to quote from Larkin's 'The Old Fools', from *High Windows*, has been given by Faber & Faber Ltd., and by Farrar Straus Giroux, for Larkin's *Collected Poems*, 1988.

Permission to quote from Robert Lowell's 'Mr. Edwards and the Spider' has been given by Faber & Faber Ltd.

Permission to quote from Dudley Fitts's *From the Greek Anthology* has been given by Laurence Pollinger, and by New Directions Publishing Corporation.

I am grateful to Michael Prince, who read the typescript of *Beckett's Dying Words* with imaginative care and then gave me good advice.

C.R.

INDEX